UNCTAD/DITE/4(Vol. XIV)

United Nations Conference on Trade and Development
Division on Investment, Technology and Enterprise Development

International Investment Instruments: A Compendium

Volume XIV

United Nations
New York and Geneva, 2005

Note

UNCTAD serves as the focal point within the United Nations Secretariat for all matters related to foreign direct investment and transnational corporations. In the past, the Programme on Transnational Corporations was carried out by the United Nations Centre on Transnational Corporations (1975-1992) and the Transnational Corporations and Management Division of the United Nations Department of Economic and Social Development (1992-1993). In 1993, the Programme was transferred to the United Nations Conference on Trade and Development. UNCTAD seeks to further the understanding of the nature of transnational corporations and their contribution to development and to create an enabling environment for international investment and enterprise development. UNCTAD's work is carried out through intergovernmental deliberations, technical assistance activities, seminars, workshops and conferences.

The term "country", as used in the boxes added by the UNCTAD secretariat at the beginning of the instruments reproduced in this volume, also refers, as appropriate, to territories or areas; the designations employed and the presentation of the material do not imply the expression of any opinion whatsoever on the part of the Secretariat of the United Nations concerning the legal status of any country, territory, city or area or of its authorities, or concerning the delimitation of its frontiers or boundaries. Moreover, the country or geographical terminology used in the boxes may occasionally depart from standard United Nations practice when this is made necessary by the nomenclature used at the time of negotiation, signature, ratification or accession of a given international instrument.

To preserve the integrity of the texts of the instruments reproduced in this volume, references to the sources of the instruments that are not contained in their original text are identified as "note added by the editor".

The texts of the instruments included in this volume are reproduced as they were written in one of their original languages or as an official translation thereof. When an obvious linguistic mistake has been found, the word "sic" has been added in brackets.

The materials contained in this volume have been reprinted with special permission of the relevant institutions. For those materials under copyright protection, all rights are reserved by the copyright holders.

It should be further noted that this collection of instruments has been prepared for documentation purposes only, and its contents do not engage the responsibility of UNCTAD.

UNCTAD/DITE/4 Vol. XIV

UNITED NATIONS PUBLICATION

Sales No. E.05.II.D.8

ISBN 92-1-112665-7

MAY 13 2005

PREFACE

International Investment Instruments: A Compendium contains a collection of international instruments relating to foreign direct investment (FDI) and transnational corporations (TNCs). The collection is presented in fourteen volumes. The first three volumes were published in 1996. *Volumes IV* and *V* were published in 2000 followed by *Volume VI* in 2001. *Volumes* VII, VIII, IX and X were published in 2002. *Volumes XI* and *XII* were published in 2003 bringing the collection up to date. The present publication comprises *volumes XIII* and *XIV.*

The collection has been prepared to make the texts of international investment instruments conveniently available to interested policy-makers, scholars and business executives. The need for such a collection has increased in recent years as bilateral, regional, interregional and multilateral instruments dealing with various aspects of FDI have proliferated, and as new investment instruments are being negotiated or discussed at all levels.

While by necessity selective, the *Compendium* seeks to provide a faithful record of the evolution and present status of intergovernmental cooperation concerning FDI and TNCs. Although the emphasis of the collection is on relatively recent documents, it was deemed useful to include important older instruments as well, with a view to providing some indications of the historical development of international concerns about FDI in the decades since the end of the Second World War.

The core of this collection consists of legally binding international instruments, mainly multilateral conventions, regional agreements, and bilateral treaties that have entered into force. In addition, a number of "soft law" documents, such as guidelines, declarations and resolutions adopted by intergovernmental bodies, have been included since these instruments also play a role in the evolution of international agreements concerning FDI. In an effort to enhance the understanding of this evolution, certain draft instruments that never entered into force, or texts of instruments on which the negotiations were not concluded, are also included; prototypes of bilateral investment treaties are reproduced as well. Included also are a number of influential documents prepared by business, consumer and labour organizations, as well as by other non-governmental organizations. It is clear from the foregoing that no conclusions concerning the legal status or the legal effect of an instrument can be drawn from its inclusion in this collection.

In view of the great diversity of the instruments in this *Compendium* -- in terms of subject matter, approach, legal form and extent of participation of States -- the simplest possible method of presentation was deemed the most appropriate. With regard to previous volumes, the structure and content are indicated in the table of content which is included below (see pp. ix-xli). As far as volumes XIII and XIV are concerned relevant instruments are distributed as follows:

Volume XIII is divided into the following three parts:

- Part One contains additional regional instruments, including agreements and other texts from regional organizations with an inclusive geographical context.

- Part Two reproduces investment-related provisions in a number of additional free trade, economic partnership arrangements and framework frame-work agreements not covered in previous volumes.

- Part Three contains the texts of a number of additional prototype BITs not covered in previous volumes.

Volume XIV is divided into the following two parts:

- Part One reproduces investment-related provisions in three free trade agreements and a framework agreement not covered in previous volumes.

- Part Two contains the text of a number of an additional prototype BIT not covered in previous volumes.

Within each of these subdivisions and in previous volumes, instruments are reproduced in chronological order, except for the sections dedicated to prototype instruments.

The multilateral and regional instruments covered are widely differing in scope and coverage. Some are designed to provide an overall, general framework for FDI and cover many, although rarely all, aspects of investment operations. Most instruments deal with particular aspects and issues concerning FDI. A significant number address core FDI issues, such as the promotion and protection of investment, investment liberalization, dispute settlement and insurance and guarantees. Others cover specific issues, of direct but not exclusive relevance to FDI and TNCs, such as transfer of technology, intellectual property, avoidance of double taxation, competition and the protection of consumers and the environment. A relatively small number of instruments of this last category has been reproduced, since each of these specific issues often constitutes an entire system of legal regulation of its own, whose proper coverage would require an extended exposition of many kinds of instruments and arrangements.[a]

The *Compendium* is meant to be a collection of instruments, not an anthology of relevant provisions. Indeed, to understand a particular instrument, it is normally necessary to take its entire text into consideration. An effort has been made, therefore, to reproduce complete instruments, even though, in a number of cases, reasons of space and relevance have dictated the inclusion of excerpts. Owing to their size, annexes containing the list of reservations and exceptions are also excluded in many cases. The excerpts are meant to reflect all provisions directly relevant to investment in an international agreement. There are other provisions that have an indirect bearing on investment but are not covered in the *Compendium*. The mark "[...]" has been inserted to indicate missing text.

The UNCTAD secretariat has deliberately refrained from adding its own commentary to the texts reproduced in the *Compendium*. The only exception to this rule is the boxes added to each instrument. They provide some basic facts, such as its date of adoption and date of entry into force and, where appropriate, signatory countries. Also, a list of agreements containing investment-related provisions signed by the EFTA countries and by the EC countries with third

---

[a]   For a collection of instruments (or excerpts therefrom) dealing with transfer of technology, see UNCTAD, *Compendium of International Arrangements on Transfer of Technology: Selected Instruments* (Geneva: United Nations), United Nations publication, Sales No. E.01.II.D.28.

countries or regional groups are reproduced in the *Compendium*. Moreover, to facilitate the identification of each instrument in the table of contents, additional information has been added, in brackets, next to each title, on the year of its signature and the name of the relevant institution involved.

Carlos Fortin
Officer-in-Charge of UNCTAD

Geneva, February 2005

ACKNOWLEDGEMENTS

Volume XIV of the *Compendium* was prepared by Abraham Negash under the supervision of Torbjörn Fredriksson and the overall guidance of Anne Miroux and Karl P. Sauvant. Comments and inputs were received from James Zhan, Amare Bekele, Hamid El-Khadi, Gabriele Koehler, Moritz Meier-Ewert and Elisabeth Tuerk. The cooperation of the relevant countries and organizations from which the instruments originate is acknowledged with gratitude.

VOLUME XIV

PART ONE
BILATERAL INSTRUMENTS

PART TWO
PROTOTYPE INSTRUMENTS

CONTENTS OF OTHER VOLUMES

VOLUME I

MULTILATERAL INSTRUMENTS

VOLUME II

REGIONAL INSTRUMENTS

REGIONAL INSTRUMENTS

VOLUME III

REGIONAL INTEGRATION, BILATERAL AND NON-GOVERNMENTAL INSTRUMENTS

ANNEX C. NON-GOVERNMENTAL INSTRUMENTS

VOLUME IV

MULTILATERAL AND REGIONAL INSTRUMENTS

PART ONE

MULTILATERAL INSTRUMENTS

PART TWO

REGIONAL INSTRUMENTS

VOLUME V

REGIONAL INTEGRATION, BILATERAL AND NON-GOVERNMENTAL INSTRUMENTS

PART ONE

INVESTMENT-RELATED PROVISIONS IN FREE TRADE AND ECONOMIC INTEGRATION AGREEMENTS

PART TWO

INVESTMENT-RELATED PROVISIONS IN ASSOCIATION AGREEMENTS, BILATERAL AND INTERREGIONAL COOPERATION AGREEMENTS

ANNEX C. OTHER BILATERAL INVESTMENT-RELATED AGREEMENTS

PART THREE

PROTOTYPE BILATERAL INVESTMENT TREATIES AND LIST OF BILATERAL INVESTMENT TREATIES (MID-1995 — END-1998)

PART FOUR

NON-GOVERNMENTAL INSTRUMENTS

VOLUME VI

PART ONE

MULTILATERAL INSTRUMENTS

PART TWO

INTERREGIONAL AND REGIONAL INSTRUMENTS

PART THREE

INVESTMENT-RELATED PROVISIONS IN FREE TRADE AND ECONOMIC INTEGRATION AGREEMENTS

PART FOUR

INVESTMENT-RELATED PROVISIONS IN ASSOCIATION AGREEMENTS, BILATERAL AND INTERREGIONAL COOPERATION AGREEMENTS

PART FIVE

PROTOTYPE BILATERAL INVESTMENT TREATIES

VOLUME VII

PART ONE

MULTILATERAL INSTRUMENTS

PART TWO

BILATERAL INSTRUMENTS

PART THREE

PROTOTYPE INSTRUMENTS

VOLUME VIII

PART ONE

INTERREGIONAL AND REGIONAL INSTRUMENTS

PART TWO

BILATERAL INSTRUMENTS

PART THREE

PROTOTYPE INSTRUMENTS

VOLUME IX

PART ONE

INTERREGIONAL AND REGIONAL INSTRUMENTS

PART TWO

BILATERAL INSTRUMENTS

PART THREE

PROTOTYPE INSTRUMENTS

VOLUME X

PART ONE

BILATERAL INSTRUMENTS

PART TWO

PROTOTYPE INSTRUMENTS

VOLUME XI

PART ONE

MULTILATERAL INSTRUMENTS

PART TWO

REGIONAL AND INTERREGIONAL INSTRUMENTS

PART THREE

BILATERAL INSTRUMENTS

VOLUME XII

PART ONE

BILATERAL INSTRUMENTS

PART TWO

PROTOTYPE INSTRUMENTS

Selected UNCTAD publications on transnational corporations and

VOLUME XIII

PART ONE
REGIONAL AND INTERREGIONAL INSTRUMENTS

PART TWO
BILATERAL INSTRUMENTS

PART THREE
PROTOTYPE INSTRUMENTS

PART ONE
BILATERAL INSTRUMENTS

UNITED STATES - MOROCCO FREE TRADE AGREEMENT*
[excerpts]

The United States - Morocco Free Trade Agreement was signed on 16 June 2004.

[…]

CHAPTER TEN
INVESTMENT

Section A: Investment

ARTICLE 10.1: SCOPE AND COVERAGE

This Chapter applies to measures adopted or maintained by a Party relating to:

(a)   investors of the other Party;

(b)   covered investments; and

(c)   with respect to Articles 10.8 and 10.10, all investments in the territory of the Party.

ARTICLE 10.2: RELATION TO OTHER CHAPTERS

1.   In the event of any inconsistency between this Chapter and another Chapter, the other Chapter shall prevail to the extent of the inconsistency.

2.   A requirement by a Party that a service supplier of the other Party post a bond or other form of financial security as a condition of the cross-border supply of a service does not of itself make this Chapter applicable to measures adopted or maintained by the Party relating to such cross-border supply of the service. This Chapter applies to measures adopted or maintained by the Party relating to the posted bond or financial security, to the extent that such bond or financial security is a covered investment.

3.   This Chapter does not apply to measures adopted or maintained by a Party to the extent that they are covered by Chapter Twelve (Financial Services).

ARTICLE 10.3: NATIONAL TREATMENT

1.   Each Party shall accord to investors of the other Party treatment no less favourable than that it accords, in like circumstances, to its own investors with respect to the establishment,

* *Source*: The Government of the United States of America and the Government of the Kingdom of Morocco (2004). "United States - Morocco Free Trade Agreement", available on the Internet (http://www.ustr.gov/Trade_Agreements/Bilateral/Morocco_FTA/FInal_Text/Section_Index.html). [Note added by the editor.]

acquisition, expansion, management, conduct, operation, and sale or other disposition of investments in its territory.

2.   Each Party shall accord to covered investments treatment no less favorable than that it accords, in like circumstances, to investments in its territory of its own investors with respect to the establishment, acquisition, expansion, management, conduct, operation, and sale or other disposition of investments.

3.   The treatment to be accorded by a Party under paragraphs 1 and 2 means, with respect to a regional level of government, treatment no less favorable than the most favorable treatment accorded, in like circumstances, by that regional level of government to investors, and to investments of investors, of the Party of which it forms a part.

ARTICLE 10.4: MOST-FAVORED-NATION TREATMENT

1.   Each Party shall accord to investors of the other Party treatment no less favourable than that it accords, in like circumstances, to investors of any non-Party with respect to the establishment, acquisition, expansion, management, conduct, operation, and sale or other disposition of investments in its territory.

2.   Each Party shall accord to covered investments treatment no less favorable than that it accords, in like circumstances, to investments in its territory of investors of any non- Party with respect to the establishment, acquisition, expansion, management, conduct, operation, and sale or other disposition of investments.

ARTICLE 10.5: MINIMUM STANDARD OF TREATMENT[1]

1.   Each Party shall accord to covered investments treatment in accordance with customary international law, including fair and equitable treatment and full protection and security.

2.   For greater certainty, paragraph 1 prescribes the customary international law minimum standard of treatment of aliens as the minimum standard of treatment to be afforded to covered investments. The concepts of "fair and equitable treatment" and "full protection and security" do not require treatment in addition to or beyond that which is required by that standard, and do not create additional substantive rights. The obligation in paragraph 1 to provide:

   (a)   "fair and equitable treatment" includes the obligation not to deny justice in criminal, civil, or administrative adjudicatory proceedings in accordancewith the principle of due process embodied in the principal legal systems of the world; and

   (b)   "full protection and security" requires each Party to provide the level of police protection required under customary international law.

3.   A determination that there has been a breach of another provision of this Agreement, or of a separate international agreement, does not establish that there has been a breach of this Article.

---

[1] Article 10.5 shall be interpreted in accordance with Annex 10-A.

4.   Notwithstanding Article 10.12.5(b), each Party shall accord to investors of the other Party, and to covered investments, non-discriminatory treatment with respect to measures it adopts or maintains relating to losses suffered by investments in its territory owing to armed conflict or civil strife.

5.   Notwithstanding paragraph 4, if an investor of a Party, in the situations referred to in paragraph 4, suffers a loss in the territory of the other Party resulting from:

(a)   requisitioning of its covered investment or part thereof by the latter's forces or authorities; or

(b)   destruction of its covered investment or part thereof by the latter's forces or authorities, which was not required by the necessity of the situation, the latter Party shall provide the investor restitution, compensation, or both, as appropriate, for such loss. Any compensation shall be prompt, adequate, and effective in accordance with Article 10.6.2 through 10.6.4, mutatis mutandis.

6.   Paragraph 4 does not apply to existing measures relating to subsidies or grants that would be inconsistent with Article 10.3 but for Article 10.12.5(b).

ARTICLE 10.6: EXPROPRIATION AND COMPENSATION[2]

1.   Neither Party may expropriate or nationalize a covered investment either directly or indirectly through measures equivalent to expropriation or nationalization ("expropriation"), except:

(a)   for a public purpose;

(b)   in a non-discriminatory manner;

(c)   on payment of prompt, adequate, and effective compensation; and

(d)   in accordance with due process of law and Article 10.5.1 through 10.5.3.

2.   The compensation referred to in paragraph 1(c) shall:

(a)   be paid without delay;

(b)   be equivalent to the fair market value of the expropriated investment immediately before the expropriation took place ("the date of expropriation");

(c)   not reflect any change in value occurring because the intended expropriation had become known earlier; and

(d)   be fully realizable and freely transferable.

3.   If the fair market value is denominated in a freely usable currency, the compensation referred to in paragraph 1(c) shall be no less than the fair market value on the date of

---

[2] Article 10.6 shall be interpreted in accordance with Annexes 10-A and 10-B.

expropriation, plus interest at a commercially reasonable rate for that currency, accrued from the date of expropriation until the date of payment.

4.   If the fair market value is denominated in a currency that is not freely usable, the compensation referred to in paragraph 1(c) – converted into the currency of payment at the market rate of exchange prevailing on the date of payment – shall be no less than:

(a)   the fair market value on the date of expropriation, converted into a freely usable currency at the market rate of exchange[3] prevailing on that date, plus

(b)   interest, at a commercially reasonable rate for that freely usable currency, accrued from the date of expropriation until the date of payment.

5.   This Article does not apply to the issuance of compulsory licenses granted in relation to intellectual property rights in accordance with the TRIPS Agreement, or to the revocation, limitation, or creation of intellectual property rights, to the extent that such issuance, revocation, limitation, or creation is consistent with Chapter Fifteen (Intellectual Property Rights).[4]

ARTICLE 10.7: TRANSFERS

1.   Each Party shall permit all transfers relating to a covered investment to be made freely and without delay into and out of its territory. Such transfers include:

(a)   contributions to capital;

(b)   profits, dividends, capital gains, and proceeds from the sale of all or any part of the covered investment or from the partial or complete liquidation of the covered investment;

(c)   interest, royalty payments, management fees, and technical assistance and other fees;

(d)   payments made under a contract, including a loan agreement;

(e)   payments made pursuant to Article 10.5.4 and 10.5.5 and Article 10.6; and

(f)   payments arising out of a dispute.

2.   Each Party shall permit transfers relating to a covered investment to be made in a freely usable currency at the market rate of exchange prevailing at the time of transfer.

3.   Each Party shall permit returns in kind relating to a covered investment to be made as authorized or specified in a written agreement between the Party and a covered investment or an investor of the other Party.

---

[3] For purposes of this paragraph and Article 10.7.2, Morocco's foreign exchange system in effect on the date of signature of this Agreement yields an exchange rate comparable to a "market rate of exchange."

[4] For greater certainty, the reference to the TRIPS Agreement in paragraph 5 includes any waiver in force between the Parties of any provision of that agreement granted by WTO Members in accordance with the WTO Agreement.

4.	Notwithstanding paragraphs 1 through 3, a Party may prevent a transfer through the equitable, non-discriminatory, and good faith application of its laws relating to:

(a)	bankruptcy, insolvency, or the protection of the rights of creditors;

(b)	issuing, trading, or dealing in securities, futures, options, or derivatives;

(c)	criminal or penal offenses;

(d)	financial reporting or record keeping of transfers when necessary to assist law enforcement or financial regulatory authorities; or

(e)	ensuring compliance with orders or judgments in judicial or administrative proceedings.

ARTICLE 10.8: PERFORMANCE REQUIREMENTS

1.	Neither Party may, in connection with the establishment, acquisition, expansion, management, conduct, operation, or sale or other disposition of an investment of an investor of a Party or of a non-Party in its territory, impose or enforce any requirement or enforce any commitment or undertaking:[5]

(a)	to export a given level or percentage of goods or services;

(b)	to achieve a given level or percentage of domestic content;

(c)	to purchase, use, or accord a preference to goods produced in its territory, or to purchase goods from persons in its territory;

(d)	to relate in any way the volume or value of imports to the volume or value of exports or to the amount of foreign exchange inflows associated with such investment;

(e)	to restrict sales of goods or services in its territory that such investment produces or supplies by relating such sales in any way to the volume or value of its exports or foreign exchange earnings;

(f)	to transfer a particular technology, a production process, or other proprietary knowledge to a person in its territory; or

(g)	to supply exclusively from the territory of the Party the goods that such investment produces or the services that it supplies to a specific regional market or to the world market.

2.	Neither Party may condition the receipt or continued receipt of an advantage, in connection with the establishment, acquisition, expansion, management, conduct, operation, or

---

[5] For greater certainty, a condition for the receipt or continued receipt of an advantage referred to in paragraph 2 does not constitute a "commitment or undertaking" for the purposes of paragraph 1.

sale or other disposition of an investment in its territory of an investor of a Party or of a non-Party, on compliance with any requirement:

(a)   to achieve a given level or percentage of domestic content;

(b)   to purchase, use, or accord a preference to goods produced in its territory, or to purchase goods from persons in its territory;

(c)   to relate in any way the volume or value of imports to the volume or value of exports or to the amount of foreign exchange inflows associated with such investment; or

(d)   to restrict sales of goods or services in its territory that such investment produces or supplies by relating such sales in any way to the volume or value of its exports or foreign exchange earnings.

3.   (a)   Nothing in paragraph 2 shall be construed to prevent a Party from conditioning the receipt or continued receipt of an advantage, in connection with an investment in its territory of an investor of a Party or of a non-Party, on compliance with a requirement to locate production, supply a service, train or employ workers, construct or expand particular facilities, or carry out research and development, in its territory.

(b)   Paragraph 1(f) does not apply:

(i)   when a Party authorizes use of an intellectual property right in accordance with Article 31 of the TRIPS Agreement, or to measures requiring the disclosure of proprietary information that fall within the scope of, and are consistent with, Article 39 of the TRIPS Agreement;[6] or

(ii)   when the requirement is imposed or the commitment or undertaking is enforced by a court, administrative tribunal, or competition authority to remedy a practice determined after judicial or administrative process to be anticompetitive under the Party's competition laws.[7]

(c)   Provided that such measures are not applied in an arbitrary or unjustifiable manner, and provided that such measures do not constitute a disguised restriction on international trade or investment, paragraphs 1(b), (c), and (f), and 2(a) and (b), shall not be construed to prevent a Party from adopting or maintaining measures, including environmental measures:

(i)   necessary to secure compliance with laws and regulations that are not inconsistent with this Agreement;

(ii)   necessary to protect human, animal, or plant life or health; or

---

[6] For greater certainty, the references to the TRIPS Agreement in paragraph 3(b)(i) include any waiver in force between the Parties of any provision of that agreement granted by WTO Members in accordance with the WTO Agreement.

[7] The Parties recognize that a patent does not necessarily confer market power.

(iii)   related to the conservation of living or non-living exhaustible natural resources.

(d)   Paragraphs 1(a), (b), and (c), and 2(a) and (b), do not apply to qualification requirements for goods or services with respect to export promotion and foreign aid programs.

(e)   Paragraphs 1(b), (c), (f), and (g), and 2(a) and (b), do not apply to procurement.

(f)   Paragraphs 2(a) and (b) do not apply to requirements imposed by an importing Party relating to the content of goods necessary to qualify for preferential tariffs or preferential quotas.

4.   For greater certainty, paragraphs 1 and 2 do not apply to any requirement other than the requirements set out in those paragraphs.

5.   This Article does not preclude enforcement of any commitment, undertaking, or requirement between private parties, where a Party did not impose or require the commitment, undertaking, or requirement.

ARTICLE 10.9: SENIOR MANAGEMENT AND BOARDS OF DIRECTORS

1.   Neither Party may require that an enterprise of that Party that is a covered investment appoint to senior management positions natural persons of any particular nationality.

2.   A Party may require that a majority of the board of directors, or any committee thereof, of an enterprise of that Party that is a covered investment, be of a particular nationality, or resident in the territory of the Party, provided that the requirement does not materially impair the ability of the investor to exercise control over its investment.

ARTICLE 10.10: INVESTMENT AND ENVIRONMENT

Nothing in this Chapter shall be construed to prevent a Party from adopting, maintaining, or enforcing any measure otherwise consistent with this Chapter that it considers appropriate to ensure that investment activity in its territory is undertaken in a manner sensitive to environmental concerns.

ARTICLE 10.11: DENIAL OF BENEFITS

1.   A Party may deny the benefits of this Chapter to an investor of the other Party that is an enterprise of such other Party and to investments of that investor if persons of a non- Party own or control the enterprise and the denying Party:

(a)   does not maintain diplomatic relations with the non-Party; or

(b)   adopts or maintains measures with respect to the non-Party or a person of the non-Party that prohibit transactions with the enterprise or that would be violated or circumvented if the benefits of this Chapter were accorded to the enterprise or to its investments.

2.   A Party may deny the benefits of this Chapter to an investor of the other Party that is an enterprise of such other Party and to investments of that investor if the enterprise has no substantial business activities in the territory of the other Party and persons of a non-Party, or of the denying Party, own or control the enterprise.

ARTICLE 10.12: NON-CONFORMING MEASURES

1.   Articles 10.3, 10.4, 10.8, and 10.9 do not apply to:

    (a)   any existing non-conforming measure that is maintained by a Party at:

        (i)   the central level of government, as set out by that Party in its Schedule to Annex I,

        (ii)   a regional level of government, as set out by that Party in its Schedule to Annex I, or

        (iii)   a local level of government;

    (b)   the continuation or prompt renewal of any non-conforming measure referred to in subparagraph (a); or

    (c)   an amendment to any non-conforming measure referred to in subparagraph (a) to the extent that the amendment does not decrease the conformity of the measure, as it existed immediately before the amendment, with Article 10.3, 10.4, 10.8, or 10.9.

2.   Articles 10.3, 10.4, 10.8, and 10.9 do not apply to any measure that a Party adopts or maintains with respect to sectors, subsectors, or activities, as set out in its Schedule to Annex II.

3.   Neither Party may, under any measure adopted after the date of entry into force of this Agreement and covered by its Schedule to Annex II, require an investor of the other Party, by reason of its nationality, to sell or otherwise dispose of an investment existing at the time the measure becomes effective.

4.   Articles 10.3 and 10.4 do not apply to any measure that is an exception to, or derogation from, the obligations under Article 15.1.5 (General Provisions) as specifically provided in that Article.

5.   Articles 10.3, 10.4, and 10.9 do not apply to:

    (a)   procurement; or

    (b)   subsidies or grants provided by a Party, including government-supported loans, guarantees, and insurance.

ARTICLE 10.13: SPECIAL FORMALITIES AND INFORMATION REQUIREMENTS

1.   Nothing in Article 10.3 shall be construed to prevent a Party from adopting or maintaining a measure that prescribes special formalities in connection with covered

investments, such as a requirement that investors be residents of the Party or that covered investments be legally constituted under the laws or regulations of the Party, provided that such formalities do not materially impair the protections afforded by a Party to investors of the other Party and covered investments pursuant to this Chapter.

2.   Notwithstanding Articles 10.3 and 10.4, a Party may require an investor of the other Party, or a covered investment, to provide information concerning that investmentsolely for informational or statistical purposes. The Party shall protect any confidential business information from any disclosure that would prejudice the competitive position of the investor or the covered investment. Nothing in this paragraph shall be construed to prevent a Party from otherwise obtaining or disclosing information in connection with the equitable and good faith application of its law.

Section B: Investor-State Dispute Settlement

ARTICLE 10.14: CONSULTATION AND NEGOTIATION

In the event of an investment dispute, the claimant and the respondent should initially seek to resolve the dispute through consultation and negotiation, which may include the use of non-binding, third-party procedures.

ARTICLE 10.15: SUBMISSION OF A CLAIM TO ARBITRATION

1.   In the event that a disputing party considers that an investment dispute cannot be settled by consultation and negotiation:

    (a)   the claimant, on its own behalf, may submit to arbitration under this Section a claim

        (i)   that the respondent has breached

            (A)   an obligation under Section A,
            (B)   an investment authorization, or
            (C)   an investment agreement;
                     and

        (ii)   that the claimant has incurred loss or damage by reason of, or arising out of, that breach; and

    (b)   the claimant, on behalf of an enterprise of the respondent that is a juridical person that the claimant owns or controls directly or indirectly, may submit to arbitration under this Section a claim

        (i)   that the respondent has breached

            (A)   an obligation under Section A,
            (B)   an investment authorization, or
            (C)   an investment agreement;
                     and

> (ii)   that the enterprise has incurred loss or damage by reason of, or arising out of, that breach.

2.   At least 90 days before submitting any claim to arbitration under this Section, a claimant shall deliver to the respondent a written notice of its intention to submit the claim to arbitration ("notice of intent"). The notice shall specify:

>   (a)   the name and address of the claimant and, where a claim is submitted on behalf of an enterprise, the name, address, and place of incorporation of the enterprise;
>
>   (b)   for each claim, the provision of this Agreement, investment authorization, or investment agreement alleged to have been breached and any other relevant provisions;
>
>   (c)   the legal and factual basis for each claim; and
>
>   (d)   the relief sought and the approximate amount of damages claimed.

3.   Provided that six months have elapsed since the events giving rise to the claim, a claimant may submit a claim referred to in paragraph 1:

>   (a)   under the ICSID Convention and the ICSID Rules of Procedures for Arbitration Proceedings, provided that both the respondent and the nondisputing Party are parties to the ICSID Convention;
>
>   (b)   under the ICSID Additional Facility Rules, provided that either the respondent or the non-disputing Party is a party to the ICSID Convention;
>
>   (c)   under the UNCITRAL Arbitration Rules; or
>
>   (d)   if the claimant and respondent agree, to any other arbitration institution or under any other arbitration rules.

4.   A claim shall be deemed submitted to arbitration under this Section when the claimant's notice of or request for arbitration ("notice of arbitration"):

>   (a)   referred to in paragraph 1 of Article 36 of the ICSID Convention is received by the Secretary-General;
>
>   (b)   referred to in Article 2 of Schedule C of the ICSID Additional Facility Rules is received by the Secretary-General;
>
>   (c)   referred to in Article 3 of the UNCITRAL Arbitration Rules, together with the statement of claim referred to in Article 18 of the UNCITRAL Arbitration Rules, are received by the respondent; or
>
>   (d)   referred to under any other arbitral institution or arbitral rules selected under paragraph 3(d) is received by the respondent.

A claim asserted by the claimant for the first time after such notice of arbitration is submitted shall be deemed submitted to arbitration under this Section on the date of its receipt under the applicable arbitral rules.

5.   The arbitration rules applicable under paragraph 3, and in effect on the date the claim or claims were submitted to arbitration under this Section, shall govern the arbitration except to the extent modified by this Agreement.

6.   The claimant shall provide with the notice of arbitration:

(a)   the name of the arbitrator that the claimant appoints; or

(b)   the claimant's written consent for the Secretary-General to appoint that arbitrator.

ARTICLE 10.16: CONSENT OF EACH PARTY TO ARBITRATION

1.   Each Party consents to the submission of a claim to arbitration under this Section in accordance with this Agreement.

2.   The consent under paragraph 1 and the submission of a claim to arbitration under this Section shall satisfy the requirements of:

(a)   Chapter II of the ICSID Convention (Jurisdiction of the Centre) and the ICSID Additional Facility Rules for written consent of the parties to the dispute; and

(b)   Article II of the New York Convention for an "agreement in writing."

ARTICLE 10.17: CONDITIONS AND LIMITATIONS ON CONSENT OF EACH PARTY

1.   No claim may be submitted to arbitration under this Section if more than three years have elapsed from the date on which the claimant first acquired, or should have first acquired, knowledge of the breach alleged under Article 10.15.1 and knowledge that the claimant (for claims brought under Article 10.15.1(a)) or the enterprise (for claims brought under Article 10.15.1(b)) has incurred loss or damage.

2.   No claim may be submitted to arbitration under this Section unless:

(a)   the claimant consents in writing to arbitration in accordance with the procedures set out in this Agreement; and

(b)   the notice of arbitration is accompanied,

(i)   for claims submitted to arbitration under Article 10.15.1(a), by the claimant's written waiver, and

(ii)   for claims submitted to arbitration under Article 10.15.1(b), by the claimant's and the enterprise's written waivers of any right to initiate or continue before any administrative tribunal or court under the law of either Party, or other dispute settlement procedures, any proceeding with respect to any measure alleged to constitute a breach referred to in Article 10.15.

3.   Notwithstanding paragraph 2(b), the claimant (for claims brought under Article 10.15.1(a)) and the claimant or the enterprise (for claims brought under Article 10.15.1(b)) may initiate or continue an action that seeks interim injunctive relief and does not involve the payment of monetary damages before a judicial or administrative tribunal of the respondent, provided that the action is brought for the sole purpose of preserving the claimant's or the enterprise's rights and interests during the pendency of the arbitration. In no case should such relief, if granted, be dispositive of the issues in dispute before the tribunal or suspend the proceedings before the tribunal.

ARTICLE 10.18: SELECTION OF ARBITRATORS

1.   Unless the disputing parties agree otherwise, the tribunal shall comprise three arbitrators, one arbitrator appointed by each of the disputing parties and the third, who shall be the presiding arbitrator, appointed by agreement of the disputing parties.

2.   The Secretary-General shall serve as appointing authority for an arbitration under this Section.

3.   If a tribunal has not been constituted within 75 days from the date that a claim is submitted to arbitration under this Section, the Secretary-General, on the request of a disputing party, shall appoint, in his or her discretion, the arbitrator or arbitrators not yet appointed.

4.   For purposes of Article 39 of the ICSID Convention and Article 7 of Schedule C to the ICSID Additional Facility Rules, and without prejudice to an objection to an arbitrator on a ground other than nationality:

    (a)   the respondent agrees to the appointment of each individual member of a tribunal established under the ICSID Convention or the ICSID Additional Facility Rules;

    (b)   a claimant referred to in Article 10.15.1(a) may submit a claim to arbitration under this Section, or continue a claim, under the ICSID Convention or the ICSID Additional Facility Rules, only on condition that the claimant agrees in writing to the appointment of each individual member of the tribunal; and

    (c)   a claimant referred to in Article 10.15.1(b) may submit a claim to arbitration under this Section, or continue a claim, under the ICSID Convention or the ICSID Additional Facility Rules, only on condition that the claimant and the enterprise agree in writing to the appointment of each individual member of the tribunal.

ARTICLE 10.19: CONDUCT OF THE ARBITRATION

1.   The disputing parties may agree on the legal place of any arbitration under the arbitral rules applicable under Article 10.15.3. If the disputing parties fail to reach agreement, the tribunal shall determine the place in accordance with the applicable arbitral rules, provided that the place shall be in the territory of a State that is a party to the New York Convention.

2.   The non-disputing Party may make oral and written submissions to the tribunal regarding the interpretation of this Agreement.

3.   The tribunal shall have the authority to accept and consider amicus curiae submissions from a person or entity that is not a disputing party.

4.   Without prejudice to a tribunal's authority to address other objections as a preliminary question, a tribunal shall address and decide as a preliminary question any objection by the respondent that, as a matter of law, a claim submitted is not a claim for which an award in favor of the claimant may be made under Article 10.25.

   (a)   Such objection shall be submitted to the tribunal as soon as possible after the tribunal is constituted, and in no event later than the date the tribunal fixes for the respondent to submit its counter-memorial (or, in the case of an amendment to the notice of arbitration, the date the tribunal fixes for the respondent to submit its response to the amendment).

   (b)   On receipt of an objection under this paragraph, the tribunal shall suspend any proceedings on the merits, establish a schedule for considering the objection consistent with any schedule it has established for considering any other preliminary question, and issue a decision or award on the objection, stating the grounds therefor.

   (c)   In deciding an objection under this paragraph, the tribunal shall assume to be true claimant's factual allegations in support of any claim in the notice of arbitration (or any amendment thereof) and, in disputes brought under the UNCITRAL Arbitration Rules, the statement of claim referred to in Article 18 of the UNCITRAL Arbitration Rules. The tribunal may also consider any relevant facts not in dispute.

   (d)   The respondent does not waive any objection as to competence or any argument on the merits merely because the respondent did or did not raise an objection under this paragraph or make use of the expedited procedure set out in paragraph 5.

5.   In the event that the respondent so requests within 45 days after the tribunal is constituted, the tribunal shall decide on an expedited basis an objection under paragraph 4 and any objection that the dispute is not within the tribunal's competence. The tribunal shall suspend any proceedings on the merits and issue a decision or award on the objection(s), stating the grounds therefor, no later than 150 days after the date of the request. However, if a disputing party requests a hearing, the tribunal may take an additional 30 days to issue the decision or award. Regardless of whether a hearing is requested, a tribunal may, on a showing of extraordinary cause, delay issuing its decision or award by an additional brief period, which may not exceed 30 days.

6.   When it decides a respondent's objection under paragraph 4 or 5, the tribunal may, if warranted, award to the prevailing disputing party reasonable costs and attorney's fees incurred in submitting or opposing the objection. In determining whether such an award is warranted, the tribunal shall consider whether either the claimant's claim or the respondent's objection was frivolous, and shall provide the disputing parties a reasonable opportunity to comment.

7.   A respondent may not assert as a defense, counterclaim, right of set-off, or for any other reason that the claimant has received or will receive indemnification or other compensation for all or part of the alleged damages pursuant to an insurance or guarantee contract.

8.   The tribunal may order an interim measure of protection to preserve the rights of a disputing party, or to ensure that the tribunal's jurisdiction is made fully effective, including an order to preserve evidence in the possession or control of a disputing party or to protect the tribunal's jurisdiction. The tribunal may not order attachment or enjoin the application of a measure alleged to constitute a breach referred to in Article 10.15. For purposes of this paragraph, an order includes a recommendation.

9.   (a)   In any arbitration conducted under this Section, at the request of a disputing party, a tribunal shall, before issuing a decision or award on liability, transmit its proposed decision or award to the disputing parties and to the non-disputing Party. Within 60 days after the tribunal transmits its proposed decision or award, the disputing parties may submit written comments to the tribunal concerning any aspect of its proposed decision or award. The tribunal shall consider any such comments and issue its decision or award not later than 45 days after the expiration of the 60-day comment period.

        (b)   Subparagraph (a) shall not apply in any arbitration conducted pursuant to this Section for which an appeal has been made available pursuant to paragraph 10 or Annex 10-D.

10.   If a separate regional or multilateral agreement concerning investment enters into force between the Parties that establishes an appellate body for purposes of reviewing awards rendered by tribunals constituted pursuant to international trade or investment arrangements to hear investment disputes, the Parties shall strive to reach an agreement that would have such appellate body review awards rendered under Article 10.25 in arbitrations commenced after the regional or multilateral agreement enters into force between the Parties.

ARTICLE 10.20: TRANSPARENCY OF ARBITRAL PROCEEDINGS

1.   Subject to paragraphs 2 and 4, the respondent shall, after receiving the following documents, promptly transmit them to the non-disputing Party and make them available to the public:

        (a)   the notice of intent;

        (b)   the notice of arbitration;

        (c)   pleadings, memorials, and briefs submitted to the tribunal by a disputing party and any written submissions submitted pursuant to Article 10.19.2 and 10.19.3 and Article 10.24;

        (d)   minutes or transcripts of hearings of the tribunal, where available; and

        (e)   orders, awards, and decisions of the tribunal.

2.   The tribunal shall conduct hearings open to the public and shall determine, in consultation with the disputing parties, the appropriate logistical arrangements. However, any disputing party that intends to use information designated as protected information in a hearing shall so advise the tribunal. The tribunal shall make appropriate arrangements to protect the information from disclosure.

3.   Nothing in this Section requires a respondent to disclose protected information or to furnish or allow access to information that it may withhold in accordance with Article 21.2 (Essential Security) or Article 21.5 (Disclosure of Information).

4.   Any protected information that is submitted to the tribunal shall be protected from disclosure in accordance with the following procedures:

   (a)   Subject to subparagraph (d), neither the disputing parties nor the tribunal shall disclose to the non-disputing Party or to the public any protected information where the disputing party that provided the information clearly designates it in accordance with subparagraph (b);

   (b)   Any disputing party claiming that certain information constitutes protected information shall clearly designate the information at the time it issubmitted to the tribunal;

   (c)   A disputing party shall, at the time it submits a document containing information claimed to be protected information, submit a redacted version of the document that does not contain the information. Only the redacted version shall be provided to the non-disputing Party and made public in accordance with paragraph 1; and

   (d)   The tribunal shall decide any objection regarding the designation of information claimed to be protected information. If the tribunal determines that such information was not properly designated, the disputing party that submitted the information may (i) withdraw all or part of its submission containing such information, or (ii) agree to resubmit complete and redacted documents with corrected designations in accordance with the tribunal's determination and subparagraph (c). In either case, the other disputing party shall, whenever necessary, resubmit complete and redacted documents which either remove the information withdrawn under (i) by the disputing party that first submitted the information or redesignate the information consistent with the designation under (ii) of the disputing party that first submitted the information.

5.   Nothing in this Section requires a respondent to withhold from the public information required to be disclosed by its laws.

ARTICLE 10.21: GOVERNING LAW

1.   Subject to paragraph 3, when a claim is submitted under Article 10.15.1(a)(i)(A) or Article 10.15.1(b)(i)(A), the tribunal shall decide the issues in dispute in accordance with this Agreement and applicable rules of international law.

2.   Subject to paragraph 3 and the other terms of this Section, when a claim is submitted under Article 10.15.1(a)(i)(B) or (C), or Article 10.15.1(b)(i)(B) or (C), the tribunal shall apply:

(a)   the rules of law specified in the pertinent investment authorization or investment agreement, or as the disputing parties may agree otherwise; or

(b)   if the rules of law have not been specified or agreed otherwise:

(i)   the law of the respondent, including its rules on the conflict of laws;[8] and

(ii)   such rules of international law as may be applicable.

3.   A decision of the Joint Committee declaring its interpretation of a provision of this Agreement under Article 19.2 (Joint Committee) shall be binding on a tribunal, and any decision or award issued by a tribunal must be consistent with that decision.

ARTICLE 10.22: INTERPRETATION OF ANNEXES

1.   Where a respondent asserts as a defense that the measure alleged to be a breach is within the scope of an entry set out in Annex I or Annex II, the tribunal shall, on request of the respondent, request the interpretation of the Joint Committee on the issue. The Joint Committee shall submit in writing any decision declaring its interpretation under Article 19.2 (Joint Committee) to the tribunal within 60 days of delivery of the request.

2.   A decision issued by the Joint Committee under paragraph 1 shall be binding on the tribunal, and any decision or award issued by the tribunal must be consistent with that decision. If the Joint Committee fails to issue such a decision within 60 days, the tribunal shall decide the issue.

Article 10.23: EXPERT REPORTS

Without prejudice to the appointment of other kinds of experts where authorized by the applicable arbitration rules, a tribunal, at the request of a disputing party or, unless the disputing parties disapprove, on its own initiative, may appoint one or more experts to report to it in writing on any factual issue concerning environmental, health, safety, or other scientific matters raised by a disputing party in a proceeding, subject to such terms and conditions as the disputing parties may agree.

ARTICLE 10.24: CONSOLIDATION

1.   Where two or more claims have been submitted separately to arbitration under Article 10.15.1 and the claims have a question of law or fact in common and arise out of the same events or circumstances, any disputing party may seek a consolidation order in accordance with the agreement of all the disputing parties sought to be covered by the order or the terms of paragraphs 2 through 10.

2.   A disputing party that seeks a consolidation order under this Article shall deliver, in writing, a request to the Secretary-General and to all the disputing parties sought to be covered by the order and shall specify in the request:

---

[8] The **law of the respondent** means the law that a domestic court or tribunal of proper jurisdiction would apply in the same case.

(a)   the names and addresses of all the disputing parties sought to be covered by the order;

(b)   the nature of the order sought; and

(c)   the grounds on which the order is sought.

3.   Unless the Secretary-General finds within 30 days after receiving a request under paragraph 2 that the request is manifestly unfounded, a tribunal shall be established under this Article.

4.   Unless all the disputing parties sought to be covered by the order agree otherwise, a tribunal established under this Article shall comprise three arbitrators:

(a)   one arbitrator appointed by agreement of the claimants;

(b)   one arbitrator appointed by the respondent; and

(c)   the presiding arbitrator appointed by the Secretary-General, provided, however, that the presiding arbitrator shall not be a national of either Party.

5.   If, within 60 days after the Secretary-General receives a request made under paragraph 2, the respondent fails or the claimants fail to appoint an arbitrator in accordance with paragraph 4, the Secretary-General, on the request of any disputing party sought to be covered by the order, shall appoint the arbitrator or arbitrators not yet appointed. If the respondent fails to appoint an arbitrator, the Secretary-General shall appoint a national of the disputing Party, and if the claimants fail to appoint an arbitrator, the Secretary-General shall appoint a national of the non-disputing Party.

6.   Where a tribunal established under this Article is satisfied that two or more claims that have been submitted to arbitration under Article 10.15.1 have a question of law or fact in common, and arise out of the same events or circumstances, the tribunal may, in the interest of fair and efficient resolution of the claims, and after hearing the disputing parties, by order:

(a)   assume jurisdiction over, and hear and determine together, all or part of the claims;

(b)   assume jurisdiction over, and hear and determine one or more of the claims, the determination of which it believes would assist in the resolution of the others; or

(c)   instruct a tribunal previously established under Article 10.18 to assume jurisdiction over, and hear and determine together, all or part of the claims, provided that

(i)   that tribunal, at the request of any claimant not previously a disputing party before that tribunal, shall be reconstituted with its original members, except that the arbitrator for the claimants shall be appointed pursuant to paragraphs 4(a) and 5; and

(ii)   that tribunal shall decide whether any prior hearing shall be repeated.

7.   Where a tribunal has been established under this Article, a claimant that has submitted a claim to arbitration under Article 10.15.1 and that has not been named in a request made under paragraph 2 may make a written request to the tribunal that it be included in any order made under paragraph 6, and shall specify in the request:

(a)   the name and address of the claimant;

(b)   the nature of the order sought; and

(c)   the grounds on which the order is sought.

The claimant shall deliver a copy of its request to the Secretary-General.

8.   A tribunal established under this Article shall conduct its proceedings in accordance with the UNCITRAL Arbitration Rules, except as modified by this Section.

9.   A tribunal established under Article 10.18 shall not have jurisdiction to decide a claim, or a part of a claim, over which a tribunal established or instructed under this Article has assumed jurisdiction.

10.   On application of a disputing party, a tribunal established under this Article, pending its decision under paragraph 6, may order that the proceedings of a tribunal established under Article 10.18 be stayed, unless the latter tribunal has already adjourned its proceedings.

ARTICLE 10.25: AWARDS

1.   Where a tribunal makes a final award against a respondent, the tribunal may award, separately or in combination, only:

(a)   monetary damages and interest, as appropriate; and

(b)   restitution of property, in which case the award shall provide that the respondent may pay monetary damages and interest, as appropriate, in lieu of restitution.

A tribunal may also award costs and attorney's fees in accordance with this Section and he applicable arbitration rules.

2.   Subject to paragraph 1, where a claim is submitted to arbitration under Article 0.15.1(b):

(a)   an award of restitution of property shall provide that restitution be made to he enterprise;

(b)   an award of monetary damages and interest, as appropriate, shall provide that the sum be paid to the enterprise; and

(c)   the award shall provide that it is made without prejudice to any right that any person may have in the relief under applicable domestic law.

3.   A tribunal may not award punitive damages.

4.   An award made by a tribunal shall have no binding force except between the disputing parties and in respect of the particular case.

5.   Subject to paragraph 6 and the applicable review procedure for an interim award, a disputing party shall abide by and comply with an award without delay.

6.   A disputing party may not seek enforcement of a final award until:

(a)   in the case of a final award made under the ICSID Convention

(i)   120 days have elapsed from the date the award was rendered and no disputing party has requested revision or annulment of the award; or

(ii)   revision or annulment proceedings have been completed; and

(b)   in the case of a final award under the ICSID Additional Facility Rules, the UNCITRAL Arbitration Rules, or the rules selected pursuant to Article 10.15.3(d)

(i)   90 days have elapsed from the date the award was rendered and no disputing party has commenced a proceeding to revise, set aside, or annul the award; or

(ii)   a court has dismissed or allowed an application to revise, set aside, or annul the award and there is no further appeal.

7.   Each Party shall provide for the enforcement of an award in its territory.

8.   If the respondent fails to abide by or comply with a final award, on delivery of a request by the non-disputing Party, a panel shall be established under Article 20.7 (Establishment of Panel). The requesting Party may seek in such proceedings:

(a)   a determination that the failure to abide by or comply with the final award is inconsistent with the obligations of this Agreement; and

(b)   in accordance with Article 20.9.2 (Panel Report), a recommendation that the respondent abide by or comply with the final award.

9.   A disputing party may seek enforcement of an arbitration award under the ICSID Convention or the New York Convention regardless of whether proceedings have been taken under paragraph 8.

10.   A claim that is submitted to arbitration under this Section shall be considered to arise out of a commercial relationship or transaction for purposes of Article I of the New York Convention.

ARTICLE 10.26: SERVICE OF DOCUMENTS

Delivery of notice and other documents on a Party shall be made to the place named for that Party in Annex 10-C.

Section C: Definitions

ARTICLE 10.27: DEFINITIONS

For purposes of this Chapter:

Centre means the International Centre for Settlement of Investment Disputes ("ICSID") established by the ICSID Convention;

claimant means an investor of a Party that is a party to an investment dispute with the other Party;

disputing parties means the claimant and the respondent;

disputing party means either the claimant or the respondent;

enterprise means an enterprise as defined in Article 1.3 (Definitions), and a branch of an enterprise;

enterprise of a Party means an enterprise constituted or organized under the law of a Party, and a branch located in the territory of a Party and carrying out business activities there;

freely usable currency means "freely usable currency" as determined by the International Monetary Fund under its Articles of Agreement;

ICSID Additional Facility Rules means the Rules Governing the Additional Facility for the Administration of Proceedings by the Secretariat of the International Centre for

Settlement of Investment Disputes;

ICSID Convention means the Convention on the Settlement of Investment Disputes between States and Nationals of Other States, done at Washington, March 18, 1965;

investment means every asset that an investor owns or controls, directly or indirectly, that has the characteristics of an investment, including such characteristics as the commitment of capital or other resources, the expectation of gain or profit, or the assumption of risk.

Forms that an investment may take include:

    (a)   an enterprise;
    (b)   shares, stock, and other forms of equity participation in an enterprise;
    (c)   bonds, debentures, other debt instruments, and loans;[9]
    (d)   futures, options, and other derivatives;
    (e)   turnkey, construction, management, production, concession, revenuesharing, and other similar contracts;
    (f)   intellectual property rights;

---

[9] Some forms of debt, such as bonds, debentures, and long-term notes, are more likely to have the characteristics of an investment, while other forms of debt, such as claims to payment that are immediately due and result from the sale of goods or services, are less likely to have such characteristics.

    (g)   licenses, authorizations, permits, and similar rights conferred pursuant to domestic law;[10,11] and

    (h)   other tangible or intangible, movable or immovable property, and related property rights, such as leases, mortgages, liens, and pledges;

investment agreement means a written agreement[12] that takes effect on or after the date of entry into force of this Agreement between a national authority1[13] of a Party and a covered investment or an investor of the other Party that grants the covered investment or investor rights:

    (a)   with respect to natural resources or other assets that a national authority controls; and

    (b)   upon which the covered investment or the investor relies in establishing or acquiring a covered investment other than the written agreement itself;

investment authorization[14] means an authorization that the foreign investment authority of a Party grants to a covered investment or an investor of the other Party;

investor of a non-Party means, with respect to a Party, an investor that concretely attempts to make, is making, or has made an investment in the territory of that Party, that is not an investor of either Party;

investor of a Party means a Party or state enterprise thereof, or a national or an enterprise of a Party, that concretely attempts to make, is making, or has made an investment in the territory of the other Party; provided, however, that a natural person who is a dual national shall be deemed to be exclusively a national of the State of his or her dominant and effective nationality;

New York Convention means the United Nations Convention on the Recognition and Enforcement of Foreign Arbitral Awards, done at New York, June 10, 1958;

non-disputing Party means the Party that is not a party to an investment dispute;

protected information means confidential business information or information that is privileged or otherwise protected from disclosure under a Party's law;

---

[10] Whether a particular type of license, authorization, permit, or similar instrument (including a concession, to the extent that it has the nature of such an instrument) has the characteristics of an investment depends on such factors as the nature and extent of the rights that the holder has under the law of the Party. Among the licenses, authorizations, permits, and similar instruments that do not have the characteristics of an investment are those that do not create any rights protected under domestic law. For greater certainty, the foregoing is without prejudice to whether any asset associated with the license, authorization, permit, or similar instrument has the characteristics of an investment.

[11] The term "investment" does not include an order or judgment entered in a judicial or administrative action.

[12] "Written agreement" refers to an agreement in writing, executed by both parties, that creates an exchange of rights and obligations, binding on both parties under the law applicable under Article 10.21.2. For greater certainty, (a) a unilateral act of an administrative or judicial authority, such as a permit, license, or authorization issued by a Party solely in its regulatory capacity or a decree, order, or judgment; and (b) an administrative or judicial consent decree or order, shall not be considered a written agreement.

[13] For purposes of this definition, "national authority" means an authority at the central level of government.

[14] For greater certainty, actions taken by a Party to enforce laws of general application, such as competition laws, are not encompassed within this definition.

respondent means the Party that is a party to an investment dispute;

Secretary-General means the Secretary-General of ICSID; and

UNCITRAL Arbitration Rules means the arbitration rules of the United Nations Commission on International Trade Law.

ANNEX 10-A
CUSTOMARY INTERNATIONAL LAW

The Parties confirm their shared understanding that "customary international law" generally and as specifically referenced in Article 10.5 and Annex 10-B results from a general and consistent practice of States that they follow from a sense of legal obligation.

With regard to Article 10.5, the customary international law minimum standard of treatment of aliens refers to all customary international law principles that protect the economic rights and interests of aliens.

ANNEX 10-B
EXPROPRIATION

The Parties confirm their shared understanding that:

1.   Article 10.6.1 is intended to reflect customary international law concerning the obligation of States with respect to expropriation.

2.   An action or a series of actions by a Party cannot constitute an expropriation unless it interferes with a tangible or intangible property right or property interest in an investment.

3.   Article 10.6.1 addresses two situations. The first is direct expropriation, where an investment is nationalized or otherwise directly expropriated through formal transfer of title or outright seizure.

4.   The second situation addressed by Article 10.6.1 is indirect expropriation, where an action or series of actions by a Party has an effect equivalent to direct expropriation without formal transfer of title or outright seizure.

    (a)   The determination of whether an action or series of actions by a Party, in a specific fact situation, constitutes an indirect expropriation, requires a caseby-case, fact-based inquiry that considers, among other factors:

        (i)   the economic impact of the government action, although the fact that an action or series of actions by a Party has an adverse effect on the economic value of an investment, standing alone, does not establish that an indirect expropriation has occurred;

        (ii)   the extent to which the government action interferes with distinct, reasonable investment-backed expectations; and

(iii)   the character of the government action.

(b)   Except in rare circumstances, non-discriminatory regulatory actions by a Party that are designed and applied to protect legitimate public welfare objectives, such as public health, safety, and the environment, do not constitute indirect expropriations.

ANNEX 10-C
SERVICE OF DOCUMENTS ON A PARTY UNDER SECTION B

Morocco

Notices and other documents in disputes under Section B shall be served on Morocco by delivery to:

Directorate for Legal Affairs and Treaties
Ministry of Foreign Affairs and Cooperation
Rabat
Kingdom of Morocco
United States

Notices and other documents in disputes under Section B shall be served on the United States by delivery to:

Executive Director (L/EX)
Office of the Legal Adviser
Department of State
Washington, D.C. 20520
United States of America

ANNEX 10-D
POSSIBILITY OF A BILATERAL APPELLATE MECHANISM

Within three years after the date of entry into force of this Agreement, the Parties shall consider whether to establish a bilateral appellate body or similar mechanism to review awards rendered under Article 10.25 in arbitrations commenced after they establish the appellate body or similar mechanism.

ANNEX 10-E
SUBMISSION OF A CLAIM TO ARBITRATION

Morocco

If an investor of the United States, or an enterprise of Morocco that is a juridical person that the investor owns or controls directly or indirectly, initiates proceedings before a court of Morocco alleging a breach by Morocco of an obligation under Section A, an investment authorization, or an investment agreement, the investor may not submit that alleged breach to arbitration under Section B either:

(a)   on its own behalf under Article 10.15.1(a), or

(b)   on behalf of the enterprise under Article 10.15.1(b),

unless at least one year has elapsed from the date the court proceedings were initiated.

CHAPTER ELEVEN
CROSS-BORDER TRADE IN SERVICES

ARTICLE 11.1: SCOPE AND COVERAGE

1.   This Chapter applies to measures adopted or maintained by a Party affecting crossborder trade in services by service suppliers of the other Party. Such measures include measures affecting:

(a)   the production, distribution, marketing, sale, and delivery of a service;

(b)   the purchase or use of, or payment for, a service;

(c)   the access to and use of distribution, transport, or telecommunications networks and services in connection with the supply of a service;

(d)   the presence in its territory of a service supplier of the other Party; and

(e)   the provision of a bond or other form of financial security as a condition for the supply of a service.

2.   For purposes of this Chapter, measures adopted or maintained by a Party means measures adopted or maintained by:

(a)   central, regional, or local governments and authorities; and

(b)   non-governmental bodies in the exercise of powers delegated by central, regional, or local governments or authorities.

3.   Articles 11.4, 11.7, and 11.8 shall also apply to measures by a Party affecting the supply of a service in its territory by a covered investment.[1]

4.   This Chapter does not apply to:

(a)   financial services as defined in Article 12.19 (Definitions), except as provided in paragraph 3;

---

[1] The Parties understand that nothing in this Chapter, including this paragraph, shall be subject to investorstate dispute settlement pursuant to Section B of Chapter Ten (Investment).

(b) air services, including domestic and international air transportation services, whether scheduled or non-scheduled, and related services in support of air services, other than:

   (i) aircraft repair and maintenance services during which an aircraft is withdrawn from service; and

   (ii) specialty air services;

(c) government procurement; or

(d) subsidies or grants provided by a Party, including government-supported loans, guarantees, and insurance.

5. This Chapter does not impose any obligation on a Party with respect to a national of the other Party seeking access to its employment market, or employed on a permanent basis in its territory, and does not confer any right on that national with respect to that access or employment.

6. This Chapter does not apply to services supplied in the exercise of governmental authority within the territory of each respective Party.

ARTICLE 11.2: NATIONAL TREATMENT

1. Each Party shall accord to service suppliers of the other Party treatment no less favorable than that it accords, in like circumstances, to its own service suppliers.

2. The treatment to be accorded by a Party under paragraph 1 means, with respect to a regional level of government, treatment no less favorable than the most favourable treatment accorded, in like circumstances, by that regional level of government to service suppliers of the Party of which it forms a part.

ARTICLE 11.3: MOST-FAVORED-NATION TREATMENT

Each Party shall accord to service suppliers of the other Party treatment no less favourable than that it accords, in like circumstances, to service suppliers of a non-Party.

ARTICLE 11.4: MARKET ACCESS

1. Neither Party may adopt or maintain, either on the basis of a regional subdivision or on the basis of its entire territory, measures that:

(a) impose limitations on:

   (i) the number of service suppliers whether in the form of numerical quotas, monopolies, exclusive service suppliers, or the requirement of an economic needs test;

   (ii) the total value of service transactions or assets in the form of numerical quotas or the requirement of an economic needs test;

      (iii)   the total number of service operations or on the total quantity of services output expressed in terms of designated numerical units in the form of quotas or the requirement of an economic needs test;[2] or

      (iv)   the total number of natural persons that may be employed in a particular service sector or that a service supplier may employ and who are necessary for, and directly related to, the supply of a specific service in the form of numerical quotas or the requirement of an economic needs test; or

    (b)   restrict or require specific types of legal entity or joint venture through which a service supplier may supply a service.

ARTICLE 11.5: LOCAL PRESENCE

Neither Party may require a service supplier of the other Party to establish or maintain a representative office or any form of enterprise, or to be resident, in its territory as a condition for the cross-border supply of a service.

ARTICLE 11.6: NON-CONFORMING MEASURES

1.   Articles 11.2, 11.3, 11.4, and 11.5 do not apply to:

    (a)   any existing non-conforming measure that is maintained by a Party at:

      (i)   the central level of government, as set out by that Party in its Schedule to Annex I;

      (ii)   a regional level of government, as set out by that Party in its Schedule to Annex I; or

      (iii)   a local level of government;

    (b)   the continuation or prompt renewal of any non-conforming measure referred to in subparagraph (a); or

    (c)   an amendment to any non-conforming measure referred to in subparagraph (a) to the extent that the amendment does not decrease the conformity of the measure, as it existed immediately before the amendment, with Articles 11.2, 11.3, 11.4, or 11.5.

2.   Articles 11.2, 11.3, 11.4, and 11.5 do not apply to any measure that a Party adopts or maintains with respect to sectors, sub-sectors, or activities set out in its Schedule to Annex II.

3.   Annex 11-A sets out specific commitments by the Parties.

---

[2]   This paragraph does not cover measures of a Party that limit inputs for the supply of services.

ARTICLE 11.7: DOMESTIC REGULATION

1.   Where a Party requires authorization for the supply of a service, the Party's competent authorities shall, within a reasonable period after the submission of an application considered complete under its laws and regulations, inform the applicant of the decision concerning the application. At the request of the applicant, the competent authorities of the Party shall provide, without undue delay, information concerning the status of the application. This obligation shall not apply to authorization requirements that are within the scope of Article 11.6.2.

2.   With a view to ensuring that measures relating to qualification requirements and procedures, technical standards, and licensing requirements do not constitute unnecessary barriers to trade in services, each Party shall endeavor to ensure, as appropriate for individual sectors, that such measures are:

(a)   based on objective and transparent criteria, such as competence and the ability to supply the service;

(b)   not more burdensome than necessary to ensure the quality of the service; and

(c)   in the case of licensing procedures, not in themselves a restriction on the supply of the service.

3.   If the results of the negotiations related to Article VI:4 of GATS (or the results of any similar negotiations undertaken in other multilateral fora in which both Parties participate) enter into effect, this Article shall be amended, as appropriate, after consultations between the Parties, to bring those results into effect under this Agreement.

The Parties agree to coordinate on such negotiations, as appropriate.

ARTICLE 11.8: TRANSPARENCY IN DEVELOPMENT AND APPLICATION OF REGULATIONS

Further to Chapter Eighteen (Transparency):

1.   Each Party shall establish or maintain appropriate mechanisms for responding to inquiries from interested persons regarding its regulations relating to the subject matter of this Chapter.[34]

2.   If a Party does not provide advance notice of and opportunity for comment on proposed regulations relating to the subject matter of this Chapter pursuant to Article 18.1.2 (Publication), it shall, to the extent possible, address in writing the reasons therefore.

3.   At the time it adopts final regulations relating to the subject matter of this Chapter, a Party shall, to the extent possible, including on request, address in writing substantive comments received from interested persons with respect to the proposed regulations.

---

[3] For greater certainty, such regulations include regulations establishing or applying to licensing authorization or criteria.

[4] Morocco's implementation of its obligation to establish appropriate mechanisms for small administrative agencies may need to take into account resource and budget constraints.

4.   To the extent possible, each Party shall allow reasonable time between publication of final regulations relating to the subject matter of this Chapter and their effective date.

ARTICLE 11.9: MUTUAL RECOGNITION

1.   For the purposes of the fulfillment, in whole or in part, of its standards or criteria for the authorization, licensing, or certification of services suppliers, and subject to the requirements of paragraph 4, a Party may recognize the education or experience obtained, requirements met, or licenses or certifications granted in a particular country, including the other Party and non-Parties. Such recognition, which may be achieved through harmonization or otherwise, may be based on an agreement or arrangement with the country concerned or may be accorded autonomously.

2.   Where a Party recognizes, autonomously or by agreement or arrangement, the education or experience obtained, requirements met, or licenses or certifications granted in the territory of a non-Party, nothing in Article 11.3 shall be construed to require the Party to accord such recognition to the education or experience obtained, requirements met, or licenses or certifications granted in the territory of the other Party.

3.   A Party that is a party to an agreement or arrangement of the type referred to in paragraph 1, whether existing or future, shall afford adequate opportunity for the other Party, if the other Party is interested, to negotiate its accession to such an agreement or arrangement or to negotiate a comparable one with it. Where a Party accords recognition autonomously, it shall afford adequate opportunity for the other Party to demonstrate that education, experience, licenses, or certifications obtained or requirements met in that other Party's territory should be recognized.

4.   Neither Party may accord recognition in a manner that would constitute a means of discrimination between countries in the application of its standards or criteria for the authorization, licensing, or certification of services suppliers, or a disguised restriction on trade in services.

5.   Annex 11-B applies to measures adopted or maintained by a Party relating to the licensing or certification of professional service suppliers as set out in that Annex.

ARTICLE 11.10: TRANSFERS AND PAYMENTS

1.   Each Party shall permit all transfers and payments relating to the cross-border supply of services to be made freely and without delay into and out of its territory.

2.   Each Party shall permit such transfers and payments relating to the cross-border supply of services to be made in a freely usable currency at the market rate of exchange prevailing at the time of transfer.

3.   Notwithstanding paragraphs 1 and 2, a Party may prevent a transfer or payment through the equitable, non-discriminatory, and good faith application of its laws relating to:

(a)   bankruptcy, insolvency, or the protection of the rights of creditors;

(b)   issuing, trading, or dealing in securities, futures, options, or derivatives;

(c) financial reporting or record keeping of transfers, when necessary to assist law enforcement or financial regulatory authorities;

(d) criminal or penal offenses; or

(e) ensuring compliance with orders or judgments in judicial or administrative proceedings.

ARTICLE 11.11: DENIAL OF BENEFITS

1. A Party may deny the benefits of this Chapter to a service supplier of the other Party if the service is being supplied by an enterprise owned or controlled by persons of a non-Party, and the denying Party:

(a) does not maintain diplomatic relations with the non-Party, or

(b) adopts or maintains measures with respect to the non-Party or a person of the non-Party that prohibit transactions with the enterprise or that would be violated or circumvented if the benefits of this Chapter were accorded to the enterprise.

2. A Party may deny the benefits of this Chapter to a service supplier of the other Party if the service is being supplied by an enterprise that has no substantial business activities in the territory of the other Party and the enterprise is owned or controlled by persons of a non-Party or of the denying Party.

ARTICLE 11.12: IMPLEMENTATION

The Parties shall meet annually, and as otherwise agreed, on any issues of mutual interest arising from the implementation of this Chapter.

ARTICLE 11.13: DEFINITIONS

For purposes of this Chapter:

cross-border trade in services or cross-border supply of services means the supply of a service:

(a) from the territory of one Party into the territory of the other Party;

(b) in the territory of one Party by a person of that Party to a person of the other Party; or

(c) by a national of a Party in the territory of the other Party;

but does not include the supply of a service in the territory of a Party by a covered investment;

enterprise means an enterprise as defined in Article 1.3 (Definitions), and a branch of an enterprise;

enterprise of a Party means an enterprise constituted or organized under the law of a Party, and a branch located in the territory of a Party and carrying out business activities there;

professional services means services, the supply of which requires specialized postsecondary education, or equivalent training or experience, and for which the right to practice is granted or restricted by a Party, but does not include services supplied by trades-persons or vessel and aircraft crew members;

service supplied in the exercise of governmental authority means any service that is supplied neither on a commercial basis, nor in competition with one or more service suppliers;

service supplier of a Party means a person of that Party that seeks to supply or supplies a service;[5] and

specialty air services means any non-transportation air services, such as aerial firefighting, sightseeing, spraying, surveying, mapping, photography, parachute jumping, glider towing, and helicopter-lift for logging and construction, and other airborne agricultural, industrial, and inspection services.

ANNEX 11-A
EXPRESS DELIVERY SERVICES

1.   The Parties affirm that measures affecting express delivery services are subject to the provisions of this Agreement.

2.   For purposes of this Agreement, express delivery services means the collection, transport, and delivery of documents, printed matter, parcels, goods, or other items on an expedited basis, while tracking and maintaining control of these items throughout the supply of the service. Express delivery services do not include (1) air transport services, (2) services supplied in the exercise of governmental authority, or (3) maritime transport services.

3.   The Parties express their desire to maintain at least the level of market openness for express delivery services they provide on the date of signature of this Agreement.

4.   Morocco shall not adopt any new restriction on the supply of express delivery services after the date of signature of this Agreement.

5.   International express delivery services, and domestic express delivery services for letters and other materials in excess of one kilogram, are not within the scope of Morocco's postal monopoly. Morocco confirms that it does not intend to direct revenues from its postal monopoly to benefit these services.

---

[5] The Parties understand that for the purposes of Articles 11.2 and 11.3, "service suppliers" has the same meaning as "services and service suppliers" as used in Articles II and XVII of GATS.

ANNEX 11-B
PROFESSIONAL SERVICES

DEVELOPMENT OF PROFESSIONAL STANDARDS

1.   The Parties shall encourage the relevant bodies in their respective territories to develop mutually acceptable standards and criteria for licensing and certification of professional service suppliers and to provide recommendations on mutual recognition to the Joint Committee.

2.   The standards and criteria referred to in paragraph 1 may be developed with regard to the following matters:

      (a)   education – accreditation of schools or academic programs;

      (b)   examinations – qualifying examinations for licensing;

      (c)   experience – length and nature of experience required for licensing;

      (d)   conduct and ethics – standards of professional conduct and the nature of disciplinary action for non-conformity with those standards;

      (e)   professional development and re-certification – continuing education and ongoing requirements to maintain professional certification;

      (f)   scope of practice – extent of, or limitations on, permissible activities;

      (g)   local knowledge – requirements for knowledge of such matters as local laws, regulations, language, geography, or climate; and

      (h)   consumer protection – including alternatives to residency requirements, such as bonding, professional liability insurance, and client restitution funds, to provide for the protection of consumers.

3.   On receipt of a recommendation referred to in paragraph 1, the Joint Committee shall review the recommendation within a reasonable period to determine whether it is consistent with this Agreement. Based on the Joint Committee's review, each Party shall encourage its respective competent authorities, where appropriate, to implement the recommendation within a mutually agreed time.

Temporary Licensing

4.   Where the Parties agree, each Party shall encourage the relevant bodies in its territory to develop procedures for the temporary licensing of professional service suppliers of the other Party.

Review

5.   At least once every three years, or annually at either Party's request, the Joint Committee shall review the implementation of this Annex.

CHAPTER TWELVE
FINANCIAL SERVICES

ARTICLE 12.1: SCOPE AND COVERAGE

1.   This Chapter applies to measures adopted or maintained by a Party relating to:

    (a)   financial institutions of the other Party;

    (b)   investors of the other Party, and investments of such investors, in financial institutions in the Party's territory; and

    (c)   cross-border trade in financial services.

2.   Chapters Ten (Investment) and Eleven (Cross-Border Trade in Services) apply to measures described in paragraph 1 only to the extent that such Chapters or Articles of such Chapters are incorporated into this Chapter.

    (a)   Articles 10.6 (Expropriation and Compensation), 10.7 (Transfers), 10.10 (Investment and Environment), 10.11 (Denial of Benefits), 10.13 (Special Formalities and Information Requirements), and 11.11 (Denial of Benefits) are hereby incorporated into and made a part of this Chapter.

    (b)   Section B of Chapter Ten (Investor-State Dispute Settlement) is hereby incorporated into and made a part of this Chapter solely for claims that a Party has breached Articles 10.6 (Expropriation and Compensation), 10.7 (Transfers), 10.11 (Denial of Benefits), or 10.13 (Special Formalities and Information Requirements), as incorporated into this Chapter.

    (c)   Article 11.10 (Transfers and Payments) is incorporated into and made a part of this Chapter to the extent that cross-border trade in financial services is subject to obligations pursuant to Article 12.5.

3.   This Chapter does not apply to measures adopted or maintained by a Party relating to:

    (a)   activities or services forming part of a public retirement plan or statutory system of social security; or

    (b)   activities or services conducted for the account or with the guarantee or using the financial resources of the Party, including its public entities, except that this Chapter shall apply if a Party allows any of the activities or services referred to in subparagraphs (a) or (b) to be conducted by its financial institutions in competition with a public entity or a financial institution.

ARTICLE 12.2: NATIONAL TREATMENT

1.   Each Party shall accord to investors of the other Party treatment no less favourable than that it accords to its own investors, in like circumstances, with respect to the establishment, acquisition, expansion, management, conduct, operation, and sale or other disposition of financial institutions and investments in financial institutions in its territory.

2.   Each Party shall accord to financial institutions of the other Party and to investments of investors of the other Party in financial institutions treatment no less favorable than that it accords to its own financial institutions, and to investments of its own investors in financial institutions, in like circumstances, with respect to the establishment, acquisition, expansion, management, conduct, operation, and sale or other disposition of financial institutions and investments.

3.   For purposes of the national treatment obligations in Article 12.5.1, a Party shall accord to cross-border financial service suppliers of the other Party treatment no less favorable than that it accords to its own financial service suppliers, in like circumstances, with respect to the supply of the relevant service.

ARTICLE 12.3: MOST-FAVORED-NATION TREATMENT

1.   Each Party shall accord to investors of the other Party, financial institutions of the other Party, investments of investors in financial institutions, and cross-border financial service suppliers of the other Party treatment no less favorable than that it accords to the investors, financial institutions, investments of investors in financial institutions, and cross-border financial service suppliers of a non-Party, in like circumstances.

2.   A Party may recognize prudential measures of a non-Party in the application of measures covered by this Chapter. Such recognition may be:

(a)   accorded unilaterally;

(b)   achieved through harmonization or other means; or

(c)   based upon an agreement or arrangement with the non-Party.

3.   A Party according recognition of prudential measures under paragraph 2 shall provide adequate opportunity to the other Party to demonstrate that circumstances exist in which there are or would be equivalent regulation, oversight, implementation of regulation, and, if appropriate, procedures concerning the sharing of information between the Parties.

4.   Where a Party accords recognition of prudential measures under paragraph 2(c) and the circumstances set out in paragraph 3 exist, the Party shall provide adequate opportunity to the other Party to negotiate accession to the agreement or arrangement, or to negotiate a comparable agreement or arrangement.

ARTICLE 12.4: MARKET ACCESS FOR FINANCIAL INSTITUTIONS

Neither Party may adopt or maintain, with respect to financial institutions of the other Party or investors of the other Party in such institutions, either on the basis of a regional subdivision or on the basis of its entire territory, measures that:

(a)   impose limitations on

(i)   the number of financial institutions whether in the form of numerical quotas, monopolies, exclusive service suppliers, or the requirement of an economic needs test;

    (ii)   the total value of financial service transactions or assets in the form of numerical quotas or the requirement of an economic needs test;

    (iii)   the total number of financial service operations or on the total quantity of financial services output expressed in terms of designated numerical units in the form of quotas or the requirement of an economic needs test;[1] or

    (iv)   the total number of natural persons that may be employed in a particular financial service sector or that a financial institution may employ and who are necessary for, and directly related to, the supply of a specific financial service in the form of numerical quotas or the requirement of an economic needs test; or

(b)   restrict or require specific types of legal entity or joint venture through which a financial institution may supply a service.

ARTICLE 12.5: CROSS-BORDER TRADE

1.   Each Party shall permit, under terms and conditions that accord national treatment, cross-border financial service suppliers of the other Party to supply the services specified in Annex 12-A.

2.   Each Party shall permit persons located in its territory, and its nationals wherever located, to purchase financial services from cross-border financial service suppliers of the other Party located in the territory of the other Party. This obligation does not require a Party to permit such suppliers to do business or solicit in its territory. Each Party may define "doing business" and "solicitation" for purposes of this obligation, provided that those definitions are not inconsistent with paragraph 1.

3.   Without prejudice to other means of prudential regulation of cross-border trade in financial services, a Party may require the registration of cross-border financial service suppliers of the other Party and of financial instruments.

ARTICLE 12.6: NEW FINANCIAL SERVICES[2]

1.   Each Party shall permit a financial institution of the other Party, on request or notification to the relevant regulator, where required, to supply any new financial service that the Party would permit its own financial institutions, in like circumstances, to supply under its domestic law, provided that the introduction of the new financial service does not require the Party to adopt a new law or modify an existing law.

2.   A Party may determine the institutional and juridical form through which the new financial service may be supplied and may require authorization for the supply of the service. Where a Party would permit the new financial service and authorization is required, the decision

---

[1] This clause does not cover measures of a Party that limit inputs for the supply of financial services.

[2] The Parties understand that nothing in Article 12.6 prevents a financial institution of a Party from applying to the other Party to consider authorizing the supply of a financial service that is supplied in neither Party's territory. Such application shall be subject to the law of the Party to which the application is made and, for greater certainty, shall not be subject to the obligations of Article 12.6.

shall be made within a reasonable time and authorization may only be refused for prudential reasons.

ARTICLE 12.7: TREATMENT OF CERTAIN INFORMATION

Article 21.5 (Disclosure of Information) does not apply to this Chapter. Nothing in this Chapter shall be construed to require a Party to furnish or allow access to:

(a)   information related to the financial affairs and accounts of individual customers of financial institutions or cross-border financial service suppliers; or

(b)   any confidential information the disclosure of which would impede law enforcement or otherwise be contrary to the public interest or prejudice legitimate commercial interests of particular enterprises.

ARTICLE 12.8: SENIOR MANAGEMENT AND BOARDS OF DIRECTORS

1.   Neither Party may require financial institutions of the other Party to engage individuals of any particular nationality as senior managerial or other essential personnel.

2.   Neither Party may require that more than a minority of the board of directors of a financial institution of the other Party be composed of nationals of the Party, persons residing in the territory of the Party, or a combination thereof.

ARTICLE 12.9: NON-CONFORMING MEASURES

1.   Articles 12.2 through 12.5 and 12.8 do not apply to:

(a)   any existing non-conforming measure that is maintained by a Party at:

   (i)   the central level of government, as set out by that Party in Section A of its Schedule to Annex III;

   (ii)   a regional level of government, as set out by that Party in Section A of its Schedule to Annex III; or

   (iii)   a local level of government;

(b)   the continuation or prompt renewal of any non-conforming measure referred to in subparagraph (a); or

(c)   an amendment to any non-conforming measure referred to in subparagraph (a) to the extent that the amendment does not decrease the conformity of the measure, as it existed immediately before the amendment, with Articles 12.2, 12.3, 12.4, or 12.8.

2.   Articles 12.2 through 12.5 and 12.8 do not apply to any measure that a Party adopts or maintains with respect to sectors, subsectors, or activities set out in Section B of its Schedule to Annex III.

3.   Annex 12-B sets out certain specific commitments by each Party.

4.   A non-conforming measure set out in a Party's Schedule to Annex I or II as a measure to which Article 10.3 (National Treatment), 10.4 (Most-Favored-Nation Treatment), 11.2 (National Treatment), 11.3 (Most-Favored-Nation Treatment), or 11.4 (Market Access) does not apply shall be treated as a non-conforming measure to which Article 12.2, Article 12.3, or Article 12.4, as the case may be, does not apply, to the extent that the measure, sector, sub-sector, or activity set out in the Schedule of nonconforming measures is covered by this Chapter.

ARTICLE 12.10: EXCEPTIONS

1.   Notwithstanding any other provision of this Chapter or Chapters Ten (Investment), Thirteen (Telecommunications), or Fourteen (Electronic Commerce), including specifically Article 13.16 (Telecommunications, Relationship to Other Chapters), and Article 11.1 (Scope and Coverage) with respect to the supply of financial services in the territory of a Party by a covered investment, neither Party shall be prevented from adopting or maintaining measures for prudential reasons,[3] including for the protection of investors, depositors, policy holders, or persons to whom a fiduciary duty is owed by a financial institution or cross-border financial service supplier, or to ensure the integrity and stability of the financial system. Where such measures do not conform with the provisions of this Agreement referred to in this paragraph, they shall not be used as a means of avoiding the Party's commitments or obligations under such provisions.

2.   Nothing in this Chapter or Chapters Ten (Investment), Thirteen (Telecommunications), or Fourteen (Electronic Commerce), including specifically Article 13.16 (Telecommunications, Relationship to Other Chapters), and Article 11.1 (Scope and Coverage) with respect to the supply of financial services in the territory of a Party by a covered investment applies to non-discriminatory measures of general application taken by any public entity in pursuit of monetary and related credit policies or exchange rate policies. This paragraph shall not affect a Party's obligations under Article 10.8 (Performance Requirements) with respect to measures covered by Chapter Ten (Investment), or under Article 10.7 (Transfers) or Article 11.10 (Transfers and Payments).

3.   Notwithstanding Articles 10.7 (Transfers) and 11.10 (Transfers and Payments), as incorporated into this Chapter, a Party may prevent or limit transfers by a financial institution or cross-border financial service supplier to, or for the benefit of, an affiliate of or person related to such institution or supplier, through the equitable, nondiscriminatory, and good faith application of measures relating to maintenance of the safety, soundness, integrity, or financial responsibility of financial institutions or crossborder financial service suppliers. This paragraph does not prejudice any other provision of this Agreement that permits a Party to restrict transfers.

4.   For greater certainty, nothing in this Chapter shall be construed to prevent the adoption or enforcement by a Party of measures necessary to secure compliance with laws or regulations that are not inconsistent with this Chapter, including those relating to the prevention of deceptive and fraudulent practices or to deal with the effects of a default on financial services contracts, subject to the requirement that such measures are not applied in a manner that would constitute a means of arbitrary or unjustifiable discrimination between countries where like conditions prevail, or a

---

[3] It is understood that the term "prudential reasons" includes the maintenance of the safety, soundness, integrity, or financial responsibility of individual financial institutions or cross-border financial service suppliers.

disguised restrictionon investment in financial institutions or cross-border trade in financial services, as covered by this Chapter.

ARTICLE 12.11: TRANSPARENCY

1.   The Parties recognize that transparent regulations and policies governing the activities of financial institutions and cross-border financial service suppliers are important in facilitating access of foreign financial institutions and foreign cross-border financial service suppliers to, and their operations in, each other's market. Each Party commits to promote regulatory transparency in financial services.

2.   In lieu of Article 18.1.2 (Publication), each Party shall, to the extent practicable, (a) publish in advance any regulations of general application relating to the subject matter of this Chapter that it proposes to adopt; and (b) provide interested persons and the other Party a reasonable opportunity to comment on such proposed regulations.

3.   At the time it adopts final regulations of general application relating to the subject matter of this Chapter, each Party should, to the extent practicable, address in writing substantive comments received from interested persons with respect to the proposed regulations.

4.   To the extent practicable, each Party should allow reasonable time between publication of such final regulations and their effective date.

5.   Each Party shall ensure that the rules of general application adopted or maintained by self-regulatory organizations of the Party are promptly published or otherwise made available in such a manner as to enable interested persons to become acquainted with them.

6.   Each Party shall maintain or establish appropriate mechanisms for responding to inquiries from interested persons regarding measures of general application relating to the subject matter of this Chapter.

7.   Each Party's regulatory authorities shall make available to interested persons the requirements, including any documentation required, for completing applications relating to the supply of financial services.

8.   On the request of an applicant, a Party's regulatory authority shall inform the applicant of the status of its application. If the authority requires additional information from the applicant, it shall notify the applicant without undue delay.

9.   A Party's regulatory authority shall make an administrative decision on a completed application of an investor in a financial institution, a financial institution, or a cross-border financial service supplier of the other Party relating to the supply of a financial service within 120 days, and shall promptly notify the applicant of the decision.

An application shall not be considered complete until all relevant hearings are held andall necessary information is received. Where it is not practicable for a decision to be made within 120 days, the regulatory authority shall notify the applicant without unduedelay and shall endeavor to make the decision within a reasonable time thereafter.

ARTICLE 12.12: SELF-REGULATORY ORGANIZATIONS

Where a Party requires a financial institution or a cross-border financial service supplier of the other Party to be a member of, participate in, or have access to, a self-regulatory organization to provide a financial service in or into its territory, the Party shall ensure observance of the obligations of Articles 12.2 and 12.3 by such self-regulatory organization.

ARTICLE 12.13: PAYMENT AND CLEARING SYSTEMS

Under terms and conditions that accord national treatment, each Party shall grant financial institutions of the other Party access to payment and clearing systems operated by public entities, and to official funding and refinancing facilities available in the normal course of ordinary business. This paragraph is not intended to confer access to the Party's lender of last resort facilities.

ARTICLE 12.14: DOMESTIC REGULATION

Each Party shall ensure that all measures of general application to which this Chapter applies are administered in a reasonable, objective, and impartial manner.

ARTICLE 12.15: EXPEDITED AVAILABILITY OF INSURANCE SERVICES

The Parties recognize the importance of maintaining and developing regulatory procedures to expedite the offering of insurance services by licensed suppliers.

ARTICLE 12.16: CONSULTATIONS

1.	A Party may request consultations with the other Party regarding any matter arising under this Agreement that affects financial services. The other Party shall give sympathetic consideration to the request. The Parties shall report the results of their consultations to the Subcommittee on Financial Services.

2.	Consultations under this Article shall include officials of the authorities specified in Annex 12-D.

3.	Nothing in this Article shall be construed to require regulatory authorities participating in consultations under paragraph 1 to disclose information or take any action that would interfere with specific regulatory, supervisory, administrative, or enforcement matters.

4.	Nothing in this Article shall be construed to require a Party to derogate from its relevant law regarding sharing of information among financial regulators or the requirements of an agreement or arrangement between financial authorities of the Parties.

ARTICLE 12.17: DISPUTE SETTLEMENT

1.	Chapter Twenty (Dispute Settlement) applies as modified by this Article to the settlement of disputes arising under this Chapter.

2.   When a Party claims that a dispute arises under this Chapter, Article 20.7 (Establishment of Panel) shall apply, except that, unless the Parties agree otherwise, the panel shall be composed entirely of individuals meeting the qualifications in paragraph 3.

3.   Financial services panelists shall:

(a)   have expertise or experience in financial services law or practice, which may include the regulation of financial institutions;

(b)   be chosen strictly on the basis of objectivity, reliability, and sound judgment; and

(c)   meet the qualifications set out in Article 20.7.5(b) and (c) (Establishment of Panel).

4.   Notwithstanding Article 20.11 (Non-Implementation), where a panel finds a measure to be inconsistent with this Agreement and the measure under dispute affects:

(a)   only the financial services sector, the complaining Party may suspend benefits only in the financial services sector;

(b)   the financial services sector and any other sector, the complaining Party may suspend benefits in the financial services sector that have an effect equivalent to the effect of the measure in the Party's financial services sector; or

(c)   only a sector other than the financial services sector, the complaining Party may not suspend benefits in the financial services sector.

ARTICLE 12.18: INVESTOR-STATE DISPUTE SETTLEMENT IN FINANCIAL SERVICES

1.   Where an investor of a Party submits a claim under Section B of Chapter Ten (Investor-State Dispute Settlement) against the other Party and the respondent invokes Article 12.10 (Exceptions), on request of the respondent, the tribunal shall refer the matter in writing to the Subcommittee on Financial Services for a decision. The tribunal may not proceed pending receipt of a decision or report under this Article.

2.   In a referral pursuant to paragraph 1, the Subcommittee on Financial Services shall decide the issue of whether and to what extent Article 12.10 (Exceptions) is a valid defense to the claim of the investor. The Subcommittee shall transmit a copy of its decision to the tribunal and to the Joint Committee. The decision shall be binding on the tribunal.

3.   Where the Subcommittee on Financial Services has not decided the issue within 60 days of the receipt of the referral under paragraph 1, the respondent or the Party of the claimant may refer the issue to a panel under Chapter Twenty (Dispute Settlement). The panel shall be constituted in accordance with Article 12.17. The panel shall transmit its final report to the Subcommittee and to the tribunal. The report shall be binding on the tribunal.

4.   Where the issue has not been referred to a panel pursuant to paragraph 3 within 10 days of the expiration of the 60-day period referred to in paragraph 3, the tribunal may proceed to decide the matter.

5.   For purposes of this Article, tribunal means a tribunal established pursuant to Section B of Chapter Ten (Investor-State Dispute Settlement).

ARTICLE 12.19: DEFINITIONS

For purposes of this Chapter:

cross-border financial service supplier of a Party means a person of a Party that is engaged in the business of supplying a financial service within the territory of the Party and that seeks to supply or supplies a financial service through the cross-border supply of such services;

cross-border trade in financial services or cross-border supply of financial services means the supply of a financial service:

(a)   from the territory of one Party into the territory of the other Party,

(b)   in the territory of one Party by a person of that Party to a person of the other Party, or

(c)   by a national of one Party in the territory of the other Party,

but does not include the supply of a financial service in the territory of a Party by an investment in that territory;

financial institution means any financial intermediary or other enterprise that is authorized to do business and regulated or supervised as a financial institution under the law of the Party in whose territory it is located;

financial institution of the other Party means a financial institution, including a branch, located in the territory of a Party that is controlled by persons of the other Party;

financial service means any service of a financial nature. Financial services include all insurance and insurance-related services, and all banking and other financial services (excluding insurance), as well as services incidental or auxiliary to a service of a financial nature. Financial services include the following activities:

Insurance and insurance-related services

(a)   Direct insurance (including co-insurance):

(i)   life,
(ii)   non-life;

(b)   Reinsurance and retrocession;

(c)   Insurance intermediation, such as brokerage and agency; and

(d)   Services auxiliary to insurance, such as consultancy, actuarial, risk assessment, and claim settlement services.

Banking and other financial services (excluding insurance)

    (e)   Acceptance of deposits and other repayable funds from the public;

    (f)   Lending of all types, including consumer credit, mortgage credit, factoring, and financing of commercial transactions;

    (g)   Financial leasing;

    (h)   All payment and money transmission services, including credit, charge and debit cards, travelers checks, and bankers drafts;

    (i)   Guarantees and commitments;

    (j)   Trading for own account or for account of customers, whether on an exchange, in an over-the-counter market or otherwise, the following:

        (i)   money market instruments (including checks, bills, certificates of deposits);

        (ii)   foreign exchange;

        (iii)   derivative products including, but not limited to, futures and options;

        (iv)   exchange rate and interest rate instruments, including products such as swaps, forward rate agreements;

        (v)   transferable securities;

        (vi)   other negotiable instruments and financial assets, including bullion;

    (k)   Participation in issues of all kinds of securities, including underwriting and placement as agent (whether publicly or privately) and provision of services related to such issues;

    (l)   Money broking;

    (m)   Asset management, such as cash or portfolio management, all forms of collective investment management, pension fund management, custodial, depository, and trust services;

    (n)   Settlement and clearing services for financial assets, including securities, derivative products, and other negotiable instruments;

    (o)   Provision and transfer of financial information, and financial data processing and related software by suppliers of other financial services;

    (p)   Advisory, intermediation, and other auxiliary financial services on all the activities listed in subparagraphs (e) through (o), including credit reference and analysis, investment and portfolio research and advice, advice on acquisitions and on corporate restructuring and strategy;

financial service supplier of a Party means a person of a Party that is engaged in the business of supplying a financial service within the territory of that Party;

investment means "investment" as defined in Article 10.27 (Definitions), except that, with respect to "loans" and "debt instruments" referred to in that Article:

(a)   a loan to or debt instrument issued by a financial institution is an investment only where it is treated as regulatory capital by the Party in whose territory the financial institution is located; and

(b)   a loan granted by or debt instrument owned by a financial institution, other than a loan to or debt instrument of a financial institution referred to in subparagraph (a), is not an investment;

For greater certainty, a loan granted by or debt instrument owned by a cross-border financial service supplier, other than a loan to or debt instrument issued by a financial institution, is an investment if such loan or debt instrument meets the criteria for investments set out in Article 10.27 (Definitions);

investor of a Party means a Party or state enterprise thereof, or a person of a Party, that concretely attempts to make, is making, or has made an investment in the territory of the other Party; provided, however, that a natural person who is a dual national shall be deemed to be exclusively a national of the State of his or her dominant and effective nationality;

new financial service means a financial service not supplied in the Party's territory that is supplied within the territory of the other Party, and includes any new form of delivery of a financial service or the sale of a financial product that is not sold in the Party's territory;

person of a Party means "person of a Party" as defined in Article 1.3 (Definitions) and, for greater certainty, does not include a branch of an enterprise of a non-Party;

public entity means a central bank or monetary authority of a Party, or any financial institution owned or controlled by a Party; and

self-regulatory organization means any non-governmental body, including any securities or futures exchange or market, clearing agency, or other organization or association, that exercises its own or delegated regulatory or supervisory authority over financial service suppliers or financial institutions.

ANNEX 12-A
CROSS-BORDER TRADE

Insurance and insurance-related services

1.   For the United States, Article 12.5.1 applies to the cross-border supply of or trade in financial services as defined in subparagraph (a) of the definition of cross-border supply of financial services in Article 12.19 with respect to:

  (a)   insurance of risks relating to:

  (i)   maritime shipping and commercial aviation and space launching and freight (including satellites), with such insurance to cover any or all of the following: the goods being transported, the vehicle transporting the goods, and any liability arising therefrom; and

  (ii)   goods in international transit;

  (b)   reinsurance and retrocession, services auxiliary to insurance as referred to in subparagraph (d) of the definition of financial service, and insurance intermediation such as brokerage and agency as referred to in subparagraph

  (c)   of the definition of financial service.

2.   For the United States, Article 12.5.1 applies to the cross-border supply of or trade in financial services as defined in paragraph (c) of the definition of cross-border supply of financial services in Article 12.19 with respect to insurance services.

3.   For Morocco, Article 12.5.1 applies to the cross-border supply of or trade in financial services as defined in subparagraph (a) of the definition of cross-border supply of financial services in Article 12.19:

  (a)   with respect to insurance of risks relating to:

  (i)   maritime shipping and commercial aviation and space launching and freight (including satellites), with such insurance to cover any or all of the following: the goods being transported, the vehicle transporting the goods, and any liability arising therefrom;

  (ii)   goods in international transit; and

  (iii)   brokerage of insurance described in clauses (i) and (ii);

  no later than two years after the date of entry into force of this Agreement; and

  (b)   with respect to reinsurance and retrocession and brokerage of reinsurance, upon entry into force of this Agreement.

4.   For Morocco, Article 12.5.1 applies to the cross-border supply of or trade in financial services as defined in paragraph (c) of the definition of cross-border supply of financial services in Article 12.19 with respect to insurance services described in paragraph 3 on the dates indicated in paragraph 3.

Banking and other financial services (excluding insurance)

5.   For the United States, Article 12.5.1 applies with respect to the provision and transfer of financial information and financial data processing and related software as referred to in subparagraph (o) of the definition of financial service and advisory and other auxiliary services, excluding intermediation, relating to banking and other financial services as referred to in subparagraph (p) of the definition of financial service.

6.   For Morocco, Article 12.5.1 applies with respect to the provision and transfer of financial information and financial data processing and related software as referred to in subparagraph (o) of the definition of financial service and advisory and other auxiliary services, excluding intermediation and advice on acquisitions and on corporate restructuring and strategy, relating to banking and other financial services as referred to in subparagraph (p) of the definition of financial service.

ANNEX 12-B
SPECIFIC COMMITMENTS

United States – Expedited Availability of Insurance

Recognizing the principles of federalism under the U.S. Constitution, the history of state regulation of insurance in the United States, and the McCarran-Ferguson Act, the United States welcomes the efforts of the National Association of Insurance Commissioners ("NAIC") relating to the availability of insurance services as expressed in the NAIC's "Statement of Intent: The Future of Insurance Regulation," including the initiatives on speed-to-market intentions and regulatory re-engineering (under Part II of the Statement of Intent).

Morocco – Expedited Availability of Insurance

Morocco reaffirms the transparency, rapidity, and efficiency of its procedures regarding introduction and distribution of products issued by insurance companies in its territory.

In particular, Morocco deems any product to be approved unless it is disapproved within 30 days. Morocco imposes no limitations on the number or frequency of product introductions. As part of the work program of the Subcommittee on Financial Services,

Morocco will be open to further discussions of the need for continuing review of products other than those sold to individuals (including life insurance), small- or medium-sized businesses, or compulsory insurance.

Morocco – Future Consultation and Implementing Actions Regarding Non-Insurance Financial Services

To follow up on discussions that took place during the negotiation of this Agreement with respect to non-insurance financial services, Morocco and the United States agree as follows:

1.   Morocco shall begin consultations, in the context of the Subcommittee on Financial Services, and shall consider liberalizing changes with respect to the following two areas:

(a)   Morocco's current requirement that operations of banks incorporated abroad and functioning as branches in Morocco be limited by the amount of capital effectively allocated by those institutions to their operations in Morocco (dotation en capital). Morocco and the United States agree that any liberalizing change to this requirement would apply to new bankbranches established after the change becomes effective and would not apply in the case of the conversion to a branch by a foreign bank operating through a subsidiary in Morocco, where that subsidiary is systemically important.[4] Among possible approaches to liberalizing this requirement, the following two are noted:

(i)   allowing a foreign branch bank to operate based on the capital of its parent company through a multiplying coefficient of the branch's paid-in capital in Morocco, and

(ii)   allowing a foreign branch bank to operate based on the capital of its parent company, up to an amount that would be limited to the average of total capital of the banks operating in Morocco, as calculated at the end of the prior year.

(b)   Morocco's current prohibition on the holding of non-Moroccan securities by Moroccan mutual funds. Morocco and the United States agree that any such change to this prohibition would be implemented at a pace to be determined. Among possible approaches to liberalizing this prohibition, the following two examples are noted:

(i)   Morocco considers that a possible first step would be to permit five percent of the total amount of securities to be invested in non-Moroccan securities; and

(ii)   the United States considers that a possible first step would be to per..... ...... percent of the total amount of securities to be invested in non-Moroccan securities.

2.   Morocco agrees that it will decide, by no later than three years from the date of entry into force of this Agreement, to take action to implement liberalizing changes with respect to one of the above two areas.

---

[4] For example, a bank with assets comprising one percent or less of the total assets of the Moroccan banking sector would not be considered systemically important.

ANNEX 12-C
IMPLEMENTATION OF ARTICLE 12.11

The Parties recognize that Morocco's implementation of the obligations of paragraphs 2, 3, and 4 of Article 12.11 may require changes to its process for issuing regulations.

Morocco shall implement the obligations of paragraphs 2, 3, and 4 of Article 12.11 no later than two years after the date of entry into force of this Agreement. Morocco shall implement Article 12.11.2 within its constitutional framework.

ANNEX 12-D
AUTHORITIES RESPONSIBLE FOR FINANCIAL SERVICES

The authority of each Party responsible for financial services is:

(a)   for Morocco, the Ministry of Finance; and

(b)   for the United States, the Department of the Treasury for banking and other financial services and the Office of the United States Trade Representative, in coordination with the Department of Commerce and other agencies, for insurance services.

CHAPTER THIRTEEN
TELECOMMUNICATIONS

ARTICLE 13.1: SCOPE AND COVERAGE

1.   This Chapter applies to:

(a)   measures relating to access to and use of public telecommunications services;

(b)   measures relating to obligations of suppliers of public telecommunications services, including major suppliers;

(c)   other measures relating to public telecommunications networks or services; and

(d)   measures relating to the provision of value-added services.

2.   Except to ensure that enterprises operating broadcast stations and cable systems have continued access to and use of public telecommunications services, this Chapter does not apply to any measure relating to broadcast or cable distribution of radio or television programming.

3.   Nothing in this Chapter shall be construed to:

(a)   require a Party, or require a Party to compel any enterprise, to establish, construct, acquire, lease, operate, or provide telecommunications networks or services not offered to the public generally;

(b)   require a Party to compel any enterprise exclusively engaged in the broadcast or cable distribution of radio or television programming to make available its broadcast or cable facilities as a public telecommunications network; or

(c)   prevent a Party from adopting or enforcing new or existing telecommunications laws or regulations that are not inconsistent with this Chapter.

ARTICLE 13.2: ACCESS TO AND USE OF PUBLIC TELECOMMUNICATIONS SERVICES

1.   Each Party shall ensure that service suppliers of the other Party have access to and use of any public telecommunications service, including leased circuits, offered in its territory or across its borders, on reasonable and non-discriminatory terms and conditions, including as set out in paragraphs 2 through 6.

2.   Each Party shall ensure that service suppliers of the other Party are permitted to:[1]

(a)   purchase or lease and attach terminal or other equipment that interfaces with a public telecommunications network;

(b)   provide services to individual or multiple end-users over leased circuits;

(c)   connect owned[2] or leased circuits with public telecommunications networks and services in the territory, or across the borders, of that Party or with circuits leased or owned by another service supplier;

(d)   perform switching, signaling, processing, and conversion functions; and

(e)   use operating protocols of their choice in the supply of any service, other than as necessary to ensure the availability of telecommunications transport networks and services to the public generally.

3.   Each Party shall ensure that enterprises of the other Party may use public telecommunications services for the movement of information in its territory or across its borders and for access to information contained in databases or otherwise stored in machine-readable form in the territory of either Party.

4.   Notwithstanding paragraph 3, a Party may take such measures as are necessary to:

(a)   ensure the security and confidentiality of messages, or

(b)   protect the privacy of non-public personal data of subscribers to public telecommunications services, provided that such measures are not applied in a

---

[1] For Morocco, subparagraphs (b) through (e) apply only to service suppliers in its territory classified as suppliers of public telecommunications services or suppliers of value-added services.

[2] In Morocco, only a licensed telecommunications supplier is permitted to own circuits.

manner that would constitute a means of arbitrary or unjustifiable discrimination or disguised restriction on trade in services.

5.   Each Party shall ensure that no condition is imposed on access to and use of public telecommunications transport networks and services, other than as necessary to:

(a)   safeguard the public service responsibilities of suppliers of public telecommunications transport networks and services, in particular their ability to make their networks or services available to the public generally;

(b)   protect the technical integrity of public telecommunications transport networks or services; or

(c)   ensure that service suppliers of the other Party do not supply services unless permitted pursuant to commitments in this Agreement.

6.   Provided that they satisfy the criteria set out in paragraph 5, conditions for access to and use of public telecommunications transport networks and services may include:

(a)   a requirement to use specified technical interfaces, including interface protocols, for interconnection with such networks and services;

(b)   requirements, where necessary, for the inter-operability of such services;

(c)   type approval of terminal or other equipment that interfaces with the network and technical requirements relating to the attachment of such equipment to such networks;

(d)   restrictions on interconnection of private leased or owned circuits with such networks or services or with circuits leased or owned by another service supplier; or

(e)   notification, registration, and licensing.

ARTICLE 13.3: OBLIGATIONS RELATING TO SUPPLIERS OF PUBLIC TELECOMMUNICATIONS SERVICES[3]

Interconnection

1.   (a)   Each Party shall ensure that suppliers of public telecommunications services in its territory provide, directly or indirectly,[4] interconnection with the suppliers of public telecommunications services of the other Party within the same territory.

(b)   In carrying out subparagraph (a), each Party shall ensure that suppliers of public telecommunications services in its territory take reasonable steps to protect the confidentiality of commercially sensitive information of, or relating to, suppliers and end-users of public telecommunications services obtained as a result of

---

[3] This Article is subject to Annex 13-A.
[4] For Morocco, indirect interconnection means through another supplier of public telecommunications services in the same territory.

interconnection arrangements and only use such information for the purpose of providing these services.

Resale

2.   Each Party shall ensure that suppliers of public telecommunications services in its territory do not impose unreasonable or discriminatory conditions or limitations on the resale of these services.[5]

Number Portability

3.   Each Party shall ensure that suppliers of public telecommunications services in its territory provide number portability to the extent technically feasible, and on reasonable terms and conditions.[6]

Dialing Parity

4.   Each Party shall ensure that suppliers of public telecommunications services in its territory provide dialing parity to suppliers of public telecommunications services of the other Party.

ARTICLE 13.4: ADDITIONAL OBLIGATIONS RELATING TO MAJOR SUPPLIERS OF PUBLIC TELECOMMUNICATIONS SERVICES[7]

Treatment by Major Suppliers

1.   Each Party shall ensure that major suppliers in its territory accord suppliers of public telecommunications services of the other Party treatment no less favorable than such major suppliers accord to their subsidiaries, their affiliates, or non-affiliated service suppliers regarding:

(a)   the availability, provisioning, rates, or quality of like public telecommunications services; and

(b)   the availability of technical interfaces necessary for interconnection.

Competitive Safeguards

2.   (a)   Each Party shall maintain appropriate measures for the purpose of preventing suppliers that, alone or together, are a major supplier in its territory from engaging in or continuing anticompetitive practices.

(b)   The anticompetitive practices referred to in subparagraph (a) include in particular:

(i)   engaging in anticompetitive cross-subsidization;

(ii)   using information obtained from competitors with anti-competitive results; and

---

[5] For Morocco, resale is offered on a commercial basis, subject to commercially negotiated terms and conditions.
[6] Paragraph 3 shall apply to Morocco when it implements pending regulations.
[7] This Article is subject to Annex 13-B.

(iii) not making available, on a timely basis, to suppliers of public telecommunications services, technical information about essential facilities and commercially relevant information that are necessary for them to provide services.

Unbundling of Network Elements

3. Each Party shall provide its telecommunications regulatory body the authority to require major suppliers in its territory to offer access to network elements on an unbundled basis on terms and conditions, and at cost-oriented rates, that are reasonable, nondiscriminatory, and transparent for the supply of public telecommunications services.[8]

Interconnection

4. (a) General Terms and Conditions

Each Party shall ensure that major suppliers in its territory provide interconnection for the facilities and equipment of suppliers of public telecommunications services of the other Party:

(i) at any technically feasible point in the major supplier's network;

(ii) under non-discriminatory terms, conditions (including technical standards and specifications), and rates;

(iii) of a quality no less favorable than that provided by such major suppliers for their own like services, for like services of non-affiliated service suppliers, or for their subsidiaries or other affiliates;

(iv) in a timely fashion, on terms, conditions (including technical standards and specifications), and cost-oriented rates that are transparent, reasonable, having regard to economic feasibility, and sufficiently unbundled so that suppliers need not pay for network components or facilities that they do not require for the service to be provided; and

(v) on request, at points in addition to the network termination points offered to the majority of users, subject to charges that reflect the cost of construction of necessary additional facilities.

(b) Options for Interconnecting with Major Suppliers

Each Party shall ensure that suppliers of public telecommunications services of the other Party may interconnect their facilities and equipment with those of major suppliers in its territory pursuant to at least one of the following options:

(i) a reference interconnection offer or another standard interconnection offer containing the rates, terms, and conditions that the major suppliers offer generally to suppliers of public telecommunications services; or

---

[8] Paragraph 3 shall apply to Morocco when it implements pending regulations.

(ii)   the terms and conditions of an existing interconnection agreement or through negotiation of a new interconnection agreement.

(c)   Public Availability of Interconnection Offers

Each Party shall require major suppliers in its territory to make publicly available reference interconnection offers or other standard interconnection offers containing the rates, terms, and conditions that the major suppliers offer generally to suppliers of public telecommunications services.

(d)   Public Availability of Procedures for Interconnection Negotiations

Each Party shall make publicly available the applicable procedures for interconnection negotiations with major suppliers in its territory.

(e)   Public Availability of Interconnection Agreements Concluded with Major Suppliers

(i)   Each Party shall require major suppliers in its territory to file all interconnection agreements to which they are party with its telecommunications regulatory body.[9]

(ii)   Each Party shall make publicly available interconnection agreements in force between major suppliers in its territory and other suppliers of public telecommunications services in its territory.

Provisioning and Pricing of Leased Circuits Services

5.   (a)   Each Party shall ensure that major suppliers in its territory provide enterprises of the other Party leased circuits services that are public telecommunications services on terms and conditions, and at rates, that are reasonable and nondiscriminatory.

(b)   In carrying out subparagraph (a), each Party shall provide its telecommunications regulatory body the authority to require major suppliers in its territory to offer leased circuits services that are public telecommunications services to enterprises of the other Party at capacity-based, cost-oriented prices.

Co-location

6.   (a)   Subject to subparagraphs (b) and (c), each Party shall ensure that major suppliers in its territory provide to suppliers of public telecommunications services of the other Party physical co-location of equipment necessary for interconnection on terms and conditions, and at cost-oriented rates, that are reasonable, nondiscriminatory, and transparent.

(b)   Where physical co-location is not practical for technical reasons or because of space limitations, each Party shall ensure that major suppliers in its territory

---

[9] In the United States, this obligation may be satisfied by requiring filing with a state regulatory authority.

(i)   provide an alternative solution or

(ii)   facilitate virtual co-location,

on terms and conditions, and at cost-oriented rates, that are reasonable, nondiscriminatory, and transparent.

(c)   Each Party may determine through its law or regulations which premises are subject to subparagraphs (a) and (b).

Access to Rights-of-Way

7.   Each Party shall endeavor to ensure that major suppliers in its territory afford access to their poles, ducts, conduits, and rights-of-way to suppliers of public telecommunications services of the other Party on terms and conditions, and at rates, that are reasonable and nondiscriminatory.

ARTICLE 13.5: SUBMARINE CABLE SYSTEMS AND SATELLITE SERVICES

1.   Each Party shall ensure that any enterprise that it authorizes to operate a submarine cable system in its territory as a public telecommunications service accords reasonable and non-discriminatory treatment with respect to access to that system (including landing facilities) to suppliers of public telecommunications services of the other Party.

2.   Each Party shall ensure that any enterprise that it authorizes to provide satellite services in its territory as a public telecommunications service accords reasonable and non-discriminatory treatment with respect to access to those services by suppliers of public telecommunications services of the other Party.

ARTICLE 13.6: CONDITIONS FOR THE SUPPLY OF VALUE-ADDED SERVICES

1.   Neither Party may require an enterprise in its territory that it classifies as a supplier of value-added services and that supplies those services over facilities that it does not own to:

(a)   supply those services to the public generally;

(b)   cost-justify its rates for those services;

(c)   file a tariff for those services;

(d)   interconnect its networks with any particular customer for the supply of those services; or

(e)   conform with any particular standard or technical regulation for interconnection other than for interconnection to a public telecommunications network.

2.   Notwithstanding paragraph 1, a Party may take the actions described in paragraph 1 to remedy a practice of a supplier of value-added services that the Party has found in a particular

case to be anticompetitive under its law or regulations, or to otherwise promote competition or safeguard the interests of consumers.

ARTICLE 13.7: INDEPENDENT REGULATORY BODIES AND PRIVATIZATION

1.   Each Party shall ensure that its telecommunications regulatory body is separate from, and not accountable to, any supplier of public telecommunications services. To this end, each Party shall ensure that its telecommunications regulatory body does not hold a financial interest or maintain an operating role in any such supplier.

2.   Each Party shall ensure that the decisions and procedures of its telecommunications regulatory body are impartial with respect to all interested persons. To this end, each Party shall ensure that any financial interest that it holds in a supplier of public telecommunications services does not influence the decisions and procedures of its telecommunications regulatory body.

3.   Each Party shall maintain the absence of or eliminate as soon as feasible national government ownership in any supplier of public telecommunications services. Where a Party has an ownership interest in a supplier of public telecommunications services and intends to reduce or eliminate its interest, it shall notify the other Party of its intention as soon as possible.

ARTICLE 13.8: UNIVERSAL SERVICE

Each Party shall administer any universal service obligation that it maintains in a transparent, non-discriminatory, and competitively neutral manner and shall ensure that its universal service obligation is not more burdensome than necessary for the kind of universal service that it has defined.

ARTICLE 13.9: LICENSING PROCESS

1.   When a Party requires a supplier of public telecommunications services to have a license, the Party shall make publicly available:

    (a)   all the licensing criteria and procedures it applies;

    (b)   the time it normally requires to reach a decision concerning an application for a license; and

    (c)   the terms and conditions of all licenses it has issued.

2.   Each Party shall ensure that, on request, an applicant receives the reasons for its denial of a license.

ARTICLE 13.10: ALLOCATION AND USE OF SCARCE RESOURCES

1.   Each Party shall administer its procedures for the allocation and use of scarce telecommunications resources, including frequencies, numbers, and rights-of-way, in an objective, timely, transparent, and non-discriminatory manner.

2.   Each Party shall make publicly available the current state of allocated frequency bands but shall not be required to provide detailed identification of frequencies allocated for specific government uses.

3.   Decisions on allocating and assigning spectrum and frequency management are not measures that are per se inconsistent with Article 11.4 (Market Access), which is applied to Chapter Ten (Investment) through Article 11.1.3 (Scope and Coverage). Accordingly, each Party retains the right to exercise its spectrum and frequency management policies, which may affect the number of suppliers of public telecommunications services, provided that this is done in a manner that is consistent with the provisions of this Agreement. The Parties also retain the right to allocate frequency bands taking into account existing and future needs and spectrum availability.

ARTICLE 13.11: ENFORCEMENT

Each Party shall provide its competent authority with the authority to enforce the Party's measures relating to the obligations set out in Articles 13.2 through 13.5. Such authority shall include the ability to impose effective sanctions, which may include financial penalties, injunctive relief (on an interim or final basis), or the modification, suspension, and revocation of licenses.

ARTICLE 13.12: RESOLUTION OF TELECOMMUNICATIONS DISPUTES

Further to Articles 18.3 (Administrative Proceedings) and 18.4 (Review and Appeal), each Party shall ensure the following:

Recourse to Telecommunications Regulatory Bodies

(a)   (i)   Enterprises of the other Party may seek review by a telecommunications regulatory body or other relevant body of the Party to resolve disputes regarding the Party's measures relating to a matter set out in Articles 13.2 through 13.5.

(ii)   Suppliers of public telecommunications services of the other Party that have requested interconnection with a major supplier in the Party's territory may seek review, within a reasonable and publicly specified period after the supplier requests interconnection, by its telecommunications regulatory body[10] to resolve disputes regarding the terms, conditions, and rates for interconnection with such major supplier.

Reconsideration

(b)   Any enterprise that is aggrieved or whose interests are adversely affected by a determination or decision of its telecommunications regulatory body may petition the body to reconsider that determination or decision. Neither Party may permit such a petition to constitute grounds for non-compliance with the determination or decision of the telecommunications regulatory body unless an appropriate authority stays the determination or decision.

---

[10] The United States may comply with this obligation by providing for review by a state regulatory authority.

Judicial Review

(c)   Any enterprise that is aggrieved or whose interests are adversely affected by a determination or decision of its telecommunications regulatory body may obtain judicial review of the determination or decision by an impartial and independent judicial authority.

ARTICLE 13.13: TRANSPARENCY

Further to Article 18.1 (Publication), each Party shall ensure that:

(a)   rulemakings, including the basis for such rules, of its telecommunications regulatory body and end-user tariffs filed with its telecommunications regulatory body are promptly published or otherwise made available to all interested persons;

(b)   interested persons are provided with adequate advance public notice of and the opportunity to comment on any rulemaking that its telecommunications regulatory body proposes; and

(c)   its measures relating to public telecommunications services are made publicly available, including measures relating to:

     (i)   tariffs and other terms and conditions of service;

     (ii)   procedures relating to judicial and other adjudicatory proceedings;

     (iii)   specifications of technical interfaces;

     (iv)   conditions for attaching terminal or other equipment to the public telecommunications network; and

     (v)   notification, permit, registration, or licensing requirements, if any.

ARTICLE 13.14: FLEXIBILITY IN THE CHOICE OF TECHNOLOGIES

Neither Party may prevent suppliers of public telecommunications services from choosing the technologies that they use to supply their services, including commercial mobile wireless services, except that a Party shall be free to establish and apply spectrum and frequency management policies and other measures necessary to satisfy legitimate public policy interests, such as a requirement to comply with technical specifications and national frequency tables.

ARTICLE 13.15: FORBEARANCE

The Parties recognize the importance of relying on market forces to provide wide choices in the supply of telecommunications services. To this end, each Party may forbear from applying a regulation to a service that the Party classifies as a public telecommunications service, if its telecommunications regulatory body determines that:

(a)   enforcement of the regulation is not necessary to prevent unreasonable or discriminatory practices;

(b)   enforcement of the regulation is not necessary for the protection of consumers; and

(c)   forbearance is consistent with the public interest, including promoting and enhancing competition between suppliers of public telecommunications services.

ARTICLE 13.16: RELATIONSHIP TO OTHER CHAPTERS

In the event of any inconsistency between this Chapter and another Chapter, this Chapter shall prevail to the extent of the inconsistency.

ARTICLE 13.17: DEFINITIONS

For purposes of this Chapter:

co-location (physical) means physical access to space in order to install, maintain, or repair equipment at premises owned or controlled and used by a major supplier to supply public telecommunications services;

co-location (virtual) means the ability to lease and control equipment of a major supplier of public telecommunications services for the purpose of interconnecting with that supplier or accessing its unbundled network elements;

commercial mobile services means public telecommunications services supplied through mobile wireless means;

cost-oriented means based on cost, and may include a reasonable profit, and may involve different cost methodologies for different facilities or services;

dialing parity means the ability of an end-user to use an equal number of digits to access a like public telecommunications service, regardless of which public telecommunications service supplier the end-user chooses;

end-user means a final consumer of or final subscriber to a public telecommunications service;

enterprise means an enterprise as defined in Article 1.3 (Definitions), and a branch of an enterprise;

essential facilities means facilities of a public telecommunications network or service that:

(a)   are exclusively or predominantly supplied by a single or limited number of suppliers, and

(b)   cannot feasibly be economically or technically substituted in order to supply a service;

interconnection means linking with suppliers providing public telecommunications services in order to allow the users of one supplier to communicate with users of another supplier and to access services provided by another supplier;

leased circuits means facilities between designated terminating points of a public telecommunications network leased to a user by a supplier of public telecommunications services, excluding any switching functionality controlled by the user;

major supplier means a supplier of public telecommunications services that has the ability to materially affect the terms of participation (having regard to price and supply) in the relevant market for public telecommunications services as a result of:

    (a)   control over essential facilities or

    (b)   use of its position in the market;

network element means a facility or equipment used in supplying a public telecommunications service, including features, functions, and capabilities provided by means of that facility or equipment;

non-discriminatory means treatment no less favorable than that accorded to any other user of like public telecommunications services in like circumstances;

number portability means the ability of end-users of public telecommunications services to retain, at the same location, existing telephone numbers without impairment of quality, reliability, or convenience when switching between the same category of suppliers of public telecommunications services;

public telecommunications service means any telecommunications service that a Party requires, explicitly or in effect, to be offered to the public generally. Such services may include, inter alia, telephone and data transmission typically involving customer-supplied information between two or more points without any end-to-end change in the form or content of the customer's information. Public telecommunications services in the territory of the United States do not include value-added services;

reference interconnection offer means an interconnection offer extended by a major supplier and filed with or approved by a telecommunications regulatory body[11] that is sufficiently detailed to enable a supplier of public telecommunications services that is willing to accept its rates, terms, and conditions to obtain interconnection without having to engage in negotiations with the major supplier;

supplier of public telecommunications services means any supplier of public telecommunications services;[12]

telecommunications means the transmission and reception of signals by any electromagnetic means, including by photonic means;

telecommunications regulatory body means a national body responsible for the regulation of telecommunications;

---

[11] For purposes of applying this definition with respect to the United States, this body may be a state regulatory authority.

[12] For greater certainty, suppliers of public telecommunications services in the territory of Morocco are subject to the licensing regime of Dahir No. 24-96, Law for Posts and Telecommunications.

user means a service consumer or a service supplier; and value-added services means services that add value to telecommunications services through enhanced functionality. With respect to the United States, these are services as defined in 47 U.S.C. § 153 (20). With respect to Morocco, these are services as defined in Dahir No. 24-96, Law for Posts and Telecommunications.[13]

ANNEX 13-A

For purposes of this Chapter, paragraphs 2 through 4 of Article 13.3 do not apply to the United States with respect to suppliers of commercial mobile services. In addition, a state regulatory authority of the United States may exempt a rural local exchange carrier, as defined in Section 251(f)(2) of the Communications Act of 1934, as amended, from the obligations contained in paragraphs 2 through 4 of Article 13.3.

ANNEX 13-B

1.   Article 13.4 does not apply to the United States with respect to a rural telephone company, as defined in section 3(37) of the Communications Act of 1934, as amended, unless a state regulatory authority orders that the requirements described in that Article be applied to the company. In addition, a state regulatory authority may exempt a rural local exchange carrier, as defined in section 251(f)(2) of the Communications Act of 1934, as amended, from the obligations contained in Article 13.4.

2.   For purposes of this Chapter, Article 13.4 does not apply to the United States with respect to suppliers of commercial mobile services.

[…]

CHAPTER 15
INTELLECTUAL PROPERTY RIGHTS

ARTICLE 15.1: GENERAL PROVISIONS

1.   Each Party shall, at a minimum, give effect to this Chapter.

International Agreements and Recommendations

2.   Each Party shall ratify or accede to the following agreements:

(a)   the Patent Cooperation Treaty (1970), as amended in 1979;

(b)   the Convention Relating to the Distribution of Programme-Carrying Signals Transmitted by Satellite (1974);

(c)   the Protocol Relating to the Madrid Agreement Concerning the International Registration of Marks (1989);

---

[13] Suppliers of value-added services in the territory of Morocco are subject to Morocco's declaration regime.

(d)   the Budapest Treaty on the International Recognition of the Deposit of Microorganisms for the Purposes of Patent Procedure (1977), as amended in 1980;

(e)   the International Convention for the Protection of New Varieties of Plants (1991) (UPOV Convention);

(f)   the Trademark Law Treaty (1994);

(g)   the WIPO Copyright Treaty (1996); and

(h)   the WIPO Performances and Phonograms Treaty (1996).

3.   Each Party shall make all reasonable efforts to ratify or accede to the following agreements:

(a)   the Patent Law Treaty (2000); and

(b)   the Hague Agreement Concerning the International Registration of Industrial Designs (1999).

More Extensive Protection and Enforcement

4.   A Party may provide more extensive protection for, and enforcement of, intellectual property rights under its law than this Chapter requires, provided that the additional protection and enforcement is not inconsistent with this Chapter.

National Treatment

5.   In respect of all categories of intellectual property covered in this Chapter, each Party shall accord to nationals[1] of the other Party treatment no less favourable than that it accords to its own nationals with regard to the protection[2] and enjoyment of such intellectual property rights and any benefits derived from such rights.

6.   A Party may derogate from paragraph 5 in relation to its judicial and administrative procedures, including requiring a national of another Party to designate an address for service of process in its territory, or to appoint an agent in its territory, provided that such derogation:

(a)   is necessary to secure compliance with laws and regulations that are not inconsistent with this Chapter; and

(b)   is not applied in a manner that would constitute a disguised restriction on trade.

---

[1] 1 For purposes of Articles 15.1.5, 15.1.6, 15.3.1, and 15.7.1, a "national of a Party" shall also mean, in respect of the relevant right, entities of that Party that would meet the criteria for eligibility for protection provided for in the agreements listed in Article 15.1.2 and the TRIPS Agreement.

[2] For purposes of this paragraph, "protection" includes matters affecting the availability, acquisition, scope, maintenance, and enforcement of intellectual property rights, as well as matters affecting the use of intellectual property rights specifically covered by this Chapter. Further, for purposes of this paragraph, "protection" also includes the prohibition on circumvention of effective technological measures set out in Article 15.5.8 and the rights and obligations concerning rights management information set out in Article 15.5.9.

7.   Paragraph 5 does not apply to procedures provided in multilateral agreements concluded under the auspices of the World Intellectual Property Organization (WIPO) in relation to the acquisition or maintenance of intellectual property rights.

Application of Agreement to Existing Subject Matter and Prior Acts

8.   Except as it provides otherwise, including in Article 15.5.6, this Chapter gives rise to obligations in respect of all subject matter existing at the date of entry into force of this Agreement, that is protected on that date in the territory of the Party where protection is claimed, or that meets or comes subsequently to meet the criteria for protection under this Chapter.

9.   Except as otherwise provided in this Chapter, including Article 15.5.6, a Party shall not be required to restore protection to subject matter that on the date of entry into force of this Agreement has fallen into the public domain in its territory.

10.   This Chapter does not give rise to obligations in respect of acts that occurred before the date of entry into force of this Agreement.
Transparency

11.   Further to Article 18.1 (Publication), and with the object of making the protection and enforcement of intellectual property rights as transparent as possible, each Party shall ensure that all laws, regulations, and procedures concerning the protection or enforcement of intellectual property rights shall be in writing and shall be published,[3] or where publication is not practicable made publicly available, in a national language in such a manner as to enable governments and right holders to become acquainted with them. Nothing in this paragraph shall require a Party to disclose confidential information which would impede law enforcement or otherwise be contrary to the public interest or would prejudice the legitimate commercial interests of particular enterprises, public or private.

ARTICLE 15.2: TRADEMARKS

1.   Neither Party may require, as a condition of registration, that signs be visually perceptible, nor may a Party deny registration of a trademark solely on the ground that the sign of which it is composed is a sound or a scent.

2.   Each Party shall provide that trademarks shall include certification marks.

3.   Each Party shall ensure that its measures mandating the use of the term customary in common language as the common name for a good or service ("common name"), including, inter alia, requirements concerning the relative size, placement, or style of use of the trademark in relation to the common name, do not impair the use or effectiveness of trademarks used in relation to such good or service.

4.   Each Party shall provide that the owner of a registered trademark shall have the exclusive right to prevent all third parties not having the owner's consent from using in the course of trade identical or similar signs, including geographical indications, for goods or services that are related to those goods or services in respect of which the owner's trademark is registered, where

---

[3] For greater certainty, a Party may satisfy the requirement to publish a law, regulation, or procedure by making it available to the public on the Internet.

such use would result in a likelihood of confusion. In case of the use of an identical sign, including a geographical indication, for identical goods or services, a likelihood of confusion shall be presumed.

5.   Each Party may provide limited exceptions to the rights conferred by a trademark, including a geographical indication, such as fair use of descriptive terms, provided that such exceptions take account of the legitimate interest of the owner of the trademark and of third parties.

6.   Article 6bis of the Paris Convention for the Protection of Industrial Property (1967) shall apply, mutatis mutandis, to goods or services that are not identical or similar to those identified by a well-known trademark,[4] whether registered or not, provided that use of that trademark in relation to those goods or services would indicate a connection between those goods or services and the owner of the trademark and provided that the interests of the owner of the trademark are likely to be damaged by such use.

7.   Each Party shall provide a system for the registration of trademarks, which shall include:

   (a)   providing to the applicant a communication in writing, which may be provided electronically, of the reasons for a refusal to register a trademark;

   (b)   an opportunity for the applicant to respond to communications from the trademark authorities, to contest an initial refusal, and to appeal judicially a final refusal to register;

   (c)   an opportunity for interested parties to oppose a trademark application or to seek cancellation of a trademark after it has been registered; and

   (d)   a requirement that decisions in opposition or cancellation proceedings be reasoned and in writing.

8.   Each Party shall provide:

   (a)   an electronic means for applying for, processing, registering, and maintaining trademarks, and

   (b)   a publicly available electronic database, including an online database, of trademark applications and registrations.

9.   Each Party shall provide that:

   (a)   each registration, or publication that concerns a trademark application or registration, that indicates goods or services shall indicate the goods or services by their names, grouped according to the classes of the classification established by the Nice Agreement Concerning the International Classification of Goods and Services for the Purposes of the Registration of Marks (1979), as revised and amended ("Nice Classification").

---

[4] In determining whether a trademark is well known, the reputation of the trademark need not extend beyond the sector of the public that normally deals with the relevant goods or services.

(b)   goods or services may not be considered as being similar to each other solely on the ground that, in any registration or publication, they appear in the same class of the Nice Classification.

Conversely, each Party shall provide that goods or services may not be considered as being dissimilar from each other solely on the ground that, in any registration or publication, they appear in different classes of the Nice Classification.

10.   Each Party shall provide that initial registration and each renewal of registration of a trademark shall be for a term of no less than ten years.

11.   Neither Party may require recordation of trademark licenses to establish the validity of the license, to assert any rights in a trademark, or for other purposes.

ARTICLE 15.3: GEOGRAPHICAL INDICATIONS

Procedures with Respect to Geographical Indications

1.   If a Party provides the means to apply for protection or petition for recognition of geographical indications, it shall:

(a)   accept those applications and petitions without requiring intercession by a Party on behalf of its nationals;

(b)   process those applications or petitions, as relevant, with a minimum of formalities.

(c)   ensure that its regulations governing filing of those applications or petitions, as relevant, are readily available to the public and set out clearly the procedures for these actions;

(d)   make available contact information sufficient to allow the general public to obtain guidance concerning the procedures for filing applications or petitions and the processing of those applications or petitions in general; and to allow applicants, petitioners, or their representatives to ascertain the status of, and to obtain procedural guidance concerning, specific applications and petitions; and

(e)   ensure that applications or petitions, as relevant, for geographical indications are published for opposition, and provide procedures for opposing geographical indications that are the subject of applications or petitions. Each Party shall also provide procedures to cancel a registration resulting from an application or a petition.

Relationship to Trademarks

2.   Each Party shall provide that each of the following shall be a ground for refusing protection or recognition of a geographical indication:

(a)   the geographical indication is likely to be confusingly similar to a trademark that is the subject of a good-faith pending application or registration; and

(b)   the geographical indication is confusingly similar to a pre-existing trademark, the rights to which have been acquired in the territory of the Party through use in good faith.

Definition

3.   For purposes of this Chapter, geographical indications means indications that identify a good as originating in the territory of a Party, or a region or locality in that territory, where a given quality, reputation, or other characteristic of the good is essentially attributable to its geographical origin.[5] Any sign or combination of signs (such as words, including geographical and personal names, as well as letters, numerals, figurative elements, and colors, including single colors), in any form whatsoever, shall be eligible to be a geographical indication.

ARTICLE 15.4: DOMAIN NAMES ON THE INTERNET

1.   In order to address the problem of trademark cyber-piracy, each Party shall require that the management of its country-code top-level domain ("ccTLD") provide an appropriate procedure for the settlement of disputes, based on the principles established in the Uniform Domain-Name Dispute-Resolution Policy.

2.   Each Party shall require that the management of its ccTLD provide online public access to a reliable and accurate database of contact information for domainname registrants.

ARTICLE 15.5: COPYRIGHT AND RELATED RIGHTS

1.   Each Party shall provide that authors, performers, and producers of phonograms[6] have the right[7] to authorize or prohibit all reproductions of their works, performances, and phonograms,[8] in any manner or form, permanent or temporary (including temporary storage in electronic form).

2.   Each Party shall provide to authors, performers, and producers of phonograms the right to authorize or prohibit the importation into that Party's territory of copies of the work, performance, or phonogram that are made without authorization, or made outside that Party's territory with the authorization of the author, performer, or producer of the phonogram.

3.   Each Party shall provide to authors, performers, and producers of phonograms the right to authorize the making available to the public of the original and copies of their works, performances, and phonograms through sale or other transfer of ownership.

4.   In order to ensure that no hierarchy is established between rights of authors, on the one hand, and rights of performers and producers of phonograms, on the other hand, each Party shall provide that in cases where authorization is needed from both the author of a work embodied in a phonogram and a performer or producer owning rights in the phonogram, the need for the

---

[5] For greater certainty, the term "originating", as used in this Chapter, does not have the meaning ascribed to the term originating good in Article 1.3 (Definitions).

[6] "Authors, performers, and producers of phonograms" includes any successors in interest.

[7] With respect to copyrights and related rights in this Chapter, the "right to authorize or prohibit" and the "right to authorize" refer to exclusive rights.

[8] With respect to copyrights and related rights in this Chapter, a "performance" means a performance fixed in a phonogram unless otherwise specified.

authorization of the author does not cease to exist because the authorization of the performer or producer is also required. Likewise, each Party shall establish that in cases where authorization is needed from both the author of a work embodied in a phonogram and a performer or producer owning rights in the phonogram, the need for the authorization of the performer or producer does not cease to exist because the authorization of the author is also required.

5.   Each Party shall provide that, where the term of protection of a work (including a photographic work), performance, or phonogram is to be calculated:

   (a)   on the basis of the life of a natural person, the term shall be not less than the life of the author and 70 years after the author's death; and

   (b)   on a basis other than the life of a natural person, the term shall be (i) not less than 70 years from the end of the calendar year of the first authorized publication of the work, performance, or phonogram, or (ii) failing such authorized publication within 50 years from the creation of the work, performance, or phonogram, not less than 70 years from the end of the calendar year of the creation of the work, performance, or phonogram.

6.   Each Party shall apply Article 18 of the Berne Convention for the Protection of Literary and Artistic Works (1971) (Berne Convention) and Article 14.6 of the TRIPS Agreement, mutatis mutandis, to the subject matter, rights, and obligations in this Article and Articles 15.6 and 15.7.

7.   Each Party shall provide that for copyright and related rights, any person acquiring or holding any economic right in a work, performance, or phonogram:

   (a)   may freely and separately transfer that right by contract; and

   (b)   by virtue of a contract, including contracts of employment underlying the creation of works, performances, and phonograms, shall be able to exercise that right in that person's own name and enjoy fully the benefits derived from that right.

8.   (a)   In order to provide adequate legal protection and effective legal remedies against the circumvention of effective technological measures that authors, performers, and producers of phonograms use in connection with the exercise of their rights and that restrict unauthorized acts in respect of their works, performances, and phonograms, each Party shall provide that any person who:

   (i)   circumvents without authority any effective technological measure that controls access to a protected work, performance, phonogram, or other subject matter; or

   (ii)   manufactures, imports, distributes, offers to the public, provides, or otherwise traffics in devices, products, or components, or offers to the public or provides services, that:

   (A)   are promoted, advertised, or marketed for the purpose of circumvention of any effective technological measure,

(B)   have only a limited commercially significant purpose or use other than to circumvent any effective technological measure, or

(C)   are primarily designed, produced, or performed for the purpose of enabling or facilitating the circumvention of any effective technological measure, shall be liable and subject to the remedies set out in Article 15.11.14. Each Party shall provide for criminal procedures and penalties to be applied when any person, other than a nonprofit library, archive, educational institution, or public non-commercial broadcasting entity, is found to have engaged willfully and for purposes of commercial advantage or private financial gain in any of the foregoing activities.

(b)   In implementing subparagraph (a), neither Party shall be obligated to require that the design of, or the design and selection of parts and components for, a consumer electronics, telecommunications, or computing product provide for a response to any particular technological measure, so long as the product does not otherwise violate any measures implementing subparagraph (a).

(c)   Each Party shall provide that a violation of a measure implementing this paragraph is a separate civil or criminal offense, independent of any infringement that might occur under the Party's law on copyright and related rights.

(d)   Each Party shall confine exceptions and limitations to any measures implementing subparagraph (a) to the following activities, which shall be applied to relevant measures in accordance with subparagraph (e):

(i)   noninfringing reverse engineering activities with regard to a lawfully obtained copy of a computer program, carried out in good faith with respect to particular elements of that computer program that have not been readily available to the person engaged in those activities, for the sole purpose of achieving interoperability of an independently created computer program with other programs;

(ii)   noninfringing good faith activities, carried out by an appropriately qualified researcher who has lawfully obtained a copy, unfixed performance, or display of a work, performance, or phonogram and who has made a good faith effort to obtain authorization for such activities, to the extent necessary for the sole purpose of research consisting of identifying and analyzing flaws and vulnerabilities of technologies for scrambling and descrambling of information;

(iii)   the inclusion of a component or part for the sole purpose of preventing the access of minors to inappropriate online content in a technology, product, service, or device that itself is not prohibited under the measures implementing subparagraph (a)(ii);

(iv)   noninfringing good faith activities that are authorized by the owner of a computer, computer system, or computer network for the sole purpose of testing, investigating, or correcting the security of that computer, computer system, or computer network;

(v)   noninfringing activities for the sole purpose of identifying and disabling a capability to carry out undisclosed collection or dissemination of personally identifying information reflecting the online activities of a natural person in a way that has no other effect on the ability of any person to gain access to any work;

(vi)   lawfully authorized activities carried out by government employees, agents, or contractors for the purpose of law enforcement, intelligence, essential security, or similar governmental purposes; and

(vii)   access by a nonprofit library, archive, or educational institution to a work not otherwise available to it, for the sole purpose of making acquisition decisions; and

(viii)   noninfringing uses of a work, performance, or phonogram in a particular class of works, performances, or phonograms when an actual or likely adverse impact on those noninfringing uses is demonstrated in a legislative or administrative proceeding by substantial evidence; provided that any limitation or exception adopted in reliance upon this clause shall have effect for a period of not more than three years from the date of conclusion of such proceeding.

(e)   The exceptions and limitations to any measures implementing subparagraph (a) for the activities set forth in subparagraph (d) may only be applied as follows, provided that they do not impair the adequacy of legal protection or the effectiveness of legal remedies against the circumvention of effective technological measures:

(i)   Measures implementing subparagraph (a)(i) may be subject to exceptions and limitations with respect to each activity set forth in subparagraph (d).

(ii)   Measures implementing subparagraph (a)(ii), as they apply to effective technological measures that control access to a work, performance, or phonogram, may be subject to exceptions and limitations with respect to activities set forth in subparagraph (d)(i), (ii), (iii), (iv), and (vi).

(iii)   Measures implementing subparagraph (a)(ii), as they apply to effective technological measures that protect any copyright or any rights related to copyright, may be subject to exceptions and limitations with respect to activities set forth in subparagraph (d)(i) and (vi).

(f)   For purposes of this paragraph, effective technological measure means any technology, device, or component that, in the normal course of its operation, controls access to a protected work, performance, phonogram, or other protected subject matter, or protects any copyright or any rights related to copyright.

9.   In order to provide adequate and effective legal remedies to protect rights management information:

(a)   each Party shall provide that any person who without authority, and knowing, or, with respect to civil remedies, having reasonable grounds to know, that it would induce, enable, facilitate, or conceal an infringement of any copyright or related right,

(i)   knowingly removes or alters any rights management information;

(ii)   distributes or imports for distribution rights management information knowing that the rights management information has been removed or altered without authority; or

(iii)   distributes, imports for distribution, broadcasts, communicates, or makes available to the public copies of works, performances, or phonograms, knowing that rights management information has been removed or altered without authority, shall be liable and subject to the remedies set out in Article 15.11.14. Each Party shall provide for criminal procedures and penalties to be applied when any person, other than a nonprofit library, archive, educational institution, or public noncommercial broadcasting entity, is found to have engaged willfully and for purposes of commercial advantage or private financial gain in any of the foregoing activities.

(b)   Each Party shall confine exceptions and limitations to measures implementing subparagraph (a) to lawfully authorized activities carried out by government employees, agents, or contractors for the purpose of law enforcement, intelligence, essential security, or similar government purposes.

(c)   For purposes of this paragraph, rights management information means:

(i)   information that identifies a work, performance, or phonogram; the author of the work, the performer of the performance, or the producer of the phonogram; or the owner of any right in the work, performance, or phonogram;

(ii)   information about the terms and conditions of the use of the work, performance, or phonogram; or

(iii)   any numbers or codes that represent such information, when any of these items is attached to a copy of the work, performance, or phonogram or appears in connection with the communication or making available of a work, performance, or phonogram to the public.

(d)   For greater certainty, nothing in this paragraph obligates a Party to require the owner of any right in the work, performance, or phonogram to attach rights management information to copies of the work, performance, or phonogram, or to cause rights management information to appear in connection with a communication of the work, performance, or phonogram to the public.

10.   Each Party shall issue appropriate laws, orders, regulations, or administrative or executive decrees mandating that its agencies use computer software only as authorized by the right holder. These measures shall actively regulate the acquisition and management of software for government use.

11.   (a)   With respect to this Article and Articles 15.6, and 15.7, each Party shall confine limitations or exceptions to exclusive rights to certain special cases that do not conflict with a normal exploitation of the work, performance, or phonogram, and do not unreasonably prejudice the legitimate interests of the right holder.

        (b)   Notwithstanding subparagraph (a) and Article 15.7.3(b), neither Party may permit the retransmission of television signals (whether terrestrial, cable, or satellite) on the Internet without the authorization of the right holder or right holders of the content of the signal, if any, and of the signal.

ARTICLE 15.6: COPYRIGHT

Without prejudice to Articles 11(1)(ii), 11bis(1)(i) and (ii), 11ter(1)(ii), 14(1)(ii), and 14bis(1) of the Berne Convention, each Party shall provide to authors the exclusive right to authorize or prohibit the communication to the public of their works, by wire or wireless means, including the making available to the public of their works in such a way that members of the public may access these works from a place and at a time individually chosen by them.

ARTICLE 15.7: RELATED RIGHTS

1.   Each Party shall accord the rights provided for in this Chapter with respect to performers and producers of phonograms to the performers and producers of phonograms who are nationals of the other Party and to performances or phonograms first published or fixed in the territory of the other Party. A performance or phonogram shall be considered first published in the territory of a Party in which it is published within 30 days of its original publication.[9]

2.   Each Party shall provide to performers the right to authorize or prohibit:

        (a)   the broadcasting and communication to the public of their unfixed performances, except where the performance is already a broadcast performance, and

        (b)   the fixation of their unfixed performances.

3.   (a)   Each Party shall provide to performers and producers of phonograms the right to authorize or prohibit the broadcasting or any communication to the public of their performances or phonograms, by wire or wireless means, including the making available to the public of those performances and phonograms in such a way that members of the public may access them from a place and at a time individually chosen by them.

        (b)   Notwithstanding subparagraph (a) and Article 15.5.11, the application of this right to traditional free over-the-air (i.e., noninteractive) broadcasting, and exceptions or limitations to this right for such activity, shall be a matter of each Party's law.

---

[9] For purposes of this Article, "fixation" includes the finalization of the master tape or its equivalent.

(c)   Each Party may adopt limitations to this right in respect of other noninteractive transmissions in accordance with Article 15.5.11, provided that the limitations do not prejudice the right of the performer or producer of phonograms to obtain equitable remuneration.

4.   Neither Party may subject the enjoyment and exercise of the rights of performers and producers of phonograms provided for in this Chapter to any formality.

5.   For purposes of this Article and Article 15.5, the following definitions apply with respect to performers and producers of phonograms:

(a)   broadcasting means the transmission to the public by wireless means or satellite of sounds or sounds and images, or representations thereof, including wireless transmission of encrypted signals where the means for decrypting are provided to the public by the broadcasting organization or with its consent; "broadcasting" does not include transmissions over computer networks or any transmissions where the time and place of reception may be individually chosen by members of the public;

(b)   communication to the public of a performance or a phonogram means the transmission to the public by any medium, other than by broadcasting, of sounds of a performance or the sounds or the representations of sounds fixed in a phonogram. For purposes of paragraph 3, "communication to the public" includes making the sounds or representations of sounds fixed in a phonogram audible to the public;

(c)   fixation means the embodiment of sounds, or of the representations thereof, from which they can be perceived, reproduced, or communicated through a device;

(d)   performers means actors, singers, musicians, dancers, and other persons who act, sing, deliver, declaim, play in, interpret, or otherwise perform literary or artistic works or expressions of folklore;

(e)   phonogram means the fixation of the sounds of a performance or of other sounds, or of a representation of sounds, other than in the form of a fixation incorporated in a cinematographic or other audiovisual work;

(f)   producer of a phonogram means the person who, or the legal entity which, takes the initiative and has the responsibility for the first fixation of the sounds of a performance or other sounds, or the representations of sounds; and

(g)   publication of a performance or a phonogram means the offering of copies of the performance or the phonogram to the public, with the consent of the right holder, and provided that copies are offered to the public in reasonable quantity.

ARTICLE 15.8: PROTECTION OF ENCRYPTED PROGRAM-CARRYING SATELLITE SIGNALS

1.   Each Party shall make it a criminal offense:

(a)   to manufacture, assemble, modify, import, export, sell, lease, or otherwise distribute a tangible or intangible device or system, knowing or having reason to know that the device or system is primarily of assistance in decoding an encrypted program-carrying satellite signal without the authorization of the lawful distributor of such signal; and

(b)   willfully to receive or further distribute a program-carrying signal that originated as an encrypted satellite signal knowing that it has been decoded without the authorization of the lawful distributor of the signal.

2.   Each Party shall provide for civil remedies, including compensatory damages, for any person injured by any activity described in paragraph 1, including any person that holds an interest in the encrypted programming signal or its content.

ARTICLE 15.9: PATENTS

1.   Each Party may only exclude from patentability inventions, the prevention within its territory of the commercial exploitation of which is necessary to protect ordre public or morality, including to protect human, animal, or plant life or health or to avoid serious prejudice to the environment, provided that such exclusion is not made merely because the exploitation is prohibited by law.

2.   Each Party shall make patents available for the following inventions:

(a)   plants, and

(b)   animals.

In addition, the Parties confirm that patents shall be available for any new uses or methods of using a known product, including new uses of a known product for the treatment of humans and animals.

3.   Each Party may provide limited exceptions to the exclusive rights conferred by a patent, provided that such exceptions do not unreasonably conflict with a normal exploitation of the patent and do not unreasonably prejudice the legitimate interests of the patent owner, taking account of the legitimate interests of third parties.

4.   Each Party shall provide that the exclusive right of the patent owner to prevent importation of a patented product, or a product that results from patented process, without the consent of the patent owner shall not be limited by the sale or distribution of that product outside its territory.[10]

5.   Each Party shall provide that a patent may be revoked only on grounds that would have justified a refusal to grant the patent. A Party may also provide that fraud, misrepresentation, or inequitable conduct may be the basis for revoking a patent or holding a patent unenforceable. Where a Party provides proceedings that permit a third party to oppose the grant of a patent, a Party shall not make such proceedings available before the grant of the patent.

---

[10] A Party may limit application of this paragraph to cases where the patent owner has placed restrictions on importation by contract or other means.

6.   Consistent with paragraph 3, if a Party permits a third person to use the subject matter of a subsisting patent to generate information necessary to support an application for marketing approval of a pharmaceutical product, that Party shall provide that any product produced under such authority shall not be made, used, or sold in its territory other than for purposes related to generating information to meet requirements for approval to market the product, and if the Party permits exportation, the Party shall provide that the product shall only be exported outside its territory for purposes of meeting marketing approval requirements of that Party.

7.   Each Party, at the request of the patent owner, shall adjust the term of a patent to compensate for unreasonable delays that occur in granting the patent. For purposes of this paragraph, an unreasonable delay shall at least include a delay in the issuance of the patent of more than four years from the date of filing of the application in the territory of the Party, or two years after a request for examination of the application, whichever is later. Periods attributable to actions of the patent applicant need not be included in the determination of such delays.

8.   Each Party shall disregard information contained in public disclosures used to determine if an invention is novel or has an inventive step[11] if the public disclosure:

(a)   was made or authorized by, or derived from, the patent applicant, and

(b)   occurred within 12 months prior to the date of filing of the application in the territory of the Party.

9.   Each Party shall provide patent applicants with at least one opportunity to make amendments, corrections, and observations in connection with their applications.

10.   Each Party shall provide that a disclosure of a claimed invention shall be considered to be sufficiently clear and complete if it provides information that allows the invention to be made and used by a person skilled in the art, without undue experimentation, as of the filing date.

11.   Each Party shall provide that a claimed invention:

(a)   is sufficiently supported by its disclosure if the disclosure reasonably conveys to a person skilled in the art that the applicant was in possession of the claimed invention, as of the filing date, and

(b)   is industrially applicable if it has a specific, substantial, and credible utility.

ARTICLE 15.10: MEASURES RELATED TO CERTAIN REGULATED PRODUCTS

1.   If a Party requires, as a condition of approving the marketing of a new pharmaceutical or agricultural chemical product, the submission of:

(a)   safety and efficacy data, or

(b)   evidence of prior approval of the product in another territory that requires such information,

---

[11] For purposes of this Article, "inventive step" shall be treated as synonymous with the term "non-obvious."

the Party shall not permit third persons not having the consent of the person providing the information to market a product on the basis of the approval granted to the person submitting that information for at least five years for pharmaceutical products and ten years for agricultural chemical products from the date of approval in the Party's territory. For purposes of this paragraph, a new product is one that contains a new chemical entity that has not been previously approved in the Party's territory.[12]

2.   If a Party requires the submission of

    (a)   new clinical information that is essential to the approval of a pharmaceutical product (other than information related to bioequivalency), or

    (b)   evidence of prior approval of the product in another territory that requires such new information,

the Party shall not permit third persons not having the consent of the person providing the information to market a pharmaceutical product on the basis of such new information or the approval granted to the person submitting such information for at least three years from the date of approval in the Party. A Party may limit such protection to new clinical information the origination of which involves considerable effort.[13]

3.   With respect to patents covering pharmaceutical products, each Party shall make available an extension of the patent term to compensate the patent owner for unreasonable curtailment of the effective patent term as a result of the marketing approval process.

4.   With respect to any pharmaceutical product that is subject to a patent, and where a Party permits authorizations to be granted or applications to be made to market a pharmaceutical product based on information previously submitted concerning the safety and efficacy of a product, including evidence of prior marketing approval by persons other than the person that previously submitted such information, that Party:

    (a)   shall implement measures in its marketing approval process to prevent such other persons from marketing a product covered by a patent during the term of that patent, unless by consent or with the acquiescence of the patent owner,[14] and

    (b)   if it allows applications[15] to be made to market a product during the term of a patent covering that product, shall provide that the patent owner shall be notified

---

[12] As of the date of signature of this Agreement, neither Party permits third persons not having the consent of the person providing such information to market a product on the basis of such information submitted in another territory or evidence of prior approval of the product in another territory. In addition, when a product is subject to a system of marketing approval pursuant to this paragraph and is also subject to a patent in the territory of a Party, that Party may not alter the term of protection that it provides in accordance with this paragraph in the event that the patent protection terminates before the end of the term of protection specified in Article 10.1.

[13] As of the date of signature of this Agreement, neither Party permits third persons not having the consent of the person providing such new information to market a product on the basis of such information submitted in another territory or evidence of prior approval of the product in another territory. In addition, when a product is subject to a system of marketing approval pursuant to this paragraph and is also subject to a patent in the territory of a Party, that Party may not alter the term of protection that it provides in accordance with this paragraph in the event that the patent protection terminates before the end of the term of protection specified in Article 10.2.

[14] Each Party may limit such measures to patents claiming the product and patents covering approved indications.

of the identity of any such other person who requests marketing approval to enter the market during the term of a patent notified to or identified by the approving authority as covering that product.

ARTICLE 15.11: ENFORCEMENT OF INTELLECTUAL PROPERTY RIGHTS

General Obligations

1.   Further to Article 18.1 (Publication), each Party shall provide that final judicial decisions and administrative rulings of general application pertaining to the enforcement of intellectual property rights shall be in writing and shall state any relevant findings of fact and the reasoning or the legal basis on which the decisions or rulings are based. Each Party shall provide that such decisions or rulings shall be published[16] or, where publication is not practicable, otherwise made available to the public in a national language in such a manner as to enable governments and right holders to become acquainted with them.

2.   Each Party shall publicize information on its efforts to provide effective enforcement of intellectual property rights in its civil, administrative, and criminal system, including any statistical information that the Party may collect for such purpose. Nothing in this paragraph shall require a Party to disclose confidential information that would impede law enforcement or otherwise be contrary to the public interest or would prejudice the legitimate commercial interests of particular enterprises, public or private.

3.   The Parties understand that a decision that a Party makes on the distribution of enforcement resources shall not excuse that Party from complying with this Chapter.

4.   In civil, administrative, and criminal proceedings involving copyright or related rights, each Party shall provide for a presumption that, in the absence of proof to the contrary, the person whose name is indicated as the author, producer, performer, or publisher of the work, performance, or phonogram in the usual manner is the designated right holder in such work, performance, or phonogram.

Each Party shall also provide for a presumption that, in the absence of proof to the contrary, the copyright or related right subsists in such subject matter.

Civil and Administrative Procedures and Remedies

5.   Each Party shall make available to right holders[17] civil judicial procedures concerning the enforcement of any intellectual property right.

6.   Each Party shall provide that:

---

[15] The Parties understand that as of the date of signature of this Agreement Morocco does not allow such applications to be made, except in cases that are consistent with Article 15.9.6, which is commonly referred to as the "Bolar provision."

[16] For greater certainty, a Party may satisfy the requirement for publication by making the decision or ruling available to the public on the Internet.

[17] For purposes of this Article, "right holder" includes exclusive licensees as well as federations and associations having the legal standing and authority to assert such rights. "Exclusive licensee" includes the exclusive licensee of any one or more of the exclusive intellectual property rights encompassed in a given intellectual property.

(a)   in civil judicial proceedings, its judicial authorities shall have the authority to order the infringer to pay the right holder:

(i)   damages adequate to compensate for the injury the right holder has suffered as a result of the infringement and,

(ii)   at least in the case of copyright or related rights infringement and trademark counterfeiting, the profits of the infringer that are attributable to the infringement and that are not taken into account in computing the amount of the damages referred to in clause (i); and

(b)   in determining damages for infringement of intellectual property rights, its judicial authorities shall consider, inter alia, the value of the infringed-on good or service, measured by the suggested retail price or other legitimate measure of value submitted by the right holder.

7.   In civil judicial proceedings, each Party shall, at least with respect to works, phonograms, and performances protected by copyright or related rights, and in cases of trademark counterfeiting, establish or maintain pre-established damages, which shall be available on the election of the right holder. Pre-established damages shall be in an amount sufficient to constitute a deterrent to future infringements and to compensate fully the right holder for the harm caused by the infringement. In civil judicial proceedings concerning patent infringement, each Party shall provide that its judicial authorities, except in exceptional circumstances, shall have the authority to increase damages to an amount that is up to three times the amount of the injury found or assessed.

8.   Each Party shall provide that its judicial authorities, except in exceptional circumstances, shall have the authority to order, at the conclusion of civil judicial proceedings concerning copyright or related rights infringement and trademark counterfeiting, that the prevailing party shall be awarded payment of court costs or fees and reasonable attorney's fees by the losing party. Further, each Party shall provide that its judicial authorities, at least in exceptional circumstances, shall have the authority to order, at the conclusion of civil judicial proceedings concerning patent infringement, that the prevailing party shall be awarded payment of reasonable attorney's fees by the losing party.[18]

9.   In civil judicial proceedings concerning copyright or related rights infringement and trademark counterfeiting, each Party shall provide that its judicial authorities shall have the authority to order the seizure of suspected infringing goods, any related materials and implements, and, at least for trademark counterfeiting, documentary evidence relevant to the infringement.

10.   Each Party shall provide that:

(a)   in civil judicial proceedings, at the right holder's request, goods that have been found to be pirated or counterfeit shall be destroyed, except in exceptional circumstances;

---

[18] Neither Party shall be required to apply this paragraph to actions for (a) infringement by a Party, or (b) infringement authorized by a Party.

(b)   its judicial authorities shall have the authority to order that materials and implements that have been used in the manufacture or creation of the pirated or counterfeit goods be, without compensation of any sort, promptly destroyed or, in exceptional circumstances, without compensation of any sort, disposed of outside the channels of commerce in such a manner as to minimize the risks of further infringements; and

(c)   in regard to counterfeit trademarked goods, the simple removal of the trademark unlawfully affixed shall not be sufficient to permit the release of goods into the channels of commerce.

11.   Each Party shall provide that in civil judicial proceedings concerning the enforcement of intellectual property rights, its judicial authorities shall have the authority to order the infringer to provide any information that the infringer possesses regarding any person involved in any aspect of the infringement and regarding the means of production or distribution channel of such goods, including the identification of third persons involved in the production and distribution of the infringing goods or services or in their channels of distribution, and to provide this information to the right holder.

12.   Each Party shall provide that its judicial authorities have the authority to:

(a)   fine or imprison, in appropriate cases, a party to a litigation who fails to abide by valid orders issued by such authorities; and

(b)   impose sanctions on parties to a litigation, their counsel, experts, or other persons subject to the court's jurisdiction, for violation of judicial orders regarding the protection of confidential information produced or exchanged in a proceeding.

13.   To the extent that any civil remedy can be ordered as a result of administrative procedures on the merits of a case, each Party shall provide that such procedures conform to principles equivalent in substance to those set out in this Chapter.

14.   In civil judicial proceedings concerning the acts described in Articles 15.5.8 and 15.5.9, each Party shall provide that its judicial authorities shall have the authority to order or award at least:

(a)   provisional measures, including seizure of devices and products suspected of being involved in the prohibited activity;

(b)   the opportunity for the right holder to elect between actual damages it suffered (plus any profits attributable to the prohibited activity not taken into account in computing those damages) or pre-established damages;

(c)   payment to the prevailing right holder at the conclusion of civil judicial proceedings of court costs and fees, and reasonable attorney's fees, by the party engaged in the prohibited conduct; and

(d)   destruction of devices and products found to be involved in the prohibited activity.

Neither Party may make damages available against a nonprofit library, archive, educational institution, or public noncommercial broadcasting entity that sustains the burden of proving that it was not aware and had no reason to believe that its acts constituted a prohibited activity.

15.   In civil judicial proceedings concerning the enforcement of intellectual property rights, each Party shall provide that its judicial authorities shall have the authority to order a party to desist from an infringement, in order, inter alia, to prevent, immediately after they clear customs, the entry into the channels of commerce in the jurisdiction of those authorities of imported goods that involve the infringement of an intellectual property right, or to prevent their exportation.

16.   In the event that a Party's judicial or other authorities appoint technical or other experts in civil proceedings concerning the enforcement of intellectual property rights and require that the parties to the litigation bear the costs of such experts, the Party should seek to ensure that such costs are closely related, inter alia, to the quantity and nature of work to be performed and do not unreasonably deter recourse to such proceedings.

Provisional Measures

17.   Parties shall act on requests for relief inaudita altera parte expeditiously, and shall, except in exceptional circumstances, generally execute such requests within ten days.

18.   Each Party shall provide that its judicial authorities have the authority to require the plaintiff to provide any reasonably available evidence in order to satisfy themselves with a sufficient degree of certainty that the plaintiff's right is being infringed or that such infringement is imminent, and to order the plaintiff to provide a reasonable security or equivalent assurance set at a level sufficient to protect the defendant and to prevent abuse, and so as not to unreasonably deter recourse to such procedures.

19.   In proceedings concerning the grant of provisional measures in relation to enforcement of a patent, each Party shall provide for a rebuttable presumption that the patent is valid.

Special Requirements Related to Border Measures

20.   Each Party shall provide that any right holder initiating procedures for its competent authorities to suspend release of suspected counterfeit or confusingly similar trademark goods, or pirated copyright goods[19] into free circulation is required to provide adequate evidence to satisfy the competent authorities that, under the laws of the country of importation, there is prima facie an infringement of the right holder's intellectual property right and to supply sufficient information that may reasonably be expected to be within the right holder's knowledge to make the suspected goods reasonably recognizable by its competent authorities. The requirement to provide sufficient information shall not unreasonably deter recourse to these procedures. Each

---

[19] For purposes of paragraphs 20 through 25:

    (a)   counterfeit trademark goods means any goods, including packaging, bearing without authorization a trademark that is identical to the trademark validly registered in respect of such goods, or that cannot be distinguished in its essential aspects from such a trademark, and that thereby infringes the rights of the owner of the trademark in question under the law of the country of importation; and

    (b)   pirated copyright goods means any goods that are copies made without the consent of the right holder or person duly authorized by the right holder in the country of production and which are made directly or indirectly from an article where the making of that copy would have constituted an infringement of a copyright or a related right under the law of the country of importation.

Party shall provide that the application to suspend the release of goods shall remain in force for a period of not less than one year from the date of application, or the period that the good is protected by copyright or the relevant trademark registration, whichever is shorter.

21.   Each Party shall provide that its competent authorities shall have the authority to require a right holder initiating procedures to suspend the release of suspected counterfeit or confusingly similar trademark goods, or pirated copyright goods, to provide a reasonable security or equivalent assurance sufficient to protect the defendant and the competent authorities and to prevent abuse. Each Party shall provide that such security or equivalent assurance shall not unreasonably deter recourse to these procedures. Each Party may provide that such security may be in the form of a bond conditioned to hold the importer or owner of the imported merchandise harmless from any loss or damage resulting from any suspension of the release of goods in the event the competent authorities determine that the article is not an infringing good.

22.   Where its competent authorities have made a determination that goods are counterfeit or pirated, a Party shall grant its competent authorities the authority to inform the right holder of the names and addresses of the consignor, the importer, and the consignee, and of the quantity of the goods in question.

23.   Each Party shall provide that its competent authorities may initiate border measures ex officio, with respect to imported, exported, or in-transit merchandise suspected of infringing an intellectual property right, without the need for a formal complaint from a private party or right holder.

24.   Each Party shall provide that goods that have been determined to be pirated or counterfeit by its competent authorities shall be destroyed, except in exceptional circumstances. In regard to counterfeit trademark goods, the simple removal of the trademark unlawfully affixed shall not be sufficient to permit the release of the goods into the channels of commerce. In no event shall the competent authorities be authorized, except in exceptional circumstances, to permit the exportation of counterfeit or pirated goods or to permit such goods to be subject to other customs procedures.

25.   Where an application fee or merchandise storage fee is assessed in connection with border measures to enforce an intellectual property right, each Party shall provide that such fee shall not be set at an amount that unreasonably deters recourse to these measures.

Criminal Procedures and Remedies

26.   (a)   Each Party shall provide for criminal procedures and penalties to be applied at least in cases of willful trademark counterfeiting or copyright or related rights piracy on a commercial scale. Willful copyright or related rights piracy on a commercial scale includes (i) significant willful copyright or related rights infringements that have no direct or indirect motivation of financial gain, and (ii) willful infringements for purposes of commercial advantage or private financial gain.

Each Party shall treat willful importation or exportation of counterfeit or pirated goods as unlawful activities subject to criminal penalties to the same extent as the trafficking or distribution of such goods in domestic commerce.

(b)   Specifically, each Party shall provide:

(i)   remedies that include sentences of imprisonment as well as monetary fines sufficient to provide a deterrent to future infringements, consistent with a policy of removing the infringer's monetary incentive, and shall further establish policies or guidelines that encourage judicial authorities to impose those remedies at levels sufficient to provide a deterrent to future infringements;

(ii)   that its judicial authorities shall have the authority to order the seizure of suspected counterfeit or pirated goods, any related materials and implements used in the commission of the offense, any assets traceable to the infringing activity, and any documentary evidence relevant to the offense. Each Party shall provide that items that are subject to seizure pursuant to any such judicial order need not be individually identified, so long as they fall within general categories specified in the order;

(iii)   that its judicial authorities shall have the authority, among other measures, to order the forfeiture of any assets traceable to the infringing activity and shall, except in exceptional cases, order the forfeiture and destruction of all counterfeit or pirated goods, and, at least with respect to wilful copyright or related rights piracy, order the forfeiture and destruction of materials and implements that have been used in the creation of infringing goods. Each Party shall further provide that such forfeiture and destruction shall occur without compensation of any kind to the defendant; and

(iv)   that its authorities may initiate legal action ex officio with respect to the offenses described in this Chapter, without the need for a formal complaint by a private party or right holder.

27.   Each Party shall also provide for criminal procedures and penalties to be applied in the following cases, even absent willful trademark counterfeiting or copyright piracy:

(a)   knowing trafficking in counterfeit labels affixed or designed to be affixed to: a phonogram, a copy of a computer program, documentation or packaging for a computer program, or a copy of a motion picture or other audiovisual work; and

(b)   knowing trafficking in counterfeit documentation or packaging for a computer program.

Limitations on Liability for Service Providers

28.   For the purpose of providing enforcement procedures that permit effective action against any act of copyright infringement covered by this Chapter, including expeditious remedies to prevent infringements and criminal and civil remedies, each Party shall provide, consistent with the framework set out in this Article:

(a) legal incentives for service providers to cooperate with copyright[20] owners in deterring the unauthorized storage and transmission of copyrighted materials; and

(b) limitations in its law regarding the scope of remedies available against service providers for copyright infringements that they do not control, initiate, or direct, and that take place through systems or networks controlled or operated by them or on their behalf, as set forth in this subparagraph.[21]

(i) These limitations shall preclude monetary relief, and provide reasonable restrictions on court-ordered relief to compel or restrain certain actions, for the following functions, and shall be confined to those functions:[22]

(A) transmitting, routing, or providing connections for material without modification of its content, or the intermediate and transient storage of such material in the course thereof;

(B) caching carried out through an automatic process;

(C) storage at the direction of a user of material residing on a system or network controlled or operated by or for the service provider; and

(D) referring or linking users to an online location by using information location tools, including hyperlinks and directories.

(ii) These limitations shall apply only where the service provider does not initiate the chain of transmission of the material and does not select the material or its recipients (except to the extent that a function described in clause (i)(D) in itself entails some form of selection).

(iii) Qualification by a service provider for the limitations as to each function in clause (i)(A) through (D) shall be considered separately from qualification for the limitations as to each other function, in accordance with the conditions for qualification set forth in clauses (iv) through (vii).

(iv) With respect to functions referred to in clause (i)(B), the limitations shall be conditioned on the service provider:

(A) permitting access to cached material in significant part only to users of its system or network who have met conditions on user access to that material;

(B) complying with rules concerning the refreshing, reloading, or other updating of the cached material when specified by the person making the material available online in accordance with a generally accepted industry standard data communications

---

[20] For purposes of this paragraph, "copyright" includes related rights.
[21] This subparagraph is without prejudice to the availability of defenses to copyright infringement that are of general applicability.
[22] Either Party may request consultations with the other Party to consider how to address under this paragraph functions of a similar nature that a Party identifies after the date of entry into force of this Agreement.

protocol for the system or network through which that person makes the material available;

(C) not interfering with technology consistent with industry standards accepted in the Party's territory used at the originating site to obtain information about the use of the material, and not modifying its content in transmission to subsequent users; and

(D) expeditiously removing or disabling access, on receipt of an effective notification of claimed infringement, to cached material that has been removed or access to which has been disabled at the originating site.

(v) With respect to functions referred to in clause (i)(C) and (D), the limitations shall be conditioned on the service provider:

(A) not receiving a financial benefit directly attributable to the infringing activity, in circumstances where it has the right and ability to control such activity;

(B) expeditiously removing or disabling access to the material residing on its system or network on obtaining actual knowledge of the infringement or becoming aware of facts or circumstances from which the infringement was apparent, such as through effective notifications of claimed infringement in accordance with clause (ix); and

(C) publicly designating a representative to receive such notifications.

(vi) Eligibility for the limitations in this subparagraph shall be conditioned on the service provider:

(A) adopting and reasonably implementing a policy that provides for termination in appropriate circumstances of the accounts of repeat infringers; and

(B) accommodating and not interfering with standard technical measures accepted in the Party's territory that protect and identify copyrighted material, that are developed through an open, voluntary process by a broad consensus of copyright owners and service providers, that are available on reasonable and nondiscriminatory terms, and that do not impose substantial costs on service providers or substantial burdens on their systems or networks.

(vii) Eligibility for the limitations in this subparagraph may not be conditioned on the service provider monitoring its service, or affirmatively seeking facts indicating infringing activity, except to the extent consistent with such technical measures.

(viii)   If the service provider qualifies for the limitations with respect to the function referred to in clause (i)(A), courtordered relief to compel or restrain certain actions shall be limited to terminating specified accounts, or to taking reasonable steps to block access to a specific, non-domestic online location. If the service provider qualifies for the limitations with respect to any other function in clause (i), court-ordered relief to compel or restrain certain actions shall be limited to removing or disabling access to the infringing material, terminating specified accounts, and other remedies that a court may find necessary, provided that such other remedies are the least burdensome to the service provider among comparably effective forms of relief. Each Party shall provide that any such relief shall be issued with due regard for the relative burden to the service provider and harm to the copyright owner, the technical feasibility and effectiveness of the remedy and whether less burdensome, comparably effective enforcement methods are available.

Except for orders ensuring the preservation of evidence, or other orders having no material adverse effect on the operation of the service provider's communications network, each Party shall provide that such relief shall be available only where the service provider has received notice of the court order proceedings referred to in this subparagraph and an opportunity to appear before the judicial authority.

(ix)   For purposes of the notice and take down process for the functions referred to in clauses (i)(C) and (D), each Party shall establish appropriate procedures for effective notifications of claimed infringement, and effective counternotifications by those whose material is removed or disabled through mistake or misidentification. Each Party shall also provide for monetary remedies against any person who makes a knowing material misrepresentation in a notification or counter-notification that causes injury to any interested party as a result of a service provider relying on the misrepresentation.

(x)   If the service provider removes or disables access to material in good faith based on claimed or apparent infringement, each Party shall provide that the service provider shall be exempted from liability for any resulting claims, provided that, in the case of material residing on its system or network, it takes reasonable steps promptly to notify the person making the material available on its system or network that it has done so and, if such person makes an effective counter-notification and is subject to jurisdiction in an infringement suit, to restore the material online unless the person giving the original effective notification seeks judicial relief within a reasonable time.

(xi)   Each Party shall establish an administrative or judicial procedure enabling copyright owners who have given effective notification of claimed infringement to obtain expeditiously from a service provider information in its possession identifying the alleged infringer.

(xii)   For purposes of the function referred to in clause (i)(A), **service provider** means a provider of transmission, routing, or connections for digital online communications without modification of their content between or among points specified by the user of material of the user's choosing, and for purposes of the functions referred to in clause (i)(B) through (D), **service provider** means a provider or operator of facilities for online services or network access.

ARTICLE 15.12: TRANSITIONAL PROVISIONS

Each Party shall:

(a)   implement the obligations set out in Article 15.4 within one year of the date of entry into force of this Agreement, and shall implement the obligations set out in Article 15.11.28 by January 1, 2006, and

(b)   ratify or accede to the agreements listed in paragraph 2(d), (e), and (f) of Article 15.1 by January 1, 2006.

[…]

*

DOMINICAN REPUBLIC-CENTRAL AMERICA-UNITED STATES FREE TRADE AGREEMENT[*]
[excerpts]

The Dominican Republic-Central America-United States Free Trade Agreement was signed on 5 August 2004.

[...]

Chapter Ten
Investment

Section A: Investment

Article 10.1: Scope and Coverage

1.   This Chapter applies to measures adopted or maintained by a Party relating to:

(a)   investors of another Party;

(b)   covered investments; and

(c)   with respect to Articles 10.9 and 10.11, all investments in the territory of the Party.

2.   A Party's obligations under this Section shall apply to a state enterprise or other person when it exercises any regulatory, administrative, or other governmental authority delegated to it by that Party.

3.   For greater certainty, this Chapter does not bind any Party in relation to any act or fact that took place or any situation that ceased to exist before the date of entry into force of this Agreement.

Article 10.2: Relation to Other Chapters

1.   In the event of any inconsistency between this Chapter and another Chapter, the other Chapter shall prevail to the extent of the inconsistency.

2.   A requirement by a Party that a service supplier of another Party post a bond or other form of financial security as a condition of the cross-border supply of a service does not of itself make this Chapter applicable to measures adopted or maintained by the Party relating to such cross-border supply of the service. This Chapter applies to measures adopted or maintained by the Party relating to the posted bond or financial security, to the extent that such bond or financial security is a covered investment.

---

[*] *Source*: The Government of the United States of America (2004). "Dominican Republic-Central America-United States Free Trade Agreement", available on the Internet (http://www.ustr.gov/Trade_Agreements/Bilateral/DR-CAFTA/DR-CAFTA_Final_Texts/Section_Index.html). [Note added by the editor.]

3.   This Chapter does not apply to measures adopted or maintained by a Party to the extent that they are covered by Chapter Twelve (Financial Services).

Article 10.3: National Treatment

1.   Each Party shall accord to investors of another Party treatment no less favorable than that it accords, in like circumstances, to its own investors with respect to the establishment, acquisition, expansion, management, conduct, operation, and sale or other disposition of investments in its territory.

2.   Each Party shall accord to covered investments treatment no less favorable than that it accords, in like circumstances, to investments in its territory of its own investors with respect to the establishment, acquisition, expansion, management, conduct, operation, and sale or other disposition of investments.

3.   The treatment to be accorded by a Party under paragraphs 1 and 2 means, with respect to a regional level of government, treatment no less favorable than the most favorable treatment accorded, in like circumstances, by that regional level of government to investors, and to investments of investors, of the Party of which it forms a part.

Article 10.4: Most-Favored-Nation Treatment

1.   Each Party shall accord to investors of another Party treatment no less favorable than that it accords, in like circumstances, to investors of any other Party or of any non-Party with respect to the establishment, acquisition, expansion, management, conduct, operation, and sale or other disposition of investments in its territory.

2.   Each Party shall accord to covered investments treatment no less favorable than that it accords, in like circumstances, to investments in its territory of investors of any other Party or of any non-Party with respect to the establishment, acquisition, expansion, management, conduct, operation, and sale or other disposition of investments.

Article 10.5: Minimum Standard of Treatment[1]

1.   Each Party shall accord to covered investments treatment in accordance with customary international law, including fair and equitable treatment and full protection and security.

2.   For greater certainty, paragraph 1 prescribes the customary international law minimum standard of treatment of aliens as the minimum standard of treatment to be afforded to covered investments. The concepts of "fair and equitable treatment" and "full protection and security" do not require treatment in addition to or beyond that which is required by that standard, and do not create additional substantive rights. The obligation in paragraph 1 to provide:

(a)   "fair and equitable treatment" includes the obligation not to deny justice in criminal, civil, or administrative adjudicatory proceedings in accordance with the principle of due process embodied in the principal legal systems of the world; and

---

[1] Article 10.5 shall be interpreted in accordance with Annex 10-B.

(b)   "full protection and security" requires each Party to provide the level of police protection required under customary international law.

3.   A determination that there has been a breach of another provision of this Agreement, or of a separate international agreement, does not establish that there has been a breach of this Article.

Article 10.6: Treatment in Case of Strife

1.   Notwithstanding Article 10.13.5(b), each Party shall accord to investors of another Party, and to covered investments, non-discriminatory treatment with respect to measures it adopts or maintains relating to losses suffered by investments in its territory owing to armed conflict or civil strife.

2.   Notwithstanding paragraph 1, if an investor of a Party, in the situations referred to in paragraph 1, suffers a loss in the territory of another Party resulting from:

(a)   requisitioning of its covered investment or part thereof by the latter's forces or authorities; or

(b)   destruction of its covered investment or part thereof by the latter's forces or authorities, which was not required by the necessity of the situation, the latter Party shall provide the investor restitution or compensation, which in either case shall be in accordance with customary international law and, with respect to compensation, shall be in accordance with Article 10.7.2 through 10.7.4.[2]

3.   Paragraph 1 does not apply to existing measures relating to subsidies or grants that would be inconsistent with Article 10.3 but for Article 10.13.5(b).

Article 10.7: Expropriation and Compensation[3]

1.   No Party may expropriate or nationalize a covered investment either directly or indirectly through measures equivalent to expropriation or nationalization ("expropriation"), except:

(a)   for a public purpose;

(b)   in a non-discriminatory manner;

(c)   on payment of prompt, adequate, and effective compensation in accordance with paragraphs 2 through 4; and

(d)   in accordance with due process of law and Article 10.5.

2.   Compensation shall:

(a)   be paid without delay;

---

[2] The limitations set out in Annex 10-D apply to the submission to arbitration under Section B of a claim alleging a breach of this paragraph.

[3] Article 10.7 shall be interpreted in accordance with Annexes 10-B and 10-C.

(b)   be equivalent to the fair market value of the expropriated investment immediately before the expropriation took place ("the date of expropriation");

(c)   not reflect any change in value occurring because the intended expropriation had become known earlier; and

(d)   be fully realizable and freely transferable.

3.   If the fair market value is denominated in a freely usable currency, the compensation paid shall be no less than the fair market value on the date of expropriation, plus interest at a commercially reasonable rate for that currency, accrued from the date of expropriation until the date of payment.

4.   If the fair market value is denominated in a currency that is not freely usable, the compensation paid – converted into the currency of payment at the market rate of exchange prevailing on the date of payment – shall be no less than:

(a)   the fair market value on the date of expropriation, converted into a freely usable currency at the market rate of exchange prevailing on that date, plus

(b)   interest, at a commercially reasonable rate for that freely usable currency, accrued from the date of expropriation until the date of payment.

5.   This Article does not apply to the issuance of compulsory licenses granted in relation to intellectual property rights in accordance with the TRIPS Agreement, or to the revocation, limitation, or creation of intellectual property rights, to the extent that such issuance, revocation, limitation, or creation is consistent with Chapter Fifteen (Intellectual Property Rights).[4]

Article 10.8: Transfers

1.   Each Party shall permit all transfers relating to a covered investment to be made freely and without delay into and out of its territory. Such transfers include:

(a)   contributions to capital;

(b)   profits, dividends, capital gains, and proceeds from the sale of all or any part of the covered investment or from the partial or complete liquidation of the covered investment;

(c)   interest, royalty payments, management fees, and technical assistance and other fees;

(d)   payments made under a contract, including a loan agreement;

(e)   payments made pursuant to Article 10.6.1 and 10.6.2 and Article 10.7; and

(f)   payments arising out of a dispute.

---

[4] For greater certainty, the reference to "the TRIPS Agreement" in paragraph 5 includes any waiver in force between the Parties of any provision of that Agreement granted by WTO Members in accordance with the WTO Agreement.

2.   Each Party shall permit transfers relating to a covered investment to be made in a freely usable currency at the market rate of exchange prevailing at the time of transfer.

3.   Each Party shall permit returns in kind relating to a covered investment to be made as authorized or specified in a written agreement between the Party and a covered investment or an investor of another Party.

4.   Notwithstanding paragraphs 1 through 3, a Party may prevent a transfer through the equitable, nondiscriminatory, and good faith application of its laws relating to:

(a)   bankruptcy, insolvency, or the protection of the rights of creditors;

(b)   issuing, trading, or dealing in securities, futures, options, or derivatives;

(c)   criminal or penal offenses;

(d)   financial reporting or record keeping of transfers when necessary to assist law enforcement or financial regulatory authorities; or

(e)   ensuring compliance with orders or judgments in judicial or administrative proceedings.

Article 10.9: Performance Requirements

1.   No Party may, in connection with the establishment, acquisition, expansion, management, conduct, operation, or sale or other disposition of an investment of an investor of a Party or of a non-Party in its territory, impose or enforce any of the following requirements, or enforce any commitment or undertaking:

(a)   to export a given level or percentage of goods or services;

(b)   to achieve a given level or percentage of domestic content;

(c)   to purchase, use, or accord a preference to goods produced in its territory, or to purchase goods from persons in its territory;

(d)   to relate in any way the volume or value of imports to the volume or value of exports or to the amount of foreign exchange inflows associated with such investment;

(e)   to restrict sales of goods or services in its territory that such investment produces or supplies by relating such sales in any way to the volume or value of its exports or foreign exchange earnings;

(f)   to transfer a particular technology, a production process, or other proprietary knowledge to a person in its territory; or

(g)   to supply exclusively from the territory of the Party the goods that such investment produces or the services that it supplies to a specific regional market or to the world market.

2.   No Party may condition the receipt or continued receipt of an advantage, in connection with the establishment, acquisition, expansion, management, conduct, operation, or sale or other disposition of an investment in its territory of an investor of a Party or of a non-Party, on compliance with any of the following requirements:

   (a)   to achieve a given level or percentage of domestic content;

   (b)   to purchase, use, or accord a preference to goods produced in its territory, or to purchase goods from persons in its territory;

   (c)   to relate in any way the volume or value of imports to the volume or value of exports or to the amount of foreign exchange inflows associated with such investment; or

   (d)   to restrict sales of goods or services in its territory that such investment produces or supplies by relating such sales in any way to the volume or value of its exports or foreign exchange earnings.

3.   (a)   Nothing in paragraph 2 shall be construed to prevent a Party from conditioning the receipt or continued receipt of an advantage, in connection with an investment in its territory of an investor of a Party or of a non-Party, on compliance with a requirement to locate production, supply a service, train or employ workers, construct or expand particular facilities, or carry out research and development, in its territory.

   (b)   Paragraph 1(f) does not apply:

   (i)   when a Party authorizes use of an intellectual property right in accordance with Article 31 of the TRIPS Agreement, or to measures requiring the disclosure of proprietary information that fall within the scope of, and are consistent with, Article 39 of the TRIPS Agreement;[5]s or

   (ii)   when the requirement is imposed or the commitment or undertaking is enforced by a court, administrative tribunal, or competition authority to remedy a practice determined after judicial or administrative process to be anticompetitive under the Party's competition laws.[6]

   (c)   Provided that such measures are not applied in an arbitrary or unjustifiable manner, and provided that such measures do not constitute a disguised restriction on international trade or investment, paragraphs 1(b), (c), and (f), and 2(a) and (b), shall not be construed to prevent a Party from adopting or maintaining measures, including environmental measures:

   (i)   necessary to secure compliance with laws and regulations that are not inconsistent with this Agreement;

---

[5] For greater certainty, the references to "the TRIPS Agreement" in paragraph 3(b)(i) include any waiver in force between the Parties of any provision of that Agreement granted by WTO Members in accordance with the WTO Agreement.

[6] The Parties recognize that a patent does not necessarily confer market power.

        (ii)   necessary to protect human, animal, or plant life or health; or

        (iii)   related to the conservation of living or non-living exhaustible natural resources.

(d)   Paragraphs 1(a), (b), and (c), and 2(a) and (b), do not apply to qualification requirements for goods or services with respect to export promotion and foreign aid programs.

(e)   Paragraphs 1(b), (c), (f), and (g), and 2(a) and (b), do not apply to procurement.

(f)   Paragraphs 2(a) and (b) do not apply to requirements imposed by an importing Party relating to the content of goods necessary to qualify for preferential tariffs or preferential quotas.

4.   For greater certainty, paragraphs 1 and 2 do not apply to any requirement other than the requirements set out in those paragraphs.

5.   This Article does not preclude enforcement of any commitment, undertaking, or requirement between private parties, where a Party did not impose or require the commitment, undertaking, or requirement.

Article 10.10: Senior Management and Boards of Directors

1.   No Party may require that an enterprise of that Party that is a covered investment appoint to senior management positions natural persons of any particular nationality.

2.   A Party may require that a majority of the board of directors, or any committee thereof, of an enterprise of that Party that is a covered investment, be of a particular nationality, or resident in the territory of the Party, provided that the requirement does not materially impair the ability of the investor to exercise control over its investment.

Article 10.11: Investment and Environment

Nothing in this Chapter shall be construed to prevent a Party from adopting, maintaining, or enforcing any measure otherwise consistent with this Chapter that it considers appropriate to ensure that investment activity in its territory is undertaken in a manner sensitive to environmental concerns.

Article 10.12: Denial of Benefits

1.   A Party may deny the benefits of this Chapter to an investor of another Party that is an enterprise of such other Party and to investments of that investor if persons of a non-Party own or control the enterprise and the denying Party:

(a)   does not maintain diplomatic relations with the non-Party; or

(b)   adopts or maintains measures with respect to the non-Party or a person of the non-Party that prohibit transactions with the enterprise or that would be violated or circumvented if the benefits of this Chapter were accorded to the enterprise or to its investments.

2.   Subject to Articles 18.3 (Notification and Provision of Information) and 20.4 (Consultations), a Party may deny the benefits of this Chapter to an investor of another Party that is an enterprise of such other Party and to investments of that investor if the enterprise has no substantial business activities in the territory of any Party, other than the denying Party, and persons of a non-Party, or of the denying Party, own or control the enterprise.

Article 10.13: Non-Conforming Measures

1.   Articles 10.3, 10.4, 10.9, and 10.10 do not apply to:

(a)   any existing non-conforming measure that is maintained by a Party at:

   (i)   the central level of government, as set out by that Party in its Schedule to Annex I,

   (ii)   a regional level of government, as set out by that Party in its Schedule to Annex I, or

   (iii)   a local level of government;

(b)   the continuation or prompt renewal of any non-conforming measure referred to in subparagraph (a); or

(c)   an amendment to any non-conforming measure referred to in subparagraph (a) to the extent that the amendment does not decrease the conformity of the measure, as it existed immediately before the amendment, with Article 10.3, 10.4, 10.9, or

2.   Articles 10.3, 10.4, 10.9, and 10.10 do not apply to any measure that a Party adopts or maintains with respect to sectors, subsectors, or activities, as set out in its Schedule to Annex II.

3.   No Party may, under any measure adopted after the date of entry into force of this Agreement and covered by its Schedule to Annex II, require an investor of another Party, by reason of its nationality, to sell or otherwise dispose of an investment existing at the time the measure becomes effective.

4.   Articles 10.3 and 10.4 do not apply to any measure that is an exception to, or derogation from, the obligations under Article 15.1.8 (General Provisions) as specifically provided in that Article.

5.   Articles 10.3, 10.4, and 10.10 do not apply to:

(a)   procurement; or

(b)   subsidies or grants provided by a Party, including government-supported loans, guarantees, and insurance.

Article 10.14: Special Formalities and Information Requirements

1.   Nothing in Article 10.3 shall be construed to prevent a Party from adopting or maintaining a measure that prescribes special formalities in connection with covered investments, such as a requirement that investors be residents of the Party or that covered investments be legally constituted under the laws or regulations of the Party, provided that such formalities do not materially impair the protections afforded by a Party to investors of another Party and covered investments pursuant to this Chapter.

2.   Notwithstanding Articles 10.3 and 10.4, a Party may require an investor of another Party, or a covered investment, to provide information concerning that investment solely for informational or statistical purposes. The Party shall protect any confidential business information from any disclosure that would prejudice the competitive position of the investor or the covered investment. Nothing in this paragraph shall be construed to prevent a Party from otherwise obtaining or disclosing information in connection with the equitable and good faith application of its law.

Section B: Investor-State Dispute Settlement

Article 10.15: Consultation and Negotiation

In the event of an investment dispute, the claimant and the respondent should initially seek to resolve the dispute through consultation and negotiation, which may include the use of non-binding, third-party procedures such as conciliation and mediation.

Article 10.16: Submission of a Claim to Arbitration

1.   In the event that a disputing party considers that an investment dispute cannot be settled by consultation and negotiation:

    (a)   the claimant, on its own behalf, may submit to arbitration under this Section a claim

        (i)   that the respondent has breached

            (A)   an obligation under Section A,

            (B)   an investment authorization, or

            (C)   an investment agreement; and

        (ii)   that the claimant has incurred loss or damage by reason of, or arising out of, that breach; and

    (b)   the claimant, on behalf of an enterprise of the respondent that is a juridical person that the claimant owns or controls directly or indirectly, may submit to arbitration under this Section a claim

        (i)   that the respondent has breached

> (A) an obligation under Section A,
>
> (B) an investment authorization, or
>
> (C) an investment agreement; and
>
> (ii) that the enterprise has incurred loss or damage by reason of, or arising out of, that breach.

2. At least 90 days before submitting any claim to arbitration under this Section, a claimant shall deliver to the respondent a written notice of its intention to submit the claim to arbitration ("notice of intent"). The notice shall specify:

> (a) the name and address of the claimant and, where a claim is submitted on behalf of an enterprise, the name, address, and place of incorporation of the enterprise;
>
> (b) for each claim, the provision of this Agreement, investment authorization, or investment agreement alleged to have been breached and any other relevant provisions;
>
> (c) the legal and factual basis for each claim; and
>
> (d) the relief sought and the approximate amount of damages claimed.

3. Provided that six months have elapsed since the events giving rise to the claim, a claimant may submit a claim referred to in paragraph 1:

> (a) under the ICSID Convention and the ICSID Rules of Procedures for Arbitration Proceedings, provided that both the respondent and the Party of the claimant are parties to the ICSID Convention;
>
> (b) under the ICSID Additional Facility Rules, provided that either the respondent or the Party of the claimant is a party to the ICSID Convention; or
>
> (c) under the UNCITRAL Arbitration Rules.

4. A claim shall be deemed submitted to arbitration under this Section when the claimant's notice of or request for arbitration ("notice of arbitration"):

> (a) referred to in paragraph 1 of Article 36 of the ICSID Convention is received by the Secretary-General;
>
> (b) referred to in Article 2 of Schedule C of the ICSID Additional Facility Rules is received by the Secretary-General; or
>
> (c) referred to in Article 3 of the UNCITRAL Arbitration Rules, together with the statement of claim referred to in Article 18 of the UNCITRAL Arbitration Rules, are received by the respondent.

A claim asserted for the first time after such notice of arbitration is submitted shall be deemed submitted to arbitration under this Section on the date of its receipt under the applicable arbitral rules.

5.   The arbitration rules applicable under paragraph 3, and in effect on the date the claim or claims were submitted to arbitration under this Section, shall govern the arbitration except to the extent modified by this Agreement.

6.   The claimant shall provide with the notice of arbitration:

   (a)   the name of the arbitrator that the claimant appoints; or

   (b)   the claimant's written consent for the Secretary-General to appoint such arbitrator.

Article 10.17: Consent of Each Party to Arbitration

1.   Each Party consents to the submission of a claim to arbitration under this Section in accordance with this Agreement.

2.   The consent under paragraph 1 and the submission of a claim to arbitration under this Section shall satisfy the requirements of:

   (a)   Chapter II of the ICSID Convention (Jurisdiction of the Centre) and the ICSID Additional Facility Rules for written consent of the parties to the dispute;

   (b)   Article II of the New York Convention for an "agreement in writing;" and

   (c)   Article I of the Inter-American Convention for an "agreement."

Article 10.18: Conditions and Limitations on Consent of Each Party

1.   No claim may be submitted to arbitration under this Section if more than three years have elapsed from the date on which the claimant first acquired, or should have first acquired, knowledge of the breach alleged under Article 10.16.1 and knowledge that the claimant (for claims brought under Article 10.16.1(a)) or the enterprise (for claims brought under Article 10.16.1(b)) has incurred loss or damage.

2.   No claim may be submitted to arbitration under this Section unless:

   (a)   the claimant consents in writing to arbitration in accordance with the procedures set out in this Agreement; and

   (b)   the notice of arbitration is accompanied,

      (i)   for claims submitted to arbitration under Article 10.16.1(a), by the claimant's written waiver, and

      (ii)   for claims submitted to arbitration under Article 10.16.1(b), by the claimant's and the enterprise's written waivers of any right to initiate or continue before any administrative tribunal or court under the law of any Party, or other dispute settlement procedures, any proceeding with respect to any measure alleged to constitute a breach referred to in Article 10.16.

3.   Notwithstanding paragraph 2(b), the claimant (for claims brought under Article 10.16.1(a)) and the claimant or the enterprise (for claims brought under Article 10.16.1(b)) may initiate or continue an action that seeks interim injunctive relief and does not involve the payment of monetary damages before a judicial or administrative tribunal of the respondent, provided that the action is brought for the sole purpose of preserving the claimant's or the enterprise's rights and interests during the pendency of the arbitration.

4.   No claim may be submitted to arbitration:

(a)   for breach of an investment authorization under Article 10.16.1(a)(i)(B) or Article 10.16.1(b)(i)(B), or

(b)   for breach of an investment agreement under Article 10.16.1(a)(i)(C) or Article 10.16.1(b)(i)(C), if the claimant (for claims brought under Article 10.16.1(a)) or the claimant or the enterprise (for claims brought under Article 10.16.1(b)) has previously submitted the same alleged breach to an administrative tribunal or court of the respondent, or to any other binding dispute settlement procedure, for adjudication or resolution.

Article 10.19: Selection of Arbitrators

1.   Unless the disputing parties otherwise agree, the tribunal shall comprise three arbitrators, one arbitrator appointed by each of the disputing parties and the third, who shall be the presiding arbitrator, appointed by agreement of the disputing parties.

2.   The Secretary-General shall serve as appointing authority for an arbitration under this Section.

3.   If a tribunal has not been constituted within 75 days from the date that a claim is submitted to arbitration under this Section, the Secretary-General, on the request of a disputing party, shall appoint, in his or her discretion, the arbitrator or arbitrators not yet appointed.

4.   For purposes of Article 39 of the ICSID Convention and Article 7 of Schedule C to the ICSID Additional Facility Rules, and without prejudice to an objection to an arbitrator on a ground other than nationality:

(a)   the respondent agrees to the appointment of each individual member of a tribunal established under the ICSID Convention or the ICSID Additional Facility Rules;

(b)   a claimant referred to in Article 10.16.1(a) may submit a claim to arbitration under this Section, or continue a claim, under the ICSID Convention or the ICSID Additional Facility Rules, only on condition that the claimant agrees in writing to the appointment of each individual member of the tribunal; and

(c)   a claimant referred to in Article 10.16.1(b) may submit a claim to arbitration under this Section, or continue a claim, under the ICSID Convention or the ICSID

Additional Facility Rules, only on condition that the claimant and the enterprise agree in writing to the appointment of each individual member of the tribunal.

Article 10.20: Conduct of the Arbitration

1.   The disputing parties may agree on the legal place of any arbitration under the arbitral rules applicable under Article 10.16.3. If the disputing parties fail to reach agreement, the tribunal shall determine the place in accordance with the applicable arbitral rules, provided that the place shall be in the territory of a State that is a party to the New York Convention.

2.   A non-disputing Party may make oral and written submissions to the tribunal regarding the interpretation of this Agreement.

3.   The tribunal shall have the authority to accept and consider *amicus curiae* submissions from a person or entity that is not a disputing party.

4.   Without prejudice to a tribunal's authority to address other objections as a preliminary question, a tribunal shall address and decide as a preliminary question any objection by the respondent that, as a matter of law, a claim submitted is not a claim for which an award in favor of the claimant may be made under Article 10.26.

>   (a)   Such objection shall be submitted to the tribunal as soon as possible after the tribunal is constituted, and in no event later than the date the tribunal fixes for the respondent to submit its counter-memorial (or, in the case of an amendment to the notice of arbitration, the date the tribunal fixes for the respondent to submit its response to the amendment).

>   (b)   On receipt of an objection under this paragraph, the tribunal shall suspend any proceedings on the merits, establish a schedule for considering the objection consistent with any schedule it has established for considering any other preliminary question, and issue a decision or award on the objection, stating the grounds therefor.

>   (c)   In deciding an objection under this paragraph, the tribunal shall assume to be true claimant's factual allegations in support of any claim in the notice of arbitration (or any amendment thereof) and, in disputes brought under the UNCITRAL Arbitration Rules, the statement of claim referred to in Article 18 of the UNCITRAL Arbitration Rules. The tribunal may also consider any relevant facts not in dispute.

>   (d)   The respondent does not waive any objection as to competence or any argument on the merits merely because the respondent did or did not raise an objection under this paragraph or make use of the expedited procedure set out in paragraph 5.

5.   In the event that the respondent so requests within 45 days after the tribunal is constituted, the tribunal shall decide on an expedited basis an objection under paragraph 4 and any objection that the dispute is not within the tribunal's competence. The tribunal shall suspend any proceedings on the merits and issue a decision or award on the objection(s), stating the grounds therefor, no later than 150 days after the date of the request. However, if a disputing

party requests a hearing, the tribunal may take an additional 30 days to issue the decision or award. Regardless of whether a hearing is requested, a tribunal may, on a showing of extraordinary cause, delay issuing its decision or award by an additional brief period, which may not exceed 30 days.

6.   When it decides a respondent's objection under paragraph 4 or 5, the tribunal may, if warranted, award to the prevailing disputing party reasonable costs and attorney's fees incurred in submitting or opposing the objection. In determining whether such an award is warranted, the tribunal shall consider whether either the claimant's claim or the respondent's objection was frivolous, and shall provide the disputing parties a reasonable opportunity to comment.

7.   A respondent may not assert as a defense, counterclaim, right of set-off, or for any other reason that the claimant has received or will receive indemnification or other compensation for all or part of the alleged damages pursuant to an insurance or guarantee contract.

8.   A tribunal may order an interim measure of protection to preserve the rights of a disputing party, or to ensure that the tribunal's jurisdiction is made fully effective, including an order to preserve evidence in the possession or control of a disputing party or to protect the tribunal's jurisdiction. A tribunal may not order attachment or enjoin the application of a measure alleged to constitute a breach referred to in Article 10.16. For purposes of this paragraph, an order includes a recommendation.

9.   (a)   In any arbitration conducted under this Section, at the request of a disputing party, a tribunal shall, before issuing a decision or award on liability, transmit its proposed decision or award to the disputing parties and to the non-disputing Parties. Within 60 days after the tribunal transmits its proposed decision or award, the disputing parties may submit written comments to the tribunal concerning any aspect of its proposed decision or award. The tribunal shall consider any such comments and issue its decision or award not later than 45 days after the expiration of the 60-day comment period.

        (b)   Subparagraph (a) shall not apply in any arbitration conducted pursuant to this Section for which an appeal has been made available pursuant to paragraph 10 or Annex 10-F.

10.   If a separate multilateral agreement enters into force as between the Parties that establishes an appellate body for purposes of reviewing awards rendered by tribunals constituted pursuant to international trade or investment arrangements to hear investment disputes, the Parties shall strive to reach an agreement that would have such appellate body review awards rendered under Article 10.26 in arbitrations commenced after the multilateral agreement enters into force as between the Parties.

Article 10.21: Transparency of Arbitral Proceedings

1.   Subject to paragraphs 2 and 4, the respondent shall, after receiving the following documents, promptly transmit them to the non-disputing Parties and make them available to the public:

        (a)   the notice of intent;

(b)   the notice of arbitration;

(c)   pleadings, memorials, and briefs submitted to the tribunal by a disputing party and any written submissions submitted pursuant to Article 10.20.2 and 10.20.3 and Article 10.25;

(d)   minutes or transcripts of hearings of the tribunal, where available; and

(e)   orders, awards, and decisions of the tribunal.

2.   The tribunal shall conduct hearings open to the public and shall determine, in consultation with the disputing parties, the appropriate logistical arrangements. However, any disputing party that intends to use information designated as protected information in a hearing shall so advise the tribunal. The tribunal shall make appropriate arrangements to protect the information from disclosure.

3.   Nothing in this Section requires a respondent to disclose protected information or to furnish or allow access to information that it may withhold in accordance with Article 21.2 (Essential Security) or Article 21.5 (Disclosure of Information).

4.   Any protected information that is submitted to the tribunal shall be protected from disclosure in accordance with the following procedures:

(a)   Subject to subparagraph (d), neither the disputing parties nor the tribunal shall disclose to any non-disputing Party or to the public any protected information where the disputing party that provided the information clearly designates it in accordance with subparagraph (b);

(b)   Any disputing party claiming that certain information constitutes protected information shall clearly designate the information at the time it is submitted to the tribunal;

(c)   A disputing party shall, at the same time that it submits a document containing information claimed to be protected information, submit a redacted version of the document that does not contain the information. Only the redacted version shall be provided to the non-disputing Parties and made public in accordance with paragraph 1; and

(d)   The tribunal shall decide any objection regarding the designation of information claimed to be protected information. If the tribunal determines that such information was not properly designated, the disputing party that submitted the information may (i) withdraw all or part of its submission containing such information, or (ii) agree to resubmit complete and redacted documents with corrected designations in accordance with the tribunal's determination and subparagraph (c). In either case, the other disputing party shall, whenever necessary, resubmit complete and redacted documents which either remove the information withdrawn under (i) by the disputing party that first submitted the information or redesignate the information consistent with the designation under (ii) of the disputing party that first submitted the information.

5.   Nothing in this Section requires a respondent to withhold from the public information required to be disclosed by its laws.

Article 10.22: Governing Law

1.   Subject to paragraph 3, when a claim is submitted under Article 10.16.1(a)(i)(A) or Article 10.16.1(b)(i)(A), the tribunal shall decide the issues in dispute in accordance with this Agreement and applicable rules of international law.

2.   Subject to paragraph 3 and the other terms of this Section, when a claim is submitted under Article 10.16.1(a)(i)(B) or (C), or Article 10.16.1(b)(i)(B) or (C), the tribunal shall apply:

(a)   the rules of law specified in the pertinent investment agreement or investment authorization, or as the disputing parties may otherwise agree; or

(b)   if the rules of law have not been specified or otherwise agreed:

(i)   the law of the respondent, including its rules on the conflict of laws;[7] and

(ii)   such rules of international law as may be applicable.

3.   A decision of the Commission declaring its interpretation of a provision of this Agreement under Article 19.1.3(c) (The Free Trade Commission) shall be binding on a tribunal established under this Section, and any decision or award issued by the tribunal must be consistent with that decision.

Article 10.23: Interpretation of Annexes

1.   Where a respondent asserts as a defense that the measure alleged to be a breach is within the scope of Annex I or Annex II, the tribunal shall, on request of the respondent, request the interpretation of the Commission on the issue. The Commission shall submit in writing any decision declaring its interpretation under Article 19.1.3(c) (The Free Trade Commission) to the tribunal within 60 days of delivery of the request.

2.   A decision issued by the Commission under paragraph 1 shall be binding on the tribunal, and any decision or award issued by the tribunal must be consistent with that decision. If the Commission fails to issue such a decision within 60 days, the tribunal shall decide the issue.

Article 10.24: Expert Reports

Without prejudice to the appointment of other kinds of experts where authorized by the applicable arbitration rules, a tribunal, at the request of a disputing party or, unless the disputing parties disapprove, on its own initiative, may appoint one or more experts to report to it in writing on any factual issue concerning environmental, health, safety, or other scientific matters raised by a disputing party in a proceeding, subject to such terms and conditions as the disputing parties may agree.

---

[7] The "law of the respondent" means the law that a domestic court or tribunal of proper jurisdiction would apply in the same case.

Article 10.25: Consolidation

1.   Where two or more claims have been submitted separately to arbitration under Article 10.16.1 and the claims have a question of law or fact in common and arise out of the same events or circumstances, any disputing party may seek a consolidation order in accordance with the agreement of all the disputing parties sought to be covered by the order or the terms of paragraphs 2 through 10.

2.   A disputing party that seeks a consolidation order under this Article shall deliver, in writing, a request to the Secretary-General and to all the disputing parties sought to be covered by the order and shall specify in the request:

   (a)   the names and addresses of all the disputing parties sought to be covered by the order;

   (b)   the nature of the order sought; and

   (c)   the grounds on which the order is sought.

3.   Unless the Secretary-General finds within 30 days after receiving a request under paragraph 2 that the request is manifestly unfounded, a tribunal shall be established under this Article.

4.   Unless all the disputing parties sought to be covered by the order otherwise agree, a tribunal established under this Article shall comprise three arbitrators:

   (a)   one arbitrator appointed by agreement of the claimants;

   (b)   one arbitrator appointed by the respondent; and

   (c)   the presiding arbitrator appointed by the Secretary-General, provided, however, that the presiding arbitrator shall not be a national of any Party.

5.   If, within 60 days after the Secretary-General receives a request made under paragraph 2, the respondent fails or the claimants fail to appoint an arbitrator in accordance with paragraph 4, the Secretary-General, on the request of any disputing party sought to be covered by the order, shall appoint the arbitrator or arbitrators not yet appointed. If the respondent fails to appoint an arbitrator, the Secretary-General shall appoint a national of the disputing Party, and if the claimants fail to appoint an arbitrator, the Secretary-General shall appoint a national of a Party of the claimants.

6.   Where a tribunal established under this Article is satisfied that two or more claims that have been submitted to arbitration under Article 10.16.1 have a question of law or fact in common, and arise out of the same events or circumstances, the tribunal may, in the interest of fair and efficient resolution of the claims, and after hearing the disputing parties, by order:

   (a)   assume jurisdiction over, and hear and determine together, all or part of the claims;

(b)   assume jurisdiction over, and hear and determine one or more of the claims, the determination of which it believes would assist in the resolution of the others; or

(c)   instruct a tribunal previously established under Article 10.19 to assume jurisdiction over, and hear and determine together, all or part of the claims, provided that

(i)   that tribunal, at the request of any claimant not previously a disputing party before that tribunal, shall be reconstituted with its original members, except that the arbitrator for the claimants shall be appointed pursuant to paragraphs 4(a) and 5; and

(ii)   that tribunal shall decide whether any prior hearing shall be repeated.

7.   Where a tribunal has been established under this Article, a claimant that has submitted a claim to arbitration under Article 10.16.1 and that has not been named in a request made under paragraph 2 may make a written request to the tribunal that it be included in any order made under paragraph 6, and shall specify in the request:

(a)   the name and address of the claimant;

(b)   the nature of the order sought; and

(c)   the grounds on which the order is sought.

The claimant shall deliver a copy of its request to the Secretary-General.

8.   A tribunal established under this Article shall conduct its proceedings in accordance with the UNCITRAL Arbitration Rules, except as modified by this Section.

9.   A tribunal established under Article 10.19 shall not have jurisdiction to decide a claim, or a part of a claim, over which a tribunal established or instructed under this Article has assumed jurisdiction.

10.   On application of a disputing party, a tribunal established under this Article, pending its decision under paragraph 6, may order that the proceedings of a tribunal established under Article 10.19 be stayed, unless the latter tribunal has already adjourned its proceedings.

Article 10.26: Awards

1.   Where a tribunal makes a final award against a respondent, the tribunal may award, separately or in combination, only:

(a)   monetary damages and any applicable interest;

(b)   restitution of property, in which case the award shall provide that the respondent may pay monetary damages and any applicable interest in lieu of restitution.

A tribunal may also award costs and attorney's fees in accordance with this Section and the applicable arbitration rules.

2.   Subject to paragraph 1, where a claim is submitted to arbitration under Article 10.16.1(b):

(a)   an award of restitution of property shall provide that restitution be made to the enterprise;

(b)   an award of monetary damages and any applicable interest shall provide that the sum be paid to the enterprise; and

(c)   the award shall provide that it is made without prejudice to any right that any person may have in the relief under applicable domestic law.

3.   A tribunal is not authorized to award punitive damages.

4.   An award made by a tribunal shall have no binding force except between the disputing parties and in respect of the particular case.

5.   Subject to paragraph 6 and the applicable review procedure for an interim award, a disputing party shall abide by and comply with an award without delay.

6.   A disputing party may not seek enforcement of a final award until:

(a)   in the case of a final award made under the ICSID Convention

(i)   120 days have elapsed from the date the award was rendered and no disputing party has requested revision or annulment of the award; or

(ii)   revision or annulment proceedings have been completed; and

(b)   in the case of a final award under the ICSID Additional Facility Rules or the UNCITRAL Arbitration Rules

(i)   90 days have elapsed from the date the award was rendered and no disputing party has commenced a proceeding to revise, set aside, or annul the award; or

(ii)   a court has dismissed or allowed an application to revise, set aside, or annul the award and there is no further appeal.

7.   Each Party shall provide for the enforcement of an award in its territory.

8.   If the respondent fails to abide by or comply with a final award, on delivery of a request by the Party of the claimant, a panel shall be established under Article 20.6 (Request for an Arbitral Panel). The requesting Party may seek in such proceedings:

(a)   a determination that the failure to abide by or comply with the final award is inconsistent with the obligations of this Agreement; and

(b)   in accordance with Article 20.13 (Initial Report), a recommendation that the respondent abide by or comply with the final award.

9.   A disputing party may seek enforcement of an arbitration award under the ICSID Convention, the New York Convention, or the Inter-American Convention regardless of whether proceedings have been taken under paragraph 8.

10.   A claim that is submitted to arbitration under this Section shall be considered to arise out of a commercial relationship or transaction for purposes of Article I of the New York Convention and Article I of the Inter-American Convention.

Article 10.27: Service of Documents

Delivery of notice and other documents on a Party shall be made to the place named for that Party in Annex 10-G.

Section C: Definitions

Article 10.28: Definitions

For purposes of this Chapter:

Centre means the International Centre for Settlement of Investment Disputes ("ICSID") established by the ICSID Convention;

claimant means an investor of a Party that is a party to an investment dispute with another Party;

disputing parties means the claimant and the respondent;

disputing party means either the claimant or the respondent;

enterprise means an enterprise as defined in Article 2.1 (Definitions of General Application), and a branch of an enterprise;

enterprise of a Party means an enterprise constituted or organized under the law of a Party, and a branch located in the territory of a Party and carrying out business activities there;

freely usable currency means "freely usable currency" as determined by the International Monetary Fund under its *Articles of Agreement*;

ICSID Additional Facility Rules means the *Rules Governing the Additional Facility for the Administration of Proceeding by the Secretariat of the International Centre for Settlement of Investment Disputes*;

ICSID Convention means the *Convention on the Settlement of Investment Disputes between States and Nationals of Other States,* done at Washington, March 18, 1965;

Inter-American Convention means the *Inter-American Convention on International Commercial Arbitration,* done at Panama, January 30, 1975;

investment means every asset that an investor owns or controls, directly or indirectly, that has the characteristics of an investment, including such characteristics as the commitment of capital or other resources, the expectation of gain or profit, or the assumption of risk. Forms that an investment may take include:

    (a)   an enterprise;

    (b)   shares, stock, and other forms of equity participation in an enterprise;

    (c)   bonds, debentures, other debt instruments, and loans;[8,9]

    (d)   futures, options, and other derivatives;

    (e)   turnkey, construction, management, production, concession, revenue-sharing, and other similar contracts;

    (f)   intellectual property rights;

    (g)   licenses, authorizations, permits, and similar rights conferred pursuant to domestic law;[10,11] and

    (h)   other tangible or intangible, movable or immovable property, and related property rights, such as leases, mortgages, liens, and pledges;

investment agreement means a written agreement[12] that takes effect on or after the date of entry into force of this Agreement between a national authority[13] of a Party and a covered investment or an investor of another Party that grants the covered investment or investor rights:

    (a)   with respect to natural resources or other assets that a national authority controls; and

    (b)   upon which the covered investment or the investor relies in establishing or acquiring a covered investment other than the written agreement itself;

investment authorization[14] means an authorization that the foreign investment authority of a Party grants to a covered investment or an investor of another Party;

---

[8] Some forms of debt, such as bonds, debentures, and long-term notes, are more likely to have the characteristics of an investment, while other forms of debt are less likely to have such characteristics.

[9] For purposes of this Agreement, claims to payment that are immediately due and result from the sale of goods or services are not investments.

[10] Whether a particular type of license, authorization, permit, or similar instrument (including a concession, to the extent that it has the nature of such an instrument) has the characteristics of an investment depends on such factors as the nature and extent of the rights that the holder has under the law of the Party. Among the licenses, authorizations, permits, and similar instruments that do not have the characteristics of an investment are those that do not create any rights protected under domestic law. For greater certainty, the foregoing is without prejudice to whether any asset associated with the license, authorization, permit, or similar instrument has the characteristics of an investment.

[11] The term "investment" does not include an order or judgment entered in a judicial or administrative action.

[12] "Written agreement" refers to an agreement in writing, executed by both parties, that creates an exchange of rights and obligations, binding on both parties under the law applicable under Article 10.22.2. For greater certainty, (a) a unilateral act of an administrative or judicial authority, such as a permit, license, or authorization issued by a Party solely in its regulatory capacity or a decree, order, or judgment; and (b) an administrative or judicial consent decree or order, shall not be considered a written agreement.

[13] For purposes of this definition, "national authority" means an authority at the central level of government.

investor of a non-Party means, with respect to a Party, an investor that attempts to make, is making, or has made an investment in the territory of that Party, that is not an investor of a Party;

investor of a Party means a Party or state enterprise thereof, or a national or an enterprise of a Party, that attempts to make, is making, or has made an investment in the territory of another Party; provided, however, that a natural person who is a dual national shall be deemed to be exclusively a national of the State of his or her dominant and effective nationality;

national means a natural person who has the nationality of a Party according to Annex 2.1 (Country-Specific Definitions);

New York Convention means the *United Nations Convention on the Recognition and Enforcement of Foreign Arbitral Awards,* done at New York, June 10, 1958;

non-disputing Party means a Party that is not a party to an investment dispute;

protected information means confidential business information or information that is privileged or otherwise protected from disclosure under a Party's law;

respondent means the Party that is a party to an investment dispute;

Secretary-General means the Secretary-General of ICSID;

tribunal means an arbitration tribunal established under Article 10.19 or 10.25; and

UNCITRAL Arbitration Rules means the arbitration rules of the United Nations Commission on International Trade Law.

Annex 10-A
Public Debt

The rescheduling of the debts of a Central American Party or the Dominican Republic, or of such Party's institutions owned or controlled through ownership interests by such Party, owed to the United States and the rescheduling of any of such Party's debts owed to creditors in general are not subject to any provision of Section A other than Articles 10.3 and 10.4.

Annex 10-B
Customary International Law

The Parties confirm their shared understanding that "customary international law" generally and as specifically referenced in Articles 10.5, 10.6, and Annex 10-C results from a general and consistent practice of States that they follow from a sense of legal obligation. With regard to Article 10.5, the customary international law minimum standard of treatment of aliens refer to all customary international law principles that protect the economic rights and interests of aliens.

---

[14] For greater certainty, actions taken by a Party to enforce laws of general application, such as competition laws, are not encompassed within this definition.

Annex 10-C
Expropriation

The Parties confirm their shared understanding that:

1.   Article 10.7.1 is intended to reflect customary international law concerning the obligation of States with respect to expropriation.

2.   An action or a series of actions by a Party cannot constitute an expropriation unless it interferes with a tangible or intangible property right or property interest in an investment.

3.   Article 10.7.1 addresses two situations. The first is direct expropriation, where an investment is nationalized or otherwise directly expropriated through formal transfer of title or outright seizure.

4.   The second situation addressed by Article 10.7.1 is indirect expropriation, where an action or series of actions by a Party has an effect equivalent to direct expropriation without formal transfer of title or outright seizure.

> (a)   The determination of whether an action or series of actions by a Party, in a specific fact situation, constitutes an indirect expropriation, requires a case-bycase, fact-based inquiry that considers, among other factors:
>
> > (i)   the economic impact of the government action, although the fact that an action or series of actions by a Party has an adverse effect on the economic value of an investment, standing alone, does not establish that an indirect expropriation has occurred;
> >
> > (ii)   the extent to which the government action interferes with distinct, reasonable investment-backed expectations; and
> >
> > (iii)   the character of the government action.
>
> (b)   Except in rare circumstances, nondiscriminatory regulatory actions by a Party that are designed and applied to protect legitimate public welfare objectives, such as public health, safety, and the environment, do not constitute indirect expropriations.

Annex 10-D
Treatment in Case of Strife

1.   No investor may submit to arbitration under Section B a claim alleging that Guatemala has breached Article 10.6.2 as a result of an armed movement or civil disturbance and that the investor or the investor's enterprise has incurred loss or damage by reason of or arising out of such movement or disturbance.

2.   No investor of Guatemala may submit to arbitration under Section B a claim alleging that any other Party has breached Article 10.6.2(b).

3.   The limitation set out in paragraph 1 is without prejudice to other limitations existing in Guatemala's law with respect to an investor's claim that Guatemala has breached Article 10.6.2.

Annex 10-E
Submission of a Claim to Arbitration

1.   An investor of the United States may not submit to arbitration under Section B a claim that a Central American Party or the Dominican Republic has breached an obligation under Section A either:

> (a)   on its own behalf under Article 10.16.1(a), or
>
> (b)   on behalf of an enterprise of a Central American Party or the Dominican Republic that is a juridical person that the investor owns or controls directly or indirectly under Article 10.16.1(b),

if the investor or the enterprise, respectively, has alleged that breach of an obligation under Section A in proceedings before a court or administrative tribunal of a Central American Party or the Dominican Republic.

2.   For greater certainty, if an investor of the United States elects to submit a claim of the type described in paragraph 1 to a court or administrative tribunal of a Central American Party or the Dominican Republic, that election shall be definitive, and the investor may not thereafter submit the claim to arbitration under Section B.

3.   Notwithstanding Article 10.18, an investor of the United States may not submit to arbitration under Section B a claim relating to an investment in sovereign debt instruments with a maturity of less than one year unless one year has elapsed from the date of the events giving rise to the claim.

Annex 10-F
Appellate Body or Similar Mechanism

1.   Within three months of the date of entry into force of this Agreement, the Commission shall establish a Negotiating Group to develop an appellate body or similar mechanism to review awards rendered by tribunals under this Chapter. Such appellate body or similar mechanism shall be designed to provide coherence to the interpretation of investment provisions in the Agreement. The Commission shall direct the Negotiating Group to take into account the following issues, among others:

> (a)   the nature and composition of an appellate body or similar mechanism;
>
> (b)   the applicable scope and standard of review;
>
> (c)   transparency of proceedings of an appellate body or similar mechanism;
>
> (d)   the effect of decisions by an appellate body or similar mechanism;
>
> (e)   the relationship of review by an appellate body or similar mechanism to the arbitral rules that may be selected under Articles 10.16 and 10.25; and

(f)   the relationship of review by an appellate body or similar mechanism to existing domestic laws and international law on the enforcement of arbitral awards.

2.   The Commission shall direct the Negotiating Group to provide to the Commission, within one year of establishment of the Negotiating Group, a draft amendment to the Agreement that establishes an appellate body or similar mechanism. On approval of the draft amendment by the Parties, in accordance with Article 22.2 (Amendments), the Agreement shall be so amended.

Annex 10-G
Service of Documents on a Party Under Section B

Costa Rica

Notices and other documents in disputes under Section B shall be served on Costa Rica by delivery to:

Dirección de Aplicación de Acuerdos
Comerciales Internacionales
Ministerio de Comercio Exterior
San José, Costa Rica

The Dominican Republic

Notices and other documents in disputes under Section B shall be served on the Dominican Republic by delivery to:

Dirección de Comercio Exterior y Administración de Tratados Comerciales Internacionales
Secretaría de Estado de Industria y Comercio
Santo Domingo, República Dominicana

El Salvador

Notices and other documents in disputes under Section B shall be served on El Salvador by delivery to:

Dirección de Administración de Tratados Comerciales
Ministerio de Economía
Alameda Juan Pablo II y Calle Guadalupe
Edificio C1-C2, Plan Maestro Centro de Gobierno
San Salvador, El Salvador

Guatemala

Notices and other documents in disputes under Section B shall be served on Guatemala by delivery to:

Ministerio de Economía
Ciudad de Guatemala, Guatemala

Honduras

Notices and other documents in disputes under Section B shall be served on Honduras by delivery to:

Dirección General de Integración Económica y Política Comercial
Secretaría de Estado en los Despachos de Industria y Comercio
Boulevard José Cecilio del Valle
Edificio San José, antiguo edificio de Fenaduanah
Tegucigalpa, Honduras

Nicaragua

Notices and other documents in disputes under Section B shall be served on Nicaragua by delivery to:

Dirección de Integración y Administración de Tratados, or its successor
Ministerio de Fomento, Industria y Comercio
Managua, Nicaragua

United States

Notices and other documents in disputes under Section B shall be served on the United States by delivery to:

Executive Director (L/EX)
Office of the Legal Adviser
Department of State
Washington, D.C. 20520
United States of America

Chapter Eleven
Cross-Border Trade in Services

Article 11.1: Scope and Coverage

1.   This Chapter applies to measures adopted or maintained by a Party affecting cross-border trade in services by service suppliers of another Party. Such measures include measures affecting:

   (a)   the production, distribution, marketing, sale, and delivery of a service;

   (b)   the purchase or use of, or payment for, a service;

   (c)   the access to and use of distribution, transport, or telecommunications networks and services in connection with the supply of a service;

   (d)   the presence in its territory of a service supplier of another Party; and

    (e)   the provision of a bond or other form of financial security as a condition for the supply of a service.

2.   For purposes of this Chapter, "measures adopted or maintained by a Party" means measures adopted or maintained by:

    (a)   central, regional, or local governments and authorities; and

    (b)   non-governmental bodies in the exercise of powers delegated by central, regional, or local governments or authorities.

3.   Articles 11.4, 11.7, and 11.8 also apply to measures by a Party affecting the supply of a service in its territory by an investor of another Party as defined in Article 10.28 (Definitions) or a covered investment.[1]

4.   This Chapter does not apply to:

    (a)   financial services, as defined in Article 12.20 (Definitions), except as provided in paragraph 3;

    (b)   air services, including domestic and international air transportation services, whether scheduled or non-scheduled, and related services in support of air services, other than:

        (i)   aircraft repair and maintenance services during which an aircraft is withdrawn from service, and

        (ii)   specialty air services;

    (c)   procurement; or

    (d)   subsidies or grants provided by a Party, including government-supported loans, guarantees and insurance.

5.   This Chapter does not impose any obligation on a Party with respect to a national of another Party seeking access to its employment market, or employed on a permanent basis in its territory, and does not confer any right on that national with respect to that access or employment.

6.   This Chapter does not apply to services supplied in the exercise of governmental authority. A "service supplied in the exercise of governmental authority" means any service that is supplied neither on a commercial basis, nor in competition with one or more service suppliers.

Article 11.2: National Treatment

1.   Each Party shall accord to service suppliers of another Party treatment no less favorable than that it accords, in like circumstances, to its own service suppliers.

---

[1] The Parties understand that nothing in this Chapter, including this paragraph, is subject to investor-state dispute settlement pursuant to Section B of Chapter Ten (Investment).

2.   The treatment to be accorded by a Party under paragraph 1 means, with respect to a regional level of government, treatment no less favorable than the most favorable treatment accorded, in like circumstances, by that regional level of government to service suppliers of the Party of which it forms a part.

Article 11.3: Most-Favored-Nation Treatment

Each Party shall accord to service suppliers of another Party treatment no less favorable than that it accords, in like circumstances, to service suppliers of any other Party or a non-Party.

Article 11.4: Market Access

No Party may adopt or maintain, either on the basis of a regional subdivision or on the basis of its entire territory, measures that:

(a)   impose limitations on:

   (i)   the number of service suppliers whether in the form of numerical quotas, monopolies, exclusive service suppliers, or the requirement of an economic needs test,

   (ii)   the total value of service transactions or assets in form of numerical quotas or the requirement of an economic needs test,

   (iii)   the total number of service operations or on the total quantity of services output expressed in terms of designated numerical units in the form of quotas or the requirement of an economic needs test,[2] or

   (iv)   the total number of natural persons that may be employed in a particular service sector or that a service supplier may employ and who are necessary for, and directly related to, the supply of a specific service in the form of numerical quotas or the requirement of an economic needs test; or

(b)   restrict or require specific types of legal entity or joint venture through which a service supplier may supply a service.

Article 11.5: Local Presence

No Party may require a service supplier of another Party to establish or maintain a representative office or any form of enterprise, or to be resident, in its territory as a condition for the cross-border supply of a service.

Article 11.6: Non-conforming Measures

1.   Articles 11.2, 11.3, 11.4, and 11.5 do not apply to:

(a)   any existing non-conforming measure that is maintained by a Party at:

---

[2] This clause does not cover measures of a Party that limit inputs for the supply of services.

        (i)   the central level of government, as set out by that Party in its Schedule to Annex I;

        (ii)   a regional level of government, as set out by that Party in its Schedule to Annex I; or

        (iii)   a local level of government;

    (b)   the continuation or prompt renewal of any non-conforming measure referred to in subparagraph (a); or

    (c)   an amendment to any non-conforming measure referred to in subparagraph (a) to the extent that the amendment does not decrease the conformity of the measure, as it existed immediately before the amendment, with Articles 11.2, 11.3, 11.4, and

2.   Articles 11.2, 11.3, 11.4, and 11.5 do not apply to any measure that a Party adopts or maintains with respect to sectors, sub-sectors or activities as set out in its Schedule to Annex II.

Article 11.7: Transparency in Developing and Applying Regulations[3]

Further to Chapter Eighteen (Transparency):

    (a)   each Party shall maintain or establish appropriate mechanisms for responding to inquiries from interested persons regarding its regulations relating to the subject matter of this Chapter;

    (b)   at the time it adopts final regulations relating to the subject matter of this Chapter, each Party shall, to the extent possible, including on request, address in writing substantive comments received from interested persons with respect to the proposed regulations; and

    (c)   to the extent possible, each Party shall allow a reasonable time between publication of final regulations and their effective date.

Article 11.8: Domestic Regulation

1.   Where a Party requires authorization for the supply of a service, the Party's competent authorities shall, within a reasonable time after the submission of an application considered complete under its laws and regulations, inform the applicant of the decision concerning the application. At the request of the applicant, the Party's competent authorities shall provide, without undue delay, information concerning the status of the application. This obligation shall not apply to authorization requirements that are within the scope of Article 11.6.2.

2.   With a view to ensuring that measures relating to qualification requirements and procedures, technical standards, and licensing requirements do not constitute unnecessary

---

[3] For greater certainty, "regulations" includes regulations establishing or applying to licensing authorization or criteria.

barriers to trade in services, each Party shall endeavor to ensure, as appropriate for individual sectors, that any such measures that it adopts or maintains are:

(a)   based on objective and transparent criteria, such as competence and the ability to supply the service;

(b)   not more burdensome than necessary to ensure the quality of the service; and

(c)   in the case of licensing procedures, not in themselves a restriction on the supply of the service.

3.   If the results of the negotiations related to Article VI:4 of the GATS (or the results of any similar negotiations undertaken in other multilateral fora in which the Parties participate) enter into effect for each Party, this Article shall be amended, as appropriate, after consultations between the Parties, to bring those results into effect under this Agreement. The Parties will coordinate on such negotiations as appropriate.

Article 11.9: Mutual Recognition

1.   For the purposes of the fulfillment, in whole or in part, of its standards or criteria for the authorization, licensing, or certification of services suppliers, and subject to the requirements of paragraph 4, a Party may recognize the education or experience obtained, requirements met, or licenses or certifications granted in a particular country, including another Party and a non-Party.

Such recognition, which may be achieved through harmonization or otherwise, may be based upon an agreement or arrangement with the country concerned or may be accorded autonomously.

2.   Where a Party recognizes, autonomously or by agreement or arrangement, the education or experience obtained, requirements met, or licenses or certifications granted in the territory of another Party or a non-Party, nothing in Article 11.3 shall be construed to require the Party to accord such recognition to the education or experience obtained, requirements met, or licenses or certifications granted in the territory of any other Party.

3.   A Party that is a party to an agreement or arrangement of the type referred to in paragraph 1, whether existing or future, shall afford adequate opportunity for another Party, if that other Party is interested, to negotiate its accession to such an agreement or arrangement or to negotiate a comparable one with it. Where a Party accords recognition autonomously, it shall afford adequate opportunity for another Party to demonstrate that education, experience, licenses, or certifications obtained or requirements met in that other Party's territory should be recognized.

4.   No Party may accord recognition in a manner that would constitute a means of discrimination between countries in the application of its standards or criteria for the authorization, licensing, or certification of services suppliers, or a disguised restriction on trade in services.

5.   Annex 11.9 applies to measures adopted or maintained by a Party relating to the licensing or certification of professional service suppliers as set out in that Annex.

Article 11.10: Transfers and Payments

1.   Each Party shall permit all transfers and payments relating to the cross-border supply of services to be made freely and without delay into and out of its territory.

2.   Each Party shall permit such transfers and payments relating to the cross-border supply of services to be made in a freely usable currency at the market rate of exchange prevailing at the time of transfer.

3.   Notwithstanding paragraphs 1 and 2, a Party may prevent a transfer or payment through the equitable, non-discriminatory, and good faith application of its laws relating to:

   (a)   bankruptcy, insolvency, or the protection of the rights of creditors;

   (b)   issuing, trading, or dealing in securities, futures, options, or derivatives;

   (c)   financial reporting or record keeping of transfers when necessary to assist law enforcement or financial regulatory authorities;

   (d)   criminal or penal offenses; or

   (e)   ensuring compliance with orders or judgments in judicial or administrative proceedings.

Article 11.11: Implementation

The Parties shall consult annually, or as otherwise agreed, to review the implementation of this Chapter and consider other issues of mutual interest.

Article 11.12: Denial of Benefits

1.   A Party may deny the benefits of this Chapter to a service supplier of another Party if the service is being supplied by an enterprise owned or controlled by persons of a non-Party, and the denying Party:

   (a)   does not maintain diplomatic relations with the non-Party; or

   (b)   adopts or maintains measures with respect to the non-Party that prohibit transactions with the enterprise or that would be violated or circumvented if the benefits of this Chapter were accorded to the enterprise.

2.   Subject to Articles 18.3 (Notification and Provision of Information) and 20.4 (Consultations), a Party may deny the benefits of this Chapter to a service supplier of another Party that is an enterprise of such other Party if the enterprise has no substantial business activities in the territory of any Party, other than the denying Party, and persons of a non-Party, or the denying Party, own or control the enterprise.

Article 11.13: Specific Commitments

1.   Express Delivery Services:

(a)   The Parties affirm that measures affecting express delivery services are subject to this Agreement.

(b)   For purposes of this Agreement, express delivery services means the collection, transport, and delivery, of documents, printed matter, parcels, goods, or other items on an expedited basis, while tracking and maintaining control of these items throughout the supply of the service. Express delivery services do not include (i) air transport services, (ii) services supplied in the exercise of governmental authority, or (iii) maritime transport services.[4]

(c)   The Parties express their desire to maintain at least the level of market openness they provided for express delivery services existing on the date this Agreement is signed.

(d)   Neither a Central American Party nor the Dominican Republic may adopt or maintain any restriction on express delivery services that is not in existence on the date this Agreement is signed. Each such Party confirms that it does not intend to direct revenues from its postal monopoly to benefit express delivery services as defined in subparagraph (b). Under title 39 of the United States Code, an independent government agency determines whether postal rates meet the requirement that each class of mail or type of mail service bear the direct and indirect postal costs attributable to that class or type plus that portion of all other costs of the U.S. Postal Service reasonably assignable to such class or type.

(e)   Each Party shall ensure that, where its monopoly supplier of postal services competes, either directly or through an affiliated company, in the supply of express delivery services outside the scope of its monopoly rights, such a supplier does not abuse its monopoly position to act in its territory in a manner inconsistent with the Party's obligations under Articles 11.2, 11.3, 11.4, 10.3 (National Treatment), or 10.4 (Most-Favored-Nation Treatment). The Parties also reaffirm their obligations under Article VIII of the GATS.[5]

2.   A Party's Section of Annex 11.13 sets out specific commitments by that Party.

Article 11.14: Definitions

For purposes of this Chapter:

cross-border trade in services or **cross-border supply of services** means the supply of a service:

(a)   from the territory of one Party into the territory of another Party;

(b)   in the territory of one Party by a person of that Party to a person of another Party; or

---

[4] For greater certainty, for the United States, express delivery services do not include delivery of letters subject to the *Private Express Statutes* (18 U.S.C. § 1693 *et seq.*, 39 U.S.C. § 601 *et seq.*), but do include delivery of letters subject to the exceptions to, or suspensions promulgated under, those statutes, which permit private delivery of extremely urgent letters.

[5] For greater certainty, the Parties reaffirm that nothing in this Article is subject to investor-state dispute settlement pursuant to Section B of Chapter Ten (Investment).

     (c)   by a national of a Party in the territory of another Party;

but does not include the supply of a service in the territory of a Party by an investor of another Party as defined in Article 10.28 (Definitions) or a covered investment;

enterprise means an "enterprise" as defined in Article 2.1 (Definitions of General Application), and a branch of an enterprise;

enterprise of a Party means an enterprise constituted or organized under the laws of that Party, and a branch located in the territory of that Party and carrying out business activities there;

professional services means services, the provision of which requires specialized postsecondary education, or equivalent training or experience, and for which the right to practice is granted or restricted by a Party, but does not include services provided by trades-persons or vessel and aircraft crew members;

service supplier of a Party means a person of a Party that seeks to supply or supplies a service;[6] and

specialty air services means any non-transportation air services, such as aerial fire-fighting, sightseeing, spraying, surveying, mapping, photography, parachute jumping, glider towing, and helicopter-lift for logging and construction, and other airborne agricultural, industrial, and inspection services.

Annex 11.9
Professional Services

Development of Professional Standards

1.   The Parties shall encourage the relevant bodies in their respective territories to develop mutually acceptable standards and criteria for licensing and certification of professional service suppliers and to provide recommendations on mutual recognition to the Commission.

2.   The standards and criteria referred to in paragraph 1 may be developed with regard to the following matters:

     (a)   education – accreditation of schools or academic programs;

     (b)   examinations – qualifying examinations for licensing, including alternative methods of assessment such as oral examinations and interviews;

     (c)   experience – length and nature of experience required for licensing;

     (d)   conduct and ethics – standards of professional conduct and the nature of disciplinary action for non-conformity with those standards;

---

[6] The Parties understand that for purposes of Articles 11.2 and 11.3, "service suppliers" has the same meaning as "services and service suppliers" in the GATS.

(e)   professional development and re-certification – continuing education and ongoing requirements to maintain professional certification;

(f)   scope of practice – extent of, or limitations on, permissible activities;

(g)   local knowledge – requirements for knowledge of such matters as local laws, regulations, language, geography, or climate; and

(h)   consumer protection – alternatives to residency requirements, including bonding, professional liability insurance, and client restitution funds, to provide for the protection of consumers.

3.   On receipt of a recommendation referred to in paragraph 1, the Commission shall review the recommendation within a reasonable time to determine whether it is consistent with this Agreement. Based on the Commission's review, each Party shall encourage its respective competent authorities, where appropriate, to implement the recommendation within a mutually agreed time.

Temporary licensing

4.   Where the Parties agree, each Party shall encourage the relevant bodies in its territory to develop procedures for the temporary licensing of professional service suppliers of another Party.

Review

5.   The Commission shall review the implementation of this Annex at least once every three years.

Annex 11.13
Specific Commitments

Section A: Costa Rica

1.   Costa Rica shall repeal articles 2 and 9 of Law No. 6209, entitled *Ley de Protección al Representante de Casas Extranjeras*, dated 9 March 1978, and its regulation, and item b) of article 361 of the *Código de Comercio*, Law No. 3284 of 24 April 1964, effective on the date of entry into force of this Agreement.

2.   Subject to paragraph 1, Costa Rica shall enact a new legal regime that shall become applicable to contracts of representation, distribution, or production, and:

(a)   shall apply principles of general contract law to such contracts;

(b)   shall be consistent with the obligations of this Agreement and the principle of freedom of contract;

(c)   shall treat such contracts as establishing an exclusive relationship only if the contract explicitly states that the relationship is exclusive;

(d)   shall provide that the termination of such contracts either on their termination dates or in the circumstances described in subparagraph (e) is just cause for a goods or service supplier of another Party to terminate the contract or allow the contract to expire without renewal; and

(e)   will allow contracts with no termination date to be terminated by any of the parties by giving ten months advance termination notice.

3.   The absence of an express provision for settlement of disputes in a contract of representation, distribution, or production shall give rise to a presumption that the parties intended to settle any disputes through binding arbitration. Such arbitration may take place in Costa Rica. However, the presumption of an intent to submit to arbitration shall not apply where any of the parties objects to arbitration.

4.   The United States and Costa Rica shall encourage parties to existing contracts of representation, distribution, or production to renegotiate such contracts so as to make them subject to the new legal regime enacted in accordance with paragraph 2.

5.   In any case, the repeal of articles 2 and 9 of Law No. 6209 shall not impair any vested right, when applicable, derived from that legislation and recognized under Article 34 of the *Constitución Política de la República de Costa Rica*.

6.   Costa Rica shall, to the maximum extent possible, encourage and facilitate the use of arbitration for the settlement of disputes in contracts of representation, distribution, or production. To this end, Costa Rica shall endeavor to facilitate the operation of arbitration centers and other effective means of alternative resolution of claims arising pursuant to Law No. 6209 or the new legal regime enacted in accordance with paragraph 2, and shall encourage the development of rules for such arbitrations that provide, to the greatest extent possible, for the prompt, low-cost, and fair resolution of such claims.

7.   For purposes of this Section:

(a)   **contract of representation, distribution, or production** has the same meaning as under Law No. 6209; and

(b)   **termination date** means the date provided in the contract for the contract to end, or the end of a contract extension period agreed upon by the parties to the contract.

Section B: The Dominican Republic

1.   The Dominican Republic shall not apply Law No. 173 to any covered contract signed after the date of entry into force of this Agreement unless the contract explicitly provides for the application of Law No. 173 and in place of Law No. 173 shall:

(a)   apply principles of the *Código Civil* of the Dominican Republic to the covered contract;

(b)   treat the covered contract in a manner consistent with the obligations of this Agreement and the principle of freedom of contract;

    (c)   treat the termination of the covered contract, either on its termination date or pursuant to subparagraph (d), as just cause for a goods or service supplier to terminate the contract or allow the contract to expire without renewal;

    (d)   if the covered contract has no termination date, allow it to be terminated by any of the parties by giving six months advance termination notice;

    (e)   provide that after the termination of the covered contract or the decision not to renew it:

        (i)   if the covered contract contains an indemnification provision, including a provision providing for no indemnification, the indemnification shall be based on such provision;

        (ii)   if the covered contract contains no such provision, any indemnification shall be based on actual economic damages and not on a statutory formula;

        (iii)   the principal shall honor any pending warranties; and

        (iv)   the principal shall compensate the distributor for the value of any inventory that the distributor is unable to sell by reason of the termination or decision not to renew the contract. The value of inventory shall include any customs duties, surcharges, freight expenses, internal movement costs, and inventory carrying costs paid by the distributor;

    (f)   allow disputes arising from the covered contract to be resolved through binding arbitration; and

    (g)   allow the parties to the covered contract to establish in the contract the mechanisms and forums that will be available in the case of disputes.

Nothing in subparagraph (c) shall prevent parties from demanding indemnification, when appropriate, in the form, type, and amount agreed in the contract.

2.   If Law No. 173 applies to a covered contract, either because the contract was signed before the entry into force of this Agreement or the contract explicitly provides for the application of Law No. 173, and the contract is registered with the *Banco Central* in accordance with Article 10 of Law No. 173, the Dominican Republic shall provide, consistent with articles 46 and 47 of the *Constitución de la República Dominicana*, that:

    (a)   the amount of an indemnity for termination of a covered contract based on the factors listed in Article 3 of Law No. 173 shall be no greater than would be available to the claimant under the *Código Civil* of the Dominican Republic;

    (b)   during or after the conciliation process under Article 7 of Law No. 173, the parties to a contract may agree to resolve the dispute through binding arbitration; and

(c)   the Government of the Dominican Republic and the conciliation authorities shall take all appropriate steps to encourage the resolution of disputes arising under covered contracts through binding arbitration.

3.   For all covered contracts,

(a)   a goods or service supplier shall not be required to pay damages or an indemnity for terminating a covered contract for just cause or allowing such a contract to expire without renewal for just cause; and

(b)   a contract shall be interpreted as establishing an exclusive distributorship only to the extent that the terms of the contract explicitly state that the distributor has exclusive rights to distribute a product or service.

4.   The requirement that the parties to a contract seek a negotiated settlement of any dispute through conciliation, and all other provisions of Law No. 173, shall retain all their validity and force for all contractual relations not subject to paragraph 1.

5.   For purposes of this Section:

(a)   **covered contract** means a concession contract, as defined in Law No. 173, to which a goods or service supplier of the United States or any enterprise controlled by such supplier is a party;

(b)   **Law No. 173** means Law No. 173, entitled "*Ley sobre Protección a los Agentes Importadores de Mercancías y Productos*," dated April 6, 1966, and its modifications; and

(c)   **termination date** means the date provided in the contract, or the end of a period of extension of a contract agreed upon by the parties to the contract.

Section C: El Salvador

1.   Articles 394 through 399-B of the *Código de Comercio* shall apply only to contracts that were entered into after such Articles entered into force.

2.   Articles 394 through 399-B of the *Código de Comercio* shall not apply to any distribution contract that a person of the United States enters into after the date of entry into force of this Agreement, as long as the contract so provides.

3.   Parties to a distribution contract shall be permitted to establish in the contract the mechanisms and forums that will be available in the case of disputes.

4.   If a distribution contract makes specific provision for indemnification, including a provision providing for no indemnification, Article 397 of the *Código de Comercio* shall not apply to that contract.

5.   Under Salvadoran law, a distribution contract shall be treated as exclusive only if the contract states so expressly.

6.   El Salvador shall encourage parties to distribution contracts made after the date of entry into force of this Agreement to include provisions providing for binding arbitration of disputes and specifying methods for determining any indemnity.

7.   For purposes of this Section, **distribution contract** has the same meaning as under Articles 394 through 399-B of the *Código de Comercio*.

Section D: Guatemala

1.   The Parties recognize that Guatemala, through Decree 8-98 of the *Congreso de la República*, which reformed the *Código de Comercio de Guatemala*, repealed Decree 78-71, which regulated contracts of agency, distribution, or representation, and created a new regime for agents of commerce, distributors, and representatives.

2.   During the year following the date of entry into force of this Agreement, the United States and Guatemala shall encourage parties to contracts without a fixed termination date that remain subject to Decree 78-71 to renegotiate such contracts. The new contracts shall be based on the terms and conditions established by mutual agreement of the parties and on the provisions of the *Código de Comercio de Guatemala*, which shall regulate the activities of agents of commerce, distributors, and representatives. The United States and Guatemala shall also encourage parties to other contracts of agency, distribution, or representation that remain subject to Decree 78-71 to renegotiate such contracts so as to make them subject to the new regime referenced in paragraph 1.

3.   The absence of an express provision for settlement of disputes in a contract of agency, distribution, or representation shall, to the extent consistent with the *Constitución Política de la República de Guatemala,* give rise to a rebuttable presumption that the parties intended to settle any disputes through binding arbitration.

4.   The United States and Guatemala shall encourage the parties to contracts of agency, distribution, or representation to settle any disputes through binding arbitration. In particular, if the amount and form of any indemnification payment is not established in the contract and a party wishes to terminate the contract, the parties may agree to arbitration to establish the amount, if any, of the indemnity.

5.   For purposes of this Section:

    (a)   **termination date** means the date provided in the contract for the contract to end, or the end of a contract extension period agreed upon by the parties to the contract; and

    (b)   **contract of agency, distribution, or representation** has the same meaning as under Decree 78-71.

Section E: Honduras

1.   The obligations set out in paragraphs 2, 3, and 4 shall not apply to:

(a) express conditions included in a contract of representation, distribution, or agency; or

(b) to contractual relations entered into before the date of entry into force of this Agreement.

2. Honduras may not require a goods or service supplier of another Party:

(a) to supply such goods or services in Honduras by means of a representative, agent, or distributor, except as otherwise provided by law for reasons of health, safety, or consumer protection;

(b) to offer or introduce goods or services in the territory of Honduras through existing concessionaires for such goods or services unless a contract between them requires an exclusive relationship; or

(d) to pay damages or an indemnity for terminating a contract of representation, or agency for just cause or allowing such a contract to expire without renewal for just cause.

3. Honduras may not require that a representative, agent, or distributor be a national of Honduras or an enterprise controlled by nationals of Honduras;

4. Honduras shall provide that:

(a) the fact that a contract of representation, distribution, or agency has reached its termination date shall be considered just cause for a goods or service supplier of another Party to terminate the contract or allow the contract to expire without renewal; and

(b) any damages or indemnity for terminating a contract of representation, distribution, or agency, or allowing it to expire without renewal, without just cause shall be based on the general law of contracts.

Nothing in subparagraph (b) shall be construed to require Honduras to adopt any measure that affects the right of the parties to demand indemnification, when appropriate, in the form, type, and amount agreed in the contract.

5. Honduras shall provide that:

(a) if the amount and form of any indemnification payment is not established in a contract of representation, distribution, or agency and a party wishes to terminate the contract;

(i) the parties may agree to resolve any dispute regarding such payment in the Center for Conciliation and Arbitration of Honduras, or if the parties agree otherwise, to another arbitration center; and

(ii) in such proceeding general principles of contract law will be applied;

(b)   Decree Law No. 549 shall apply to a contract only if:

  (i)   the representative, distributor, or agent has registered with the *Secretaría de Estado en los Despachos de Industria y Comercio*, which shall be possible only if it is party to a written contract of representation, distribution, or agency; and

  (ii)   the contract was entered into while such law was in effect; and

(c)   in any decision awarding an indemnity calculated under Article 14 of Decree Law No. 549, the amount shall be calculated as of the date of entry into force of this Agreement, expressed in terms of Honduran lempiras as of that date, and converted into U.S. dollars at the exchange rate in effect on the date of the decision.

6.   Under Honduran law, a contract of representation, distribution, or agency is exclusive only if the contract states so expressly.

7.   For purposes of this Section:

(a)   **termination date** means the date provided in the contract for the contract to end, at 12:00 p.m. on that day, or the end of a contract extension period agreed upon by the parties to the contract; and

(b)   **contract of representation, distribution, or agency** has the same meaning as under Decree Law No. 549.

Chapter Twelve
Financial Services

Article 12.1: Scope and Coverage

1.   This Chapter applies to measures adopted or maintained by a Party relating to:

(a)   financial institutions of another Party;

(b)   investors of another Party, and investments of such investors, in financial institutions in the Party's territory; and

(c)   cross-border trade in financial services.

2.   Chapters Ten (Investment) and Eleven (Cross-Border Trade in Services) apply to measures described in paragraph 1 only to the extent that such Chapters or Articles of such Chapters are incorporated into this Chapter.

(a)   Articles 10.7 (Expropriation and Compensation), 10.8 (Transfers), 10.11 (Investment and Environment), 10.12 (Denial of Benefits), 10.14 (Special

Formalities and Information Requirements), and 11.12 (Denial of Benefits) are hereby incorporated into and made a part of this Chapter.

(b)   Section B of Chapter Ten (Investor-State Dispute Settlement) is hereby incorporated into and made a part of this Chapter solely for claims that a Party has breached Article 10.7, 10.8, 10.12, or 10.14, as incorporated into this Chapter.

(c)   Article 11.10 (Transfers and Payments) is incorporated into and made a part of this Chapter to the extent that cross-border trade in financial services is subject to obligations pursuant to Article 12.5.

3.   This Chapter does not apply to measures adopted or maintained by a Party relating to:

(a)   activities or services forming part of a public retirement plan or statutory system of social security; or

(b)   activities or services conducted for the account or with the guarantee or using the financial resources of the Party, including its public entities, except that this Chapter shall apply if a Party allows any of the activities or services referred to in subparagraph (a) or (b) to be conducted by its financial institutions in competition with a public entity or a financial institution.

4.   (a)   Subject to subparagraph (c), for two years beginning on the date of entry into force of this Agreement, this Chapter shall not apply to:

(i)   measures adopted or maintained by the Dominican Republic relating to financial institutions of Costa Rica, El Salvador, Honduras, or Nicaragua to the extent they supply banking services; investors of Costa Rica, El Salvador, Honduras, or Nicaragua, and investments of such investors, in such financial institutions in the territory of the Dominican Republic; or cross-border trade in financial services between the Dominican Republic and Costa Rica, El Salvador, Honduras, or Nicaragua; or

(ii)   measures adopted or maintained by Costa Rica, El Salvador, Honduras, or Nicaragua relating to financial institutions of the Dominican Republic to the extent they supply banking services; investors of the Dominican Republic, and investments of such investors, in such financial institutions in the territory of Costa Rica, El Salvador, Honduras, or Nicaragua; or cross-border trade in financial services between Costa Rica, El Salvador, Honduras, or Nicaragua and the Dominican Republic;

(iii)   measures adopted or maintained by the Dominican Republic relating to financial institutions of Guatemala; investors of Guatemala, and investments of such investors, in such financial institutions in the territory of the Dominican Republic; or cross-border trade in financial services between the Dominican Republic and Guatemala; or

(iv)   measures adopted or maintained by Guatemala relating to financial institutions of the Dominican Republic; investors of the Dominican Republic, and investments of such investors, in such financial institutions in the territory of Guatemala; or cross-border trade in financial services between Guatemala and the Dominican Republic.

(b)   During the two-year period referred to in subparagraph (a), the Dominican Republic and each Central American Party shall seek to agree on those measures described in subparagraph (a) that shall be considered non-conforming measures pursuant to Article 12.9 and that shall be reflected in their respective Schedules to Annex III for purposes of modifying their rights and obligations with respect to each other under this Chapter.

(c)   If the Commission approves any such agreement during this period, each relevant Party's schedule shall be modified accordingly. Subparagraph (a) shall cease to apply as between the Dominican Republic and the relevant Central American Party on the date the modification takes effect.

Article 12.2: National Treatment

1.   Each Party shall accord to investors of another Party treatment no less favorable than that it accords to its own investors, in like circumstances, with respect to the establishment, acquisition, expansion, management, conduct, operation, and sale or other disposition of financial institutions and investments in financial institutions in its territory.

2.   Each Party shall accord to financial institutions of another Party and to investments of investors of another Party in financial institutions treatment no less favorable than that it accords to its own financial institutions, and to investments of its own investors in financial institutions, in like circumstances, with respect to the establishment, acquisition, expansion, management, conduct, operation, and sale or other disposition of financial institutions and investments.

3.   For purposes of the national treatment obligations in Article 12.5.1, a Party shall accord to cross-border financial service suppliers of another Party treatment no less favorable than that it accords to its own financial service suppliers, in like circumstances, with respect to the supply of the relevant service.

Article 12.3: Most-Favored-Nation Treatment

1.   Each Party shall accord to investors of another Party, financial institutions of another Party, investments of investors in financial institutions, and cross-border financial service suppliers of another Party treatment no less favorable than that it accords to the investors, financial institutions, investments of investors in financial institutions, and cross-border financial service suppliers of any other Party or of a non-Party, in like circumstances.

2.   A Party may recognize prudential measures of another Party or of a non-Party in the application of measures covered by this Chapter. Such recognition may be:

(a)   accorded unilaterally;

(b)   achieved through harmonization or other means; or

(c)   based upon an agreement or arrangement with another Party or a non-Party.

3.   A Party according recognition of prudential measures under paragraph 2 shall provide adequate opportunity to another Party to demonstrate that circumstances exist in which there are or would be equivalent regulation, oversight, implementation of regulation, and, if appropriate, procedures concerning the sharing of information between the relevant Parties.

4.   Where a Party accords recognition of prudential measures under paragraph 2(c) and the circumstances set out in paragraph 3 exist, the Party shall provide adequate opportunity to another Party to negotiate accession to the agreement or arrangement, or to negotiate a comparable agreement or arrangement.

Article 12.4: Market Access for Financial Institutions

No Party may adopt or maintain, with respect to financial institutions of another Party, either on the basis of a regional subdivision or on the basis of its entire territory, measures that:

(a)   impose limitations on:

(i)   the number of financial institutions whether in the form of numerical quotas, monopolies, exclusive service suppliers, or the requirements of an economic needs test;

(ii)   the total value of financial service transactions or assets in the form of numerical quotas or the requirement of an economic needs test;

(iii)   the total number of financial service operations or on the total quantity of financial services output expressed in terms of designated numerical units in the form of quotas or the requirement of an economic needs test; or

(iv)   the total number of natural persons that may be employed in a particular financial service sector or that a financial institution may employ and who are necessary for, and directly related to, the supply of a specific financial service in the form of numerical quotas or the requirement of an economic needs test; or

(b)   restrict or require specific types of legal entity or joint venture through which a financial institution may supply a service.

For purposes of this Article, "financial institutions of another Party" includes financial institutions that investors of another Party seek to establish in the territory of the Party.

Article 12.5: Cross-Border Trade

1.   Each Party shall permit, under terms and conditions that accord national treatment, crossborder financial service suppliers of another Party to supply the services specified in Annex 12.5.1.

2.   Each Party shall permit persons located in its territory, and its nationals wherever located, to purchase financial services from cross-border financial service suppliers of another Party located in the territory of that other Party or of any other Party. This obligation does not require a Party to permit such suppliers to do business or solicit in its territory. Each Party may define

"doing business" and "solicitation" for purposes of this obligation, provided that those definitions are not inconsistent with paragraph 1.

3.　　Without prejudice to other means of prudential regulation of cross-border trade in financial services, a Party may require the registration of cross-border financial service suppliers of another Party and of financial instruments.

Article 12.6: New Financial Services[1]

Each Party shall permit a financial institution of another Party to supply any new financial service that the Party would permit its own financial institutions, in like circumstances, to supply without additional legislative action by the Party. Notwithstanding Article 12.4(b), a Party may determine the institutional and juridical form through which the new financial service may be supplied and may require authorization for the supply of the service. Where a Party requires authorization to supply a new financial service, a decision shall be made within a reasonable time and the authorization may only be refused for prudential reasons.

Article 12.7: Treatment of Certain Information

Nothing in this Chapter requires a Party to furnish or allow access to:

(a)　　information related to the financial affairs and accounts of individual customers of financial institutions or cross-border financial service suppliers; or

(b)　　any confidential information the disclosure of which would impede law enforcement or otherwise be contrary to the public interest or prejudice legitimate commercial interests of particular enterprises.

Article 12.8: Senior Management and Boards of Directors

1.　　No Party may require financial institutions of another Party to engage individuals of any particular nationality as senior managerial or other essential personnel.

2.　　No Party may require that more than a minority of the board of directors of a financial institution of another Party be composed of nationals of the Party, persons residing in the territory of the Party, or a combination thereof.

Article 12.9: Non-Conforming Measures

1.　　Articles 12.2 through 12.5 and 12.8 do not apply to:

(a)　　any existing non-conforming measure that is maintained by a Party at

　　(i)　　the central level of government, as set out by that Party in its Schedule to Annex III,

---

[1] The Parties understand that nothing in Article 12.6 prevents a financial institution of a Party from applying to another Party to request it to consider authorizing the supply of a financial service that is not supplied in the territory of any Party. The application shall be subject to the law of the Party to which the application is made and, for greater certainty, shall not be subject to the obligations of Article 12.6.

(ii)   a regional level of government, as set out by that Party in its Schedule to Annex III, or

(iii)   a local level of government;

(b)   the continuation or prompt renewal of any non-conforming measure referred to in subparagraph (a); or

(c)   an amendment to any non-conforming measure referred to in subparagraph (a) to the extent that the amendment does not decrease the conformity of the measure, as it existed immediately before the amendment, with Article 12.2, 12.3, 12.4, or 12.8.[2]

2.   Annex 12.9.2 sets out certain specific commitments by each Party.

3.   Annex 12.9.3 sets out, solely for purposes of transparency, supplementary information regarding certain aspects of financial services measures of a Party that the Party considers are not inconsistent with its obligations under this Chapter.

4.   Articles 12.2 through 12.5 and 12.8 do not apply to any measure that a Party adopts or maintains with respect to sectors, subsectors, or activities, as set out in its Schedule to Annex III.

5.   A non-conforming measure set out in a Party's Schedule to Annex I or II as a measure to which Article 10.3 (National Treatment), 10.4 (Most-Favored-Nation Treatment), 11.2 (National Treatment), 11.3 (Most-Favored-Nation Treatment), or 11.4 (Market Access) does not apply shall be treated as a non-conforming measure to which Article 12.2, 12.3, or 12.4, as the case may be, does not apply, to the extent that the measure, sector, subsector, or activity set out in the Schedule is covered by this Chapter.

Article 12.10: Exceptions

1.   Notwithstanding any other provision of this Chapter or Chapters Ten (Investment), Thirteen (Telecommunications), including specifically Article 13.16 (Relationship to Other Chapters), or Fourteen (Electronic Commerce), and Article 11.1.3 (Scope and Coverage) with respect to the supply of financial services in the territory of a Party by an investor of another Party or a covered investment, a Party shall not be prevented from adopting or maintaining measures for prudential reasons,[3] including for the protection of investors, depositors, policy holders, or persons to whom a fiduciary duty is owed by a financial institution or cross-border financial service supplier, or to ensure the integrity and stability of the financial system. Where such measures do not conform with the provisions of this Agreement referred to in this paragraph, they shall not be used as a means of avoiding the Party's commitments or obligations under such provisions.

---

[2] For greater certainty, Article 12.5 does not apply to an amendment to any non-conforming measure referred to in subparagraph (a) to the extent that the amendment does not decrease the conformity of the measure, as it existed on the date of entry into force of this Agreement, with Article 12.5.

[3] It is understood that the term "prudential reasons" includes the maintenance of the safety, soundness, integrity, or financial responsibility of individual financial institutions or cross-border financial service suppliers.

2.   Nothing in this Chapter or Chapters Ten (Investment), Thirteen (Telecommunications), including specifically Article 13.16 (Relationship to Other Chapters), or Fourteen (Electronic Commerce), and Article 11.1.3 (Scope and Coverage) with respect to the supply of financial services in the territory of a Party by an investor of another Party or a covered investment, applies to non-discriminatory measures of general application taken by any public entity in pursuit of monetary and related credit policies or exchange rate policies. This paragraph shall not affect a Party's obligations under Article 10.9 (Performance Requirements) with respect to measures covered by Chapter Ten (Investment) or under Article 10.8 (Transfers) or 11.10 (Transfers and Payments).

3.   Notwithstanding Articles 10.8 (Transfers) and 11.10 (Transfers and Payments), as incorporated into this Chapter, a Party may prevent or limit transfers by a financial institution or cross-border financial service supplier to, or for the benefit of, an affiliate of or person related to such institution or supplier, through the equitable, non-discriminatory, and good faith application of measures relating to maintenance of the safety, soundness, integrity, or financial responsibility of financial institutions or cross-border financial service suppliers. This paragraph does not prejudice any other provision of this Agreement that permits a Party to restrict transfers.

4.   For greater certainty, nothing in this Chapter shall be construed to prevent the adoption or enforcement by any Party of measures necessary to secure compliance with laws or regulations that are not inconsistent with this Chapter, including those relating to the prevention of deceptive and fraudulent practices or to deal with the effects of a default on financial services contracts, subject to the requirement that such measures are not applied in a manner which would constitute a means of arbitrary or unjustifiable discrimination between countries where like conditions prevail, or a disguised restriction on investment in financial institutions or cross-border trade in financial services.

Article 12.11: Transparency

1.   The Parties recognize that transparent regulations and policies governing the activities of financial institutions and cross-border financial service suppliers are important in facilitating both access of foreign financial institutions and foreign cross-border financial service suppliers to, and their operations in, each other's markets. Each Party commits to promote regulatory transparency in financial services.

2.   In lieu of Article 18.2.2 (Publication), each Party shall, to the extent practicable:

   (a)   publish in advance any regulations of general application relating to the subject matter of this Chapter that it proposes to adopt; and

   (b)   provide interested persons and Parties a reasonable opportunity to comment on the proposed regulations.

3.   At the time it adopts final regulations, a Party should, to the extent practicable, address in writing substantive comments received from interested persons with respect to the proposed regulations.

4.   To the extent practicable, each Party should allow reasonable time between publication of final regulations and their effective date.

5.   Each Party shall ensure that the rules of general application adopted or maintained by self-regulatory organizations of the Party are promptly published or otherwise made available in such a manner as to enable interested persons to become acquainted with them.

6.   Each Party shall maintain or establish appropriate mechanisms that will respond to inquiries from interested persons regarding measures of general application covered by this Chapter.

7.   Each Party's regulatory authorities shall make available to interested persons the requirements, including any documentation required, for completing applications relating to the supply of financial services.

8.   On the request of an applicant, a Party's regulatory authority shall inform the applicant of the status of its application. If the authority requires additional information from the applicant, it shall notify the applicant without undue delay.

9.   A Party's regulatory authority shall make an administrative decision on a completed application of an investor in a financial institution, a financial institution, or a cross-border financial service supplier of another Party relating to the supply of a financial service within 120 days, and shall promptly notify the applicant of the decision. An application shall not be considered complete until all relevant hearings are held and all necessary information is received.

Where it is not practicable for a decision to be made within 120 days, the regulatory authority shall notify the applicant without undue delay and shall endeavor to make the decision within a reasonable time thereafter.

Article 12.12: Self-Regulatory Organizations

Where a Party requires a financial institution or a cross-border financial service supplier of another Party to be a member of, participate in, or have access to, a self-regulatory organization to provide a financial service in or into the territory of that Party, the Party shall ensure observance of the obligations of Articles 12.2 and 12.3 by such self-regulatory organization.

Article 12.13: Payment and Clearing Systems

Under terms and conditions that accord national treatment, each Party shall grant financial institutions of another Party established in its territory access to payment and clearing systems operated by public entities, and to official funding and refinancing facilities available in the normal course of ordinary business. This paragraph is not intended to confer access to the Party's lender of last resort facilities.

Article 12.14: Domestic Regulation

Except with respect to non-conforming measures listed in its Schedule to Annex III, each Party shall ensure that all measures of general application to which this Chapter applies are administered in a reasonable, objective, and impartial manner.

Article 12.15: Expedited Availability of Insurance Services

The Parties recognize the importance of maintaining and developing regulatory procedures to expedite the offering of insurance services by licensed suppliers.

Article 12.16: Financial Services Committee

1.   The Parties hereby establish a Financial Services Committee. The principal representative of each Party shall be an official of the Party's authority responsible for financial services set out in Annex 12.16.1.

2.   The Committee shall:

(a)   supervise the implementation of this Chapter and its further elaboration;

(b)   consider issues regarding financial services that are referred to it by a Party; and

(c)   participate in the dispute settlement procedures in accordance with Article 12.19.

All decisions of the Committee shall be taken by consensus, unless the Committee otherwise decides.

3.   The Committee shall meet annually, or as otherwise agreed, to assess the functioning of this Agreement as it applies to financial services. The Committee shall inform the Commission of the results of each meeting.

Article 12.17: Consultations

1.   A Party may request consultations with another Party regarding any matter arising under this Agreement that affects financial services. The other Party shall give sympathetic consideration to the request. The consulting Parties shall report the results of their consultations to the Committee.

2.   Consultations under this Article shall include officials of the authorities specified in Annex 12.16.1.

3.   Nothing in this Article shall be construed to require regulatory authorities participating in consultations under paragraph 1 to disclose information or take any action that would interfere with specific regulatory, supervisory, administrative, or enforcement matters.

4.   Nothing in this Article shall be construed to require a Party to derogate from its relevant law regarding sharing of information among financial regulators or the requirements of an agreement or arrangement between financial authorities of two or more Parties.

Article 12.18: Dispute Settlement

1.   Section A of Chapter Twenty (Dispute Settlement) applies as modified by this Article to the settlement of disputes arising under this Chapter.

2.   The Parties shall establish within six months after the date of entry into force of this Agreement and maintain a roster of up to 28 individuals who are willing and able to serve as financial services panelists. Unless the Parties otherwise agree, the roster shall include up to three individuals who are nationals of each Party and up to seven individuals who are not nationals of any Party. The roster members shall be appointed by consensus and may be reappointed. Once established, a roster shall remain in effect for a minimum of three years, and shall remain in effect thereafter until the Parties constitute a new roster. The Parties may appoint a replacement where a roster member is no longer available to serve.

3.   Financial services roster members, as well as financial services panelists, shall:

(a)   have expertise or experience in financial services law or practice, which may include the regulation of financial institutions;

(b)   be chosen strictly on the basis of objectivity, reliability, and sound judgment;

(c)   be independent of, and not be affiliated with or take instructions from, any Party; and

(d)   comply with a code of conduct to be established by the Commission.

4.   When a Party claims that a dispute arises under this Chapter, Article 20.9 (Panel Selection) shall apply, except that:

(a)   where the disputing Parties so agree, the panel shall be composed entirely of panelists meeting the qualifications in paragraph 3; and

(b)   in any other case,

(i)   each disputing Party may select panelists meeting the qualifications set out in paragraph 3 or in Article 20.8 (Qualifications of Panelists), and

(ii)   if the Party complained against invokes Article 12.10, the chair of the panel shall meet the qualifications set out in paragraph 3, unless the disputing Parties otherwise agree.

5.   Notwithstanding Article 20.16 (Non-Implementation – Suspension of Benefits), where a panel finds a measure to be inconsistent with this Agreement and the measure under dispute affects:

(a)   only the financial services sector, the complaining Party may suspend benefits only in the financial services sector;

(b)   the financial services sector and any other sector, the complaining Party may suspend benefits in the financial services sector that have an effect equivalent to the effect of the measure in the Party's financial services sector; or

(c)   only a sector other than the financial services sector, the complaining Party may not suspend benefits in the financial services sector.

Article 12.19: Investment Disputes in Financial Services

1.   Where an investor of a Party submits a claim under Section B of Chapter Ten (Investment) against another Party and the respondent invokes Article 12.10, on request of the respondent, the tribunal shall refer the matter in writing to the Financial Services Committee for a decision. The tribunal may not proceed pending receipt of a decision or report under this Article.

2.   In a referral pursuant to paragraph 1, the Financial Services Committee shall decide the issue of whether and to what extent Article 12.10 is a valid defense to the claim of the investor.

The Committee shall transmit a copy of its decision to the tribunal and to the Commission. The decision shall be binding on the tribunal.

3.   Where the Financial Services Committee has not decided the issue within 60 days of the receipt of the referral under paragraph 1, the respondent or the Party of the claimant may request the establishment of an arbitral panel under Article 20.6 (Request for an Arbitral Panel). The panel shall be constituted in accordance with Article 12.18. The panel shall transmit its final report to the Committee and to the tribunal. The report shall be binding on the tribunal.

4.   The Financial Services Committee may decide that, for purposes of a referral pursuant to paragraph 1, the financial services authorities of the relevant Parties shall make the decision described in paragraph 2 and transmit that decision to the tribunal and the Commission. In that case, a request may be made under paragraph 3 if the relevant Parties have not made the decision described in paragraph 2 within 60 days of their receipt of the referral under paragraph 1.

5.   Where no request for the establishment of a panel pursuant to paragraph 3 has been made within ten days of the expiration of the 60-day period referred to in paragraph 3, the tribunal may proceed to decide the matter.

6.   For purposes of this Article, **tribunal** means a tribunal established under Article 10.19 (Selection of Arbitrators).

Article 12.20: Definitions

For purposes of this Chapter:

cross-border financial service supplier of a Party means a person of a Party that is engaged in the business of supplying a financial service within the territory of the Party and that seeks to supply or supplies a financial service through the cross-border supply of such services;

cross-border trade in financial services or **cross-border supply of financial services** means the supply of a financial service:

> (a)   from the territory of one Party into the territory of another Party,

> (b)   in the territory of one Party by a person of that Party to a person of another Party, or

> (c)   by a national of one Party in the territory of another Party,

but does not include the supply of a financial service in the territory of a Party by an investment in that territory;

financial institution means any financial intermediary or other enterprise that is authorized to do business and regulated or supervised as a financial institution under the law of the Party in whose territory it is located;

financial institution of another Party means a financial institution, including a branch, located in the territory of a Party that is controlled by persons of another Party;

financial service means any service of a financial nature. Financial services include all insurance and insurance-related services, and all banking and other financial services (excluding insurance), as well as services incidental or auxiliary to a service of a financial nature. Financial services include the following activities:

Insurance and insurance-related services

   (a)   Direct insurance (including co-insurance):

   (i) life,
   (ii) non-life;

   (b)   Reinsurance and retrocession;

   (c)   Insurance intermediation, such as brokerage and agency; and

   (d)   Services auxiliary to insurance, such as consultancy, actuarial, risk assessment, and claim settlement services.

Banking and other financial services (excluding insurance)

   (e)   Acceptance of deposits and other repayable funds from the public;

   (f)   Lending of all types, including consumer credit, mortgage credit, factoring and financing of commercial transactions;

   (g)   Financial leasing;

   (h)   All payment and money transmission services, including credit, charge, and debit cards, travelers checks, and bankers drafts;

   (i)   Guarantees and commitments;

   (j)   Trading for own account or for account of customers, whether on an exchange, in an over-the-counter market, or otherwise, the following:

        (i)   money market instruments (including checks, bills, and certificates of deposits);

        (ii)   foreign exchange;

(iii)   derivative products including, but not limited to, futures and options;

(iv)   exchange rate and interest rate instruments, including products such as swaps, forward rate agreements;

(v)   transferable securities,

(vi)   other negotiable instruments and financial assets, including bullion;

(k)   Participation in issues of all kinds of securities, including underwriting and placement as agent (whether publicly or privately) and provision of services related to such issues;

(l)   Money broking;

(m)   Asset management, such as cash or portfolio management, all forms of collective investment management, pension fund management, custodial, depository, and trust services;

(n)   Settlement and clearing services for financial assets, including securities, derivative products, and other negotiable instruments;

(o)   Provision and transfer of financial information, and financial data processing and related software by suppliers of other financial services; and

(p)   Advisory, intermediation, and other auxiliary financial services on all the activities listed in subparagraphs (e) through (o), including credit reference and analysis, investment and portfolio research and advice, advice on acquisitions and on corporate restructuring and strategy;

financial service supplier of a Party means a person of a Party that is engaged in the business of supplying a financial service within the territory of that Party;

investment means "investment" as defined in Article 10.28 (Definitions), except that, with respect to "loans" and "debt instruments" referred to in that Article:

(a)   a loan to or debt instrument issued by a financial institution is an investment only where it is treated as regulatory capital by the Party in whose territory the financial institution is located; and

(b)   a loan granted by or debt instrument owned by a financial institution, other than a loan to or debt instrument of a financial institution referred to in subparagraph (a), is not an investment;

for greater certainty, a loan granted by or debt instrument owned by a cross-border financial service supplier, other than a loan to or debt instrument issued by a financial institution, is an investment if such loan or debt instrument meets the criteria for investments set out in Article 10.28;

investor of a Party means a Party or state enterprise thereof, or a person of a Party, that attempts to make, is making, or has made an investment in the territory of another Party; provided, however, that a natural person who is a dual national shall be deemed to be exclusively a national of the State of his or her dominant and effective nationality;

new financial service means a financial service not supplied in the Party's territory that is supplied within the territory of another Party, and includes any new form of delivery of a financial service or the sale of a financial product that is not sold in the Party's territory;

person of a Party means "person of a Party" as defined in Article 2.1 (Definitions of General Application) and, for greater certainty, does not include a branch of an enterprise of a non-Party;

public entity means a central bank or monetary authority of a Party, or any financial institution owned or controlled by a Party; and

self-regulatory organization means any non-governmental body, including any securities or futures exchange or market, clearing agency, or other organization or association, that exercises its own or delegated regulatory or supervisory authority over financial service suppliers or financial institutions.

Annex 12.5.1
Cross-Border Trade

Section A: Costa Rica

Banking and Other Financial Services (Excluding Insurance)

1.   For Costa Rica, Article 12.5.1 applies with respect to the provision and transfer of financial information and financial data processing and related software as referred to in subparagraph (o) of the definition of financial service, and advisory and other auxiliary services, excluding intermediation, relating to banking and other financial services as referred to in subparagraph (p) of the definition of financial service.[4]

Section B: The Dominican Republic

Insurance and Insurance-Related Services

1.   For the Dominican Republic, Article 12.5.1 applies to the cross-border supply of or trade in financial services as defined in subparagraph (a) of the definition of cross-border supply of financial services with respect to:

    (a)   insurance of risk relating to:

        (i)   maritime shipping and commercial aviation and space launching and freight (including satellites), with such insurance to cover any or all of the

---

[4] It is understood that advisory services includes portfolio management advice but not other services related to portfolio management, and that auxiliary services does not include those services referred to in subparagraphs (e) through (o) of the definition of financial service.

      following: the goods being transported, the vehicle transporting the goods and any liability arising therefrom; and

(ii)   goods in international transit;

(b)   reinsurance and retrocession;

(c)   brokerage of insurance risks relating to paragraphs (a) and (b); and

(d)   consultancy, risk assessment, actuarial, and claims settlement services.

2.   For the Dominican Republic, Article 12.5.1 applies to the cross-border supply of or trade in financial services as defined in subparagraph (c) of the definition of cross-border supply of financial services with respect to insurance services.[5]

Banking and Other Financial Services (Excluding Insurance)

3.   For the Dominican Republic, Article 12.5.1 applies with respect to the provision and transfer of financial information and financial data processing and related software as referred to in subparagraph (o) of the definition of financial service, and advisory and other auxiliary services, excluding intermediation, relating to banking and other financial services as referred to in subparagraph (p) of the definition of financial service.[6]

Section C: El Salvador

Insurance and Insurance-Related Services

1.   For El Salvador, Article 12.5.1 applies to the cross-border supply of or trade in financial services as defined in subparagraph (a) of the definition of cross-border supply of financial services with respect to:

(a)   insurance of risk relating to:

(i)   maritime shipping and commercial aviation and space launching and freight (including satellites), with such insurance to cover any or all of the following: the goods being transported, the vehicle transporting the goods, and any liability arising therefrom, and

(ii)   goods in international transit;

(b)   reinsurance and retrocession;

(c)   brokerage of insurance risks relating to paragraphs (a) and (b); and

---

[5] It is understood that the commitment for cross-border movement of persons is limited to those insurance and insurance-related services listed in paragraph 1.

[6] It is understood that advisory services includes portfolio management advice but not other services related to portfolio management, and that auxiliary services does not include those services referred to in subparagraphs (e) through (o) of the definition of financial service.

(d)   consultancy, risk assessment, actuarial, and claims settlement services.

2.   For El Salvador, Article 12.5.1 applies to the cross-border supply of or trade in financial services as defined in subparagraph (c) of the definition of cross-border supply of financial services with respect to insurance services.[7]

Banking and Other Financial Services (Excluding Insurance)

3.   For El Salvador, Article 12.5.1 applies with respect to:

(a)   provision and transfer of financial information as described in subparagraph (o) of the definition of financial service;

(b)   financial data processing as described in subparagraph (o) of the definition of financial service, subject to prior authorization from the relevant regulator, when it is required;[8] and

(c)   advisory and other auxiliary financial services, excluding intermediation, relating to banking and other financial services as described in subparagraph (p) of the definition of financial service.[9]

Section D: Guatemala

Insurance and Insurance-Related Services

1.   For Guatemala, Article 12.5.1 applies to the cross-border supply of or trade in financial services as defined in subparagraph (a) of the definition of cross-border supply of financial services with respect to:

(a)   insurance of risk relating to:

(i)   maritime shipping and commercial aviation and space launching and freight (including satellites), with such insurance to cover any or all of the following: the goods being transported, the vehicle transporting the goods, and any liability arising therefrom, and

(ii)   goods in international transit;

(b)   reinsurance and retrocession;

(c)   insurance intermediation such as brokerage and agency only for the services indicated in paragraphs (a) and (b); and

---

[7] It is understood that the commitment for cross-border movement of persons is limited to those insurance and insurance-related services listed in paragraph 1.

[8] It is understood that where the financial information or financial data referred to in subparagraphs (a) and (b) involve personal data, the treatment of such personal data shall be in accordance with El Salvador's law regulating the protection of such data.

[9] It is understood that advisory services includes portfolio management advice but not other services related to portfolio management, and that auxiliary services does not include those services referred to in subparagraphs (e) through (o) of the definition of financial service.

    (d)   services auxiliary to insurance as referred to in subparagraph (d) of the definition of financial service.

2.   For Guatemala, Article 12.5.1 applies to the cross-border supply of or trade in financial services as defined in subparagraph (c) of the definition of cross-border supply of financial services with respect to insurance services.[10]

Banking and Other Financial Services (Excluding Insurance)

3.   For Guatemala, Article 12.5.1 applies with respect to the provision and transfer of financial information and financial data processing and related software as referred to in subparagraph (o) of the definition of financial service, and advisory and other auxiliary services, excluding intermediation, relating to banking and other financial services as referred to in subparagraph (p) of the definition of financial service.[11]

Section E: Honduras

Insurance and Insurance-Related Services

1.   For Honduras, Article 12.5.1 applies to the cross-border supply of or trade in financial services as defined in subparagraph (a) of the definition of cross-border supply of financial services with respect to:

    (a)   insurance of risk relating to:

        (i)   maritime shipping and commercial aviation and space launching and freight (including satellites), with such insurance to cover any or all of the following: the goods being transported, the vehicle transporting the goods, and any liability arising therefrom, and

        (ii)   goods in international transit;

    (b)   reinsurance and retrocession;

    (c)   insurance intermediation such as brokerage and agency only for the services indicated in paragraphs (a) and (b); and

    (d)   services auxiliary to insurance as referred to in subparagraph (d) of the definition of financial service.

---

[10] It is understood that the commitment for cross-border movement of persons is limited to those insurance and insurance-related services listed in paragraph 1.

[11] It is understood that advisory services includes portfolio management advice but not other services related to portfolio management, and that auxiliary services does not include those services referred to in subparagraphs (e) through (o) of the definition of financial service.

2.   For Honduras, Article 12.5.1 applies to the cross-border supply of or trade in financial services as defined in subparagraph (c) of the definition of cross-border supply of financial services with respect to insurance services.[12]

Banking and Other Financial Services (Excluding Insurance)

3.   For Honduras, Article 12.5.1 applies with respect to the provision and transfer of financial information and financial data processing and related software as referred to in subparagraph (o) of the definition of financial service, and advisory and other auxiliary services, excluding intermediation, relating to banking and other financial services as referred to in subparagraph (p) of the definition of financial service.[13]

Section F: Nicaragua

Insurance and Insurance-Related Services

1.   For Nicaragua, Article 12.5.1 applies to the cross-border supply of or trade in financial services as defined in subparagraph (a) of the definition of cross-border supply of financial services with respect to:

     (a)   insurance of risk relating to:

          (i)   maritime shipping and commercial aviation and space launching and freight (including satellites), with such insurance to cover any or all of the following: the goods being transported, the vehicle transporting the goods, and any liability arising therefrom, and

          (ii)   goods in international transit;

     (b)   reinsurance and retrocession;

     (c)   brokerage of insurance risks relating to paragraphs (a)(i) and (a)(ii); and

     (d)   services auxiliary to insurance as referred to in subparagraph (d) of the definition of financial services.[14]

2.   For Nicaragua, Article 12.5.1 applies to the cross-border supply of or trade in financial services as defined in subparagraph (c) of the definition of cross-border supply of financial services with respect to insurance services.[15]

---

[12] It is understood that the commitment for cross-border movement of persons is limited to those insurance and insurance-related services listed in paragraph 1.

[13] It is understood that advisory services includes portfolio management advice but not other services related to portfolio management, and that auxiliary services does not include those services referred to in subparagraphs (e) through (o) of the definition of financial service.

[14] For greater certainty, it is understood that these auxiliary services will only be provided to an insurance supplier.

[15] It is understood that the commitment for cross-border movement of persons is limited to those insurance and insurance-related services listed in paragraph 1.

Banking and Other Financial Services (Excluding Insurance)

3.   For Nicaragua, Article 12.5.1 applies with respect to:

   (a)   the provision and transfer of financial information as described in subparagraph (o) of the definition of financial service;

   (b)   financial data processing as described in subparagraph (o) of the definition of financial service, subject to prior authorization from the relevant regulator, as required;[16] and

   (c)   advisory and other auxiliary financial services, excluding intermediation and credit reference and analysis, relating to banking and other financial services as described in subparagraph (p) of the definition of financial service.[17]

Section G: United States

Insurance and Insurance-Related Services

1.   For the United States, Article 12.5.1 applies to the cross-border supply of or trade in financial services as defined in subparagraph (a) of the definition of cross-border supply of financial services with respect to:

   (a)   insurance of risks relating to:

      (i)   maritime shipping and commercial aviation and space launching and freight (including satellites), with such insurance to cover any or all of the following: the goods being transported, the vehicle transporting the goods, and any liability arising therefrom, and

      (ii)   goods in international transit; and

   (b)   reinsurance and retrocession, services auxiliary to insurance as referred to in subparagraph (d) of the definition of financial service, and insurance intermediation such as brokerage and agency as referred to in subparagraph (c) of the definition of financial service.

2.   For the United States, Article 12.5.1 applies to the cross-border supply of or trade in financial services as defined in subparagraph (c) of the definition of cross-border supply of financial services with respect to insurance services.

---

[16] It is understood that Nicaragua's law regulating protection of information applies where the financial information or financial data processing referred to in subparagraphs (a) and (b) involves such protected information. Protected information includes, but is not limited to, information regulated under the concept of banking secrecy and personal information.

[17] It is understood that advisory services includes portfolio management advice but not other services related to portfolio management, and that auxiliary services does not include those services referred to in subparagraphs (e) through (o) of the definition of financial service.

Banking and Other Financial Services (Excluding Insurance)

3.   For the United States, Article 12.5.1 applies with respect to the provision and transfer of financial information and financial data processing and related software as referred to in subparagraph (o) of the definition of financial service, and advisory and other auxiliary services, excluding intermediation, relating to banking and other financial services as referred to in subparagraph (p) of the definition of financial service.[18]

Annex 12.9.2
Specific Commitments

Section A: Costa Rica

Portfolio Management

1.   Costa Rica shall allow a financial institution (other than a trust company) organized outside its territory to provide investment advice and portfolio management services, excluding (a) custodial services, (b) trustee services, and (c) execution services that are not related to managing a collective investment scheme, to a collective investment scheme located in its territory. This commitment is subject to Article 12.1 and to Article 12.5.3.

2.   Notwithstanding paragraph 1, Costa Rica may require that the ultimate responsibility for the management of a collective investment scheme be borne by a *"sociedad administradora de fondos de inversión"* constituted according to the *Ley Reguladora del Mercado de Valores*, No. 7732 of December 17, 1997 in the case of investment funds or an *"operadora de pensiones"* constituted according to the *Ley de Protección al Trabajador*, No. 7983 of February 18, 2000 in the case of pension funds and complementary pension funds.

3.   For purposes of paragraphs 1 and 2, **collective investment scheme** means an investment fund constituted according to the *Ley Reguladora del Mercado de Valores*, No. 7732 of December 17, 1997, or a pension fund or a complementary pension fund constituted according to the *Ley de Protección al Trabajador*, No. 7983 of February 18, 2000.

Expedited Availability of Insurance

4.   Costa Rica should endeavor to consider policies or procedures such as: not requiring product approval for insurance other than insurance sold to individuals or compulsory insurance; allowing introduction of products unless those products are disapproved within a reasonable period of time; and not imposing limitations on the number or frequency of product introductions.

Section B: The Dominican Republic

Portfolio Management

---

[18] It is understood that advisory services includes portfolio management advice but not other services related to portfolio management, and that auxiliary services does not include those services referred to in subparagraphs (e) through (o) of the definition of financial service.

1.   The Dominican Republic shall allow a financial institution (other than a trust company), organized outside its territory, to provide investment advice and portfolio management services, excluding (a) custodial services, (b) trustee services, and (c) execution services that are not related to managing a collective investment scheme, to a collective investment scheme located in it territory. This commitment is subject to Articles 12.1 and 12.5.3.

2.   The Parties recognize that the Dominican Republic does not currently have legislation regulating collective investment schemes. Notwithstanding paragraph 1, and no later than four years after the date of entry into force of this Agreement, the Dominican Republic shall implement paragraph 1 by adopting a Special Law regulating collective investment schemes, which shall contain a definition of collective investment scheme as specified in paragraph 3.

3.   For purposes of paragraphs 1 and 2, **collective investment scheme** will have the meaning provided under the Special Law that the Dominican Republic adopts pursuant to paragraph 2.

Expedited Availability of Insurance

4.   It is understood that the Dominican Republic requires prior product approval before the introduction of a new insurance product. The Dominican Republic shall provide that once an enterprise seeking approval for such a product files information with the Dominican Republic's regulatory authority, the regulator shall grant approval or issue disapproval in accordance with the Dominican Republic's law for the sale of the new product within 30 days. It is understood that the Dominican Republic does not maintain any limitations on the number or frequency of new product introductions.

Section C: El Salvador

Portfolio Management

1.   El Salvador shall allow a financial institution (other than a trust company), organized outside its territory, to provide investment advice and portfolio management services, excluding (a) custodial services, (b) trustee services, and (c) execution services that are not related to managing a collective investment scheme, to a collective investment scheme located in the territory of El Salvador. This commitment is subject to Article 12.1 and to Article 12.5.3.

2.   The Parties recognize that El Salvador does not currently have legislation regulating collective investment schemes. Notwithstanding paragraph 1, and no later than four years after the date of entry into force of this Agreement, El Salvador will implement paragraph 1 by adopting a Special Law regulating collective investment schemes, which shall contain a definition of collective investment scheme as specified in paragraph 3.

3.   For purposes of paragraphs 1 and 2, **collective investment scheme** will have the meaning provided under the Special Law that El Salvador adopts pursuant to paragraph 2.

Foreign Banking

4.   El Salvador shall allow banks organized under the laws of El Salvador to establish branches in the United States, subject to their compliance with relevant U.S. law. The Salvadoran regulatory agency will develop and issue prudential and other requirements that such

banks must meet in order for them to obtain authorization to apply for the establishment of branches in the United States.

Expedited Availability of Insurance

5.   It is understood that El Salvador requires prior product approval before the introduction of a new insurance product. El Salvador shall provide that once an enterprise seeking approval for such a product files information with El Salvador's supervisory authority, the regulator shall grant approval or issue disapproval in accordance with El Salvador's law for the sale of the new product within 60 days. It is understood that El Salvador does not maintain any limitations on the number or frequency of new product introductions.

Section D: Guatemala

Portfolio Management

1.   Guatemala shall allow a financial institution (other than a trust company), organized outside its territory, to provide investment advice and portfolio management services, excluding (a) custodial services, (b) trustee services, and (c) execution services not related to managing a collective investment scheme, to a collective investment scheme located in its territory. This commitment is subject to Article 12.1 and to Article 12.5.3.

2.   The Parties recognize that Guatemala does not currently allow insurance companies to manage collective investment schemes. At such time as Guatemala allows insurance companies to manage collective investment schemes, Guatemala shall comply with paragraph 1 with regard to management of such schemes by insurance companies.

3.   For purposes of paragraphs 1 and 2, **collective investment scheme** means an investment made in accordance with Articles 74, 75, 76, 77, and 79 of the *Ley del Mercado de Valores y Mercancías*, Decree No. 34-96 of the *Congreso de la República*.

Expedited Availability of Insurance

4.   It is understood that Guatemala requires prior product approval before the introduction of a new insurance product. Guatemala shall provide that once an enterprise seeking approval for such a product files the information with Guatemala's supervisory authority, the authority shall grant approval or issue disapproval in accordance with Guatemala's law for the sale of the new product within 60 days. It is understood that Guatemala does not maintain any limitations on the number or frequency of product introductions.

Section E: Honduras

Portfolio Management

1.   Honduras shall allow a financial institution (other than a trust company), organized outside its territory, to provide investment advice and portfolio management services, excluding (a) custodial services, (b) trustee services, and (c) execution services that are not related to managing a collective investment scheme, to a collective investment scheme located in its territory. This commitment is subject to Article 12.1 and to Article 12.5.3.

2.   Notwithstanding paragraph 1, Honduras may require a collective investment scheme located in its territory to retain ultimate responsibility for the management of such collective investment scheme or the funds that it manages.

3.   For purposes of paragraphs 1 and 2, **collective investment scheme** will have the meaning set out in any future laws, regulations, or guidance defining "collective investment scheme."

Expedited Availability of Insurance

4.   It is understood that Honduras requires prior product approval before the introduction of a new insurance product. Honduras shall provide that once an enterprise seeking approval for such a product files the information with the *Comisión Nacional de Bancos y Seguros*, the Commission shall grant approval according to its law or issue disapproval for the sale of the new product within 30 days. It is understood that Honduras does not maintain any limitations on the number or frequency of product introductions.

Section F: Nicaragua

Portfolio Management

1.   Nicaragua shall allow a financial institution (other than a trust company), organized outside its territory, to provide investment advice and portfolio management services, excluding (a) custodial services, (b) trustee services, and (c) execution services that are not related to managing a collective investment scheme or pension fund, to managers of a collective investment scheme or pension fund located in its territory. This commitment is subject to Article 12.1 and to Article 12.5.3.

2.   Notwithstanding paragraph 1, Nicaragua may require that the ultimate responsibility for the management of collective investment schemes and pension funds be borne, respectively, by the managers of such schemes and funds established in its territory.

3.   The Parties recognize that Nicaragua does not currently have legislation establishing collective investment schemes and that its legislation relating to pension funds is not fully implemented. Notwithstanding paragraph 1, at such time as Nicaragua adopts legislation, regulations, or administrative guidance establishing collective investment schemes, Nicaragua shall comply with paragraph 1 with respect to collective investment schemes and provide a definition of collective investment scheme to be added to paragraph 5. Notwithstanding paragraph 1, at such time as Nicaragua undertakes further implementation relating to pension funds, Nicaragua shall comply with the obligations of paragraph 1 of this provision with respect to pension funds.

4.   The Parties recognize that Nicaragua does not currently allow insurance companies to manage collective investment schemes. Notwithstanding paragraph 1, at such time as Nicaragua allows insurance companies to manage a collective investment scheme, Nicaragua shall comply with paragraph 1 with regard to management of collective investment schemes by insurance companies.

5.   For purposes of paragraphs 1 through 3, **pension fund** has the meaning established in the *Ley del Sistema de Ahorro para Pensiones*, Law No. 340 (published in *La Gaceta, Diario Oficial*, No. 72 of 11 April 2000) and its implementing regulations.

Expedited Availability of Insurance

6.   Nicaragua should endeavor to maintain existing opportunities or may wish to consider policies or procedures such as: not requiring product approval for insurance other than sold to individuals or compulsory insurance; allowing introduction of products unless those products are disapproved within a reasonable period of time; and not imposing limitations on the number or frequency of product introductions.

Insurance Branching

7.   Notwithstanding the nonconforming measures of Nicaragua in Annex III, Section B, referring to insurance market access, excluding any portion of those non-conforming measures referring to financial conglomerates and social services, no later than four years after the date of entry into force of this Agreement, Nicaragua shall allow U.S. insurance suppliers to establish in its territory through branches. Nicaragua may choose how to regulate branches, including their characteristics, structure, relationship to their parent company, capital requirements, technical reserves, and obligations regarding risk capital and their investments.

Section G: United States

Portfolio Management

1.   The United States shall allow a financial institution (other than a trust company), organized outside its territory, to provide investment advice and portfolio management services, excluding (a) custodial services, (b) trustee services, and (c) execution services that are not related to managing a collective investment scheme, to a collective investment scheme located in its territory. This commitment is subject to Article 12.1 and to Article 12.5.3.

2.   For purposes of paragraph 1, **collective investment scheme** means an investment company registered with the Securities and Exchange Commission under the *Investment Company Act of 1940*.

Expedited Availability of Insurance

3.   The United States should endeavor to maintain existing opportunities or may wish to consider policies or procedures such as: not requiring product approval for insurance other than insurance sold to individuals or compulsory insurance; allowing introduction of products unless those products are disapproved within a reasonable period of time; and not imposing limitations on the number or frequency of product introductions.

Section H: Specific Commitments of Costa Rica on Insurance Services

I.   Preamble

The Government of the Republic of Costa Rica:

reaffirming its decision to ensure that the process of opening its insurance services sector must be based on its Constitution;

emphasizing that such process shall be to the benefit of the consumer and shall be accomplished gradually and based on prudential regulation;

recognizing its commitment to modernize the *Instituto Nacional de Seguros* (INS) and the Costa Rican legal framework in the insurance sector;

undertakes through this Annex the following specific commitments on insurance services.

II.   Modernization of INS and the Costa Rican Legal Framework in the Insurance Sector

By no later than January 1, 2007, Costa Rica shall establish an independent insurance regulatory authority which shall be separate from and not accountable to any supplier of insurance services. The decisions and the procedures used by the regulatory authority shall be impartial with respect to all market participants. The insurance regulatory authority shall have adequate powers, legal protection, and financial resources to exercise its functions and powers,[19] and treat confidential information appropriately.

III.   Gradual Market Access Opening Commitments

1.   Cross-Border Commitments

Costa Rica shall allow insurance service providers of any Party, on a non-discriminatory basis, to effectively compete to supply directly to the consumer insurance services on a crossborder basis as provided below:

    A.   By no later than the date of entry into force of this Agreement, Costa Rica shall permit the following:

        (i)   pursuant to Article 12.5.2, persons located in its territory, and its nationals wherever located, to purchase any and all lines of insurance (except compulsory automobile insurance[20] and occupational risk insurance[21])[22]

---

[19] The regulatory authority shall act consistently with the core principles of the International Association of Insurance Supervisors.

[20] For purposes of this commitment, "compulsory automobile insurance" has the meaning given to that term in Article 48 of the *Ley de Tránsito por Vias Publicas Terrestres*, Law No. 7331 of 13 April 1993.

[21] As referred to in the last paragraph of Article 73 of the *Constitución Política de la República de Costa Rica*. Occupational risk insurance is a compulsory insurance that covers workers under a subordinate labor relationship for accidents or illnesses occurring as a consequence of their occupation, as well as the direct, immediate, and evident effects of such accidents and illnesses.

from cross-border insurance service suppliers of another Party located in the territory of that other Party or of another Party. This obligation will not require Costa Rica to permit such suppliers to do business or solicit in its territory. Costa Rica may define "doing business" and "solicitation" for purposes of this obligation, as long as such definitions are not inconsistent with Article 12.5.1; and

    (ii)   pursuant to Article 12.5.1, the cross-border supply of or trade in financial services as defined in subparagraph (a) of the definition of cross-border supply of financial services in Article 12.20 with respect to:

        (a)   insurance risk relating to:

            (i)   space launching of freight (including satellite), maritime shipping and commercial aviation, with such insurance to cover any or all of the following: the goods being transported, the vehicle transporting the goods and any liability arising therefrom; and

            (ii)   goods in international transit;

        (b)   retrocession and reinsurance;

        (c)   services necessary to support global accounts;[23]

        (d)   services auxiliary to insurance as referred to in subparagraph (d) of the definition of financial service;[24] and

        (e)   insurance intermediation, provided by brokers and agents outside Costa Rica, such as brokerage and agency as referred to in subparagraph (c) of the definition of financial services.[25]

B.   By July 1, 2007:

    (a)   Costa Rica shall permit the establishment of representative offices; and

    (b)   Article 12.5.1 shall apply to the cross-border supply of or trade in financial services as defined in subparagraph (a) of the definition of cross-border supply of financial services in Article 12.20 with respect to:

---

[22] For greater certainty, Costa Rica is not required to modify its regulation of compulsory automobile insurance and occupational risk insurance, provided that such regulation is consistent with the obligations undertaken in this Agreement, including this Annex.

[23] For purposes of this subclause,

(a) **services necessary to support global accounts** means that the coverage of a master (global) insurance policy written in a territory other than Costa Rica for a multinational client by an insurer of a Party extends to the operations of the multinational client in Costa Rica; and

(b) a multinational client is any foreign enterprise majority owned by a foreign manufacturer or service provider doing business in Costa Rica.

[24] This clause applies only to the lines of insurance set out in III.1.A.(ii)(a), (b), and (c).

[25] This clause applies only to the lines of insurance set out in III.1.A.(ii)(a), (b), and (c).

      (i)   services auxiliary to insurance as referred to in subparagraph (d) of the definition of financial service;[26]

      (ii)   insurance intermediation such as brokerage and agency as referred to in subparagraph (c) of the definition of financial services;[27] and

      (iii)   surplus lines.[28]

    C.   For Costa Rica, Article 12.5.1 applies to the cross-border supply of or trade in financial services as defined in subparagraph (c) of the definition of cross-border supply of financial services in Article 12.20 with respect to insurance services.

2.   <u>Right of Establishment for Insurance Providers</u>

Costa Rica shall, on a non-discriminatory basis, allow insurance service suppliers of any Party, to establish and effectively compete to supply directly to the consumer insurance services in its territory as provided below:

    (a)   any and all lines of insurance[29] (except compulsory automobile and occupational risk insurance), no later than January 1, 2008; and

    (b)   any and all lines of insurance, no later than January 1, 2011.

For purposes of this commitment Costa Rica shall allow insurance service suppliers to be established through any juridical form, as provided in Article 12.4(b). It is understood that Costa Rica may establish prudential solvency and integrity requirements, which shall be in line with comparable international regulatory practice.

Annex 12.9.3
Additional Information Regarding Financial Services Measures

Each Party indicated below has provided the following descriptive and explanatory information regarding certain aspects of its financial services measures solely for purposes of transparency.

---

[26] This clause applies to all lines of insurance.

[27] This clause applies to all lines of insurance.

[28] 28 Surplus lines of insurance means lines of insurance (products covering specific sets of risks with specific characteristics, features, and services) that meet the following criteria:

(a) lines of insurance other than those that INS supplies as of the date of signature of this Agreement, or lines of insurance that are substantially the same as such lines; and

(b) that are sold either (i) to customers with premiums in excess of 10,000 U.S. dollars per year, or (ii) to enterprises, or (iii) to customers with a particular net worth or revenues of a particular size or number of employees.

As of January 1, 2008, surplus lines shall be defined as insurance coverage not available from an admitted company in the regular market.

[29] For greater certainty, social security services referred to in the first, second, and third paragraphs of article 73 of the Constitución Política de la República de Costa Rica and provided by the Caja Costarricense de Seguro Social as of the date of signature of this Agreement are not subject to any commitment included in this Annex.

Section A: Costa Rica

Administrators of pension funds can invest up to 25 per cent of the equity of the fund in securities issued by foreign financial institutions. This limit can be increased up to 50 per cent, provided that real yields of investments of the complementary pension regime are equivalent or lower than international yields.

Section B: The Dominican Republic

Banking Services and Other Financial Services (Insurance Excluded)

1.　　Multipurpose Banks and Credit Entities

　　(a)　　In conformity with the *Ley Monetaria y Financiera,* No. 183-02, November 21, 2002, authorization for the operation of multipurpose banks (commercial banks) and credit entities (savings and credit banks and credit corporations) requires the presentation before the *Junta Monetaria* of an opinion of the *Superintendencia de Bancos* based on documents presented by the applicant entity. The *Junta Monetaria* may authorize the establishment of subsidiaries as well as branch offices, provided there is adequate coordination and exchange of information with the supervising authorities of the country of origin.

　　(b)　　Under no circumstances shall preferred shares grant their holders a greater voting right than common shares, nor shall holders of preferred shares collect dividends in advance of or independently from the results of the business year.

　　(c)　　For the purposes of opening a new entity, documentation establishing the existence and origin of the amount contributed shall be presented before the *Superintendencia de Bancos*. Such amount shall be temporarily deposited in the *Banco Central* for the execution of the initial investment plan and may be used to pay for the acquisition of fixed assets and the necessary expenses of facilities and initiation of operations.

　　(d)　　Multipurpose banks (commercial banks) and credit entities are not allowed to decrease their paid-up capital without previous authorization of the *Superintendencia de Bancos*. The payment of dividends is subject to compliance with the requirements established by the *Junta Monetaria*.

　　(e)　　Savings and Credit Banks may only contract obligations abroad and grant loans in foreign currency with the prior authorization of the *Junta Monetaria*.

　　(f)　　Representative offices of foreign banks not located in the territory of the Dominican Republic may not perform financial intermediation activities.

2.　　Exchange Agents

A prior authorization from the *Junta Monetaria* is needed to act as an Exchange Agent.

3.　　Securities and Goods Exchanges

(a)   All commodities exchanges must receive prior approval from the *Consejo Nacional de Valores*.

(b)   Securities intermediaries must be authorized to operate by the *Superintendencia de Valores*.

(c)   Securities Exchanges shall be represented in securities negotiations by natural persons known as securities brokers who are holders of a credential granted by the corresponding exchange and registered in the securities market. To register in the *Registro del Mercado de Valores*, securities and individuals must comply with Law No. 19-00. Exchanges shall be allowed to sell or rent the right to operate in an exchange, with the previous approval of the corresponding exchange and the *Superintendencia de Valores*.

(d)   Securities intermediaries existing before Law No. 19-00 went into effect, that are members of commodities exchanges and engage solely in the trading of commodities (securities representatives for commodities), must comply with the requirements of the law no later than five years from the date it went into effect.

Services of Insurance and Reinsurance

4.   According to *Ley sobre Seguros y Fianzas en la República Dominicana*, No.146-02, July 22, 2001, a foreign enterprise that wishes to or has the intention of operating in the insurance business, the reinsurance business, or both, within the Dominican Republic must formulate its request to the *Superintendencia de Seguros*, expressing the fields in which it intends to operate in the Dominican Republic, attaching the following documents:

(a)   certification regarding the enterprise's domiciles, that of its head office, and the domicile in the Dominican Republic, which must be previously established;

(b)   the profit and loss general statement of its operations during the past five years, duly approved according to the insurance legislation of the country of origin;

(c)   certification of the names and nationalities of the senior managers or directors;

(d)   copy of the proxy given to the legal representative in the Dominican Republic;

(e)   certification of the State or Government entity in charge of the operations performed by the insurance enterprise or enterprises in which their head office or head offices are located; and

(f)   certification of the agreement or agreements taken by the competent authority of the enterprise stating the decision to extend its business to the Dominican Republic, and that it shall be responsible for its obligations, whether derived from its operations in the Dominican Republic or from the law, with both the goods it owns in the territory of the Dominican Republic, and also with the goods it has in other countries as far as the laws of such countries allow; and that it will submit to the laws and courts of the Dominican Republic, expressly renouncing all rights that might oppose them. This certification must be translated into Spanish and be duly processed so that it is fully valid in the Dominican Republic.

5.   Applications for insurance, policies, certificates, provisional warrants, modifications or endorsements, renewal certificates, and other documents related to insurance contracts, as well as performance bonds, should be written in plain and simple Spanish for ease of understanding.

Reinsurance Located in the Territory of Another Party

6.   The *Superintendencia de Seguros* will communicate to the applicant within a period not to exceed 30 days, its decision with regard to the required authorization. If, after this period, the *Superintendencia de Seguros* has not reached a decision to this effect, it will be understood that no objection exists to consider the applicant entity as an accepted reinsurer.

Pensions

7.   In conformity with *Ley que Crea el Sistema Dominicano de Seguridad Social*, No. 87-01 May 9, 2001, the resources of the pension funds must be invested exclusively in the territory of the Dominican Republic. Foreign investments in this sector are subject to special rules issued by the *Consejo Nacional de Seguridad Social*.

Section C: El Salvador

With regard to banking:

(a)   Holding companies and other foreign financial institutions are subject to consolidated supervision in accordance with relevant international practice. The *Superintendencia del Sistema Financiero*, subject to the opinion of the *Banco Central*, shall issue instructions for determining eligible institutions.

(b)   Banks and other foreign financial institutions must satisfy requirements of prudential regulation and supervision in their countries of origin in accordance with relevant international practice.

(c)   To be authorized to establish a branch in El Salvador, a foreign bank must meet the following criteria:

(i)   *Establishment*: To obtain the authorization to establish a branch, a foreign bank must:

(A)   prove that its head office is legally established in accordance with the laws of the country where it is constituted, that such country subjects the bank to prudential regulation and surveillance in accordance with international usage on the issue, and that it is classified as a first-rate bank by an internationally recognized risk rating company;

(B)   prove that under the laws of the country where it is constituted and its own regulations, it can approve the establishment of branches, agencies, and offices that satisfy the requirements established by the *Ley de Bancos* and that both the head office and the government authority in charge of oversight of this entity in such country have appropriately authorized the entity's operation in El Salvador;

(C)   agree to maintain permanently in El Salvador at least one representative with full powers to perform all activities and contracts to be entered into and executed in El Salvador. The power must be granted clearly and precisely so as to bind the represented entity, so that it is wholly responsible in the country and internationally for all actions taken and contracts signed in El Salvador and so that it satisfies all the requirements established under the laws of El Salvador and the laws of the country where the foreign entity is constituted;

(D)   agree to locate and maintain in El Salvador the amount of capital and capital reserves that the *Ley de Bancos* requires of El Salvador banks;

(E)   certify that it has been in operation for at least five years and that the results of its operations have been satisfactory, based on reports of the oversight entity in the country where the foreign bank is constituted and of internationally recognized risk rating companies; and

(F)   expressly submit to the laws, courts, and authorities of El Salvador, with regard to the acts it performs and the contracts it signs, or those that have effect in El Salvador.

(ii)   In such cases, the *Superintendencia del Sistema Financiero* shall sign cooperation memoranda with the regulatory agency of the country where the investing entity is established.

(iii)   Foreign banks authorized to operate in El Salvador shall be subject to inspection and oversight by the *Superintendencia del Sistema Financiero*, shall enjoy the same rights and privileges, and will be subject to the same laws and standards that apply to domestic banks.

Section D: Honduras

1.   Banking and savings and loan associations may not provide credits to natural persons or juridical persons domiciled abroad unless the *Banco Central de Honduras* authorizes the credits.

2.   A branch of a foreign bank is not required to have its own Board of Directors or Administrative Council, but must have at least two representatives domiciled in Honduras. Such representatives are responsible for the general direction and administration of the business and have the legal authority to act in Honduras and to execute and to be responsible for the branch's own operations.

3.   The founding members of financial institutions organized under the laws of Honduras must be natural persons.

4.   The operation, function, servicing, and issuance of any new financial product with a direct and immediate relation to banking or lending must have the approval of the *Comisión Nacional de Bancos y Seguros*.

5.   Shares in a foreign investment fund may be marketed in the territory of Honduras only if there is a reciprocity agreement at the government level or at the level of the relevant supervisory authorities of the country of origin of the investment fund and the country in which its shares are marketed.

6.   Corporations that classify risk and choose to organize under Honduran law must be constituted as *sociedades anónimas* and must have in Honduras a permanent legal representative with a power of attorney sufficiently broad to undertake any legal act needed for the supply of risk classification services in Honduras.

Section E: Nicaragua

1.   Nicaragua reserves the right to deny an operating license to a financial institution or group (other than an insurance financial institution or group) in the event that another Party has denied or cancelled an operating license to such financial institution or group.

2.   To maintain a branch in Nicaragua, a bank constituted and organized in a foreign country must:

> (a)   be legally authorized and allowed by its bylaws to operate in that foreign country and to establish branches in other foreign countries;
>
> (b)   prior to establishing such branch, present a certification issued by the supervising authority of the country in which the bank is constituted and organized, indicating that authority's concurrence that the bank may establish a branch in Nicaragua; and
>
> (c)   assign the branch capital that meets minimum requirements.

Such a branch must have its domicile in Nicaragua.

3.   To maintain a branch in Nicaragua, a non-banking financial institution organized and constituted under the laws of a foreign country must:

> (a)   be legally authorized and allowed by its bylaws to operate in the country in which it is organized and constituted and to establish branches abroad;
>
> (b)   prior to establishing such branch, present a certification issued by the supervising authority of the country in which such institution is constituted and organized, indicating that authority's concurrence with the establishment of a branch in Nicaragua by such institution;
>
> (c)   assign such branch capital meeting the minimum requirements; and

    (d)   in the case of a FONCITUR, the capital and all of the funds of the FONCITUR must be invested in Nicaragua, in projects registered with the *Instituto Nicaraguense de Turismo*.

Such a branch must have its domicile in Nicaragua.

4.   For purposes of this paragraph and paragraph 3:

    (a)   **non-banking financial institution** means an institution that operates as a recipient of deposits from the public, as a stock exchange or institution related to a stock exchange; as *Almacenes Generales de Depósitos con carácter financiero*; as leasing entities; and as FONCITURs; and

    (b)   **FONCITUR** means a *Fondo de Capital de Inversión Turística*.

5.   A representative office of a foreign bank may place funds in Nicaragua in the form of loans and investments, and act as information centers for their clients, but is prohibited from accepting deposits from the public in Nicaragua.

6.   The administrator of a pension fund may invest abroad a maximum of 30 percent of the assets of the fund. However, the *Superintendencia de Pensiones* reserves the right to vary the investment limits applicable to pension funds administrators at the foreign and national level.

Annex 12.16.1
Financial Services Committee

The authority of each Party responsible for financial services is:

    (a)   in the case of Costa Rica, the *Consejo Nacional de Supervisión del Sistema Financiero* (CONASSIF) and the *Ministerio de Comercio Exterior* for banking and other financial services and for insurance;

    (b)   in the case of the Dominican Republic, the *Banco Central de la República Dominicana* in consultation with the *Superintendencia de Bancos*, the *Superintendencia de Seguros*, the *Superintendencia de Valores*, and the *Superintendencia de Pensiones*, as appropiate,

    (c)   in the case of El Salvador, the *Ministerio de Economía*, in consultation with the corresponding competent authority (*Superintendencia del Sistema Financiero, Superintendencia de Valores, Superintendencia de Pensiones* and the *Banco Central de Reserva*);

    (d)   in the case of Guatemala, the *Superintendencia de Bancos* for banking and other financial services, the *Ministerio de Economía* for insurance and securities, and any other institutions approved by those authorities to participate within the Financial Services Committee;

(e)   in the case of Honduras, the *Banco Central de Honduras*, the *Comisión Nacional de Bancos y Seguros*, and the *Secretaría de Estado en los Despachos de Industria y Comercio*;

(f)   in the case of Nicaragua, the *Ministerio de Fomento, Industria y Comercio*, the *Superintendencia de Bancos y otras Instituciones Financieras*, the *Superintendencia de Pensiones*, and the *Ministerio de Hacienda y Crédito Público*, for banking and other financial services and for insurance; and

(g)   in the case of the United States, the Department of Treasury for banking and other financial services and the Office of the United States Trade Representative, in coordination with the Department of Commerce and other agencies, for insurance,

or their successors.

Chapter Thirteen
Telecommunications[1]

Article 13.1: Scope and Coverage

1.   This Chapter applies to:

(a)   measures adopted or maintained by a Party relating to access to and use of public telecommunications services;

(b)   measures adopted or maintained by a Party relating to obligations of suppliers of public telecommunications services;

(c)   other measures relating to public telecommunications networks or services; and

(d)   measures adopted or maintained by a Party relating to the supply of information services.

2.   Except to ensure that enterprises operating broadcast stations and cable systems have continued access to and use of public telecommunications services, this Chapter does not apply to any measure adopted or maintained by a Party relating to broadcast or cable distribution of radio or television programming.

3.   Nothing in this Chapter shall be construed to:

(a)   require a Party or require a Party to compel any enterprise to establish, construct, acquire, lease, operate, or provide telecommunications networks or services where such networks or services are not offered to the public generally;

---

[1] In place of the obligations established in this Chapter, Costa Rica shall undertake the specific commitments set out in Annex 13.

    (b)   require a Party to compel any enterprise exclusively engaged in the broadcast or cable distribution of radio or television programming to make available its broadcast or cable facilities as a public telecommunications network; or

    (c)   prevent a Party from prohibiting persons operating private networks from using their networks to supply public telecommunications networks or services to third parties.

Article 13.2: Access to and Use of Public Telecommunications Services

1.   Each Party shall ensure that enterprises of another Party have access to and use of any public telecommunications service, including leased circuits, offered in its territory or across its borders, on reasonable and non-discriminatory terms and conditions, including as set out in paragraphs 2 through 6.

2.   Each Party shall ensure that such enterprises are permitted to:

    (a)   purchase or lease, and attach terminal or other equipment that interfaces with a public telecommunications network;

    (b)   provide services to individual or multiple end-users over leased or owned circuits;

    (c)   connect owned or leased circuits with public telecommunications networks and services in the territory, or across the borders, of that Party or with circuits leased or owned by another person;

    (d)   perform switching, signaling, processing, and conversion functions; and

    (e)   use operating protocols of their choice.

3.   Each Party shall ensure that enterprises of another Party may use public telecommunications services for the movement of information in its territory or across its borders and for access to information contained in databases or otherwise stored in machine-readable form in the territory of any Party.

4.   Notwithstanding paragraph 3, a Party may take such measures as are necessary to:

    (a)   ensure the security and confidentiality of messages; or

    (b)   protect the privacy of non-public personal data of subscribers to public telecommunications services, subject to the requirement that such measures are not applied in a manner that would constitute a means of arbitrary or unjustifiable discrimination or disguised restriction on trade in services.

5.   Each Party shall ensure that no condition is imposed on access to and use of public telecommunications networks or services, other than that necessary to:

    (a)   safeguard the public service responsibilities of suppliers of public telecommunications networks or services, in particular their ability to make their networks or services available to the public generally; or

(b)   protect the technical integrity of public telecommunications networks or services.

6.   Provided that conditions for access to and use of public telecommunications networks or services satisfy the criteria set out in paragraph 5, such conditions may include:

(a)   a requirement to use specified technical interfaces, including interface protocols, for interconnection with such networks or services; and

(b)   a licensing, permit, registration, or notification procedure which, if adopted or maintained, is transparent and provides for the processing of applications filed thereunder in accordance with the Party's national law or regulation.

Article 13.3: Obligations Relating to Suppliers of Public Telecommunications Services[2]

Interconnection

1.   (a)   Each Party shall ensure that suppliers of public telecommunications services in its territory provide, directly or indirectly, interconnection with the suppliers of public telecommunications services of another Party.

(b)   In carrying out subparagraph (a), each Party shall ensure that suppliers of public telecommunications services in its territory take reasonable steps to protect the confidentiality of commercially sensitive information of, or relating to, suppliers and end-users of public telecommunications services and only use such information for the purpose of providing those services.

(c)   Each Party shall provide its telecommunications regulatory body the authority to require public telecommunications suppliers to file their interconnection contracts.

Resale

2.   Each Party shall ensure that suppliers of public telecommunications services do not impose unreasonable or discriminatory conditions or limitations on the resale of those services.

Number Portability

3.   Each Party shall ensure that suppliers of public telecommunications services in its territory provide number portability to the extent technically feasible, on a timely basis, and on reasonable terms and conditions.[3]

Dialing Parity

4.   Each Party shall ensure that suppliers of public telecommunications services in its territory provide dialing parity to suppliers of public telecommunications services of another Party, and afford suppliers of public telecommunications services of another Party

---

[2] This Article is subject to Annex 13.3. Paragraphs 2 through 4 of this Article do not apply with respect to suppliers of commercial mobile services. Nothing in this Article shall be construed to preclude a Party from imposing the requirements set out in this Article on suppliers of commercial mobile services.

[3] In complying with this paragraph, the Dominican Republic, El Salvador, Guatemala, Honduras, and Nicaragua may take into account the economic feasibility of providing number portability.

nondiscriminatory access to telephone numbers and related services with no unreasonable dialing delays.

Article 13.4: Additional Obligations Relating to Major Suppliers of Public Telecommunications Services[4]

Treatment by Major Suppliers

1.   Each Party shall ensure that major suppliers in its territory accord suppliers of public telecommunications services of another Party treatment no less favorable than such major suppliers accord to their subsidiaries, their affiliates, or non-affiliated service suppliers regarding:

(a)   the availability, provisioning, rates, or quality of like public telecommunications services; and

(b)   the availability of technical interfaces necessary for interconnection.

Competitive Safeguards

2.   (a)   Each Party shall maintain[5] appropriate measures for the purpose of preventing suppliers who, alone or together, are a major supplier in its territory from engaging in or continuing anti-competitive practices.

(b)   The anti-competitive practices referred to in subparagraph (a) include in particular:

(i)   engaging in anti-competitive cross-subsidization;

(ii)   using information obtained from competitors with anti-competitive results; and

(iii)   not making available, on a timely basis, to suppliers of public telecommunications services, technical information about essential facilities and commercially relevant information which are necessary for them to provide public telecommunications services.

Resale

3.   Each Party shall ensure that major suppliers in its territory:

(a)   offer for resale, at reasonable rates,[6] to suppliers of public telecommunications services of another Party, public telecommunications services that such major

---

[4] This Article is subject to Annex 13.3. This Article does not apply with respect to suppliers of commercial mobile services. This Article is without prejudice to any rights or obligations that a Party may have under the GATS, and nothing in this Article shall be construed to preclude a Party from imposing the requirements set out in this Article on suppliers of commercial mobile services.

[5] For purposes of paragraph 2, "maintain" a measure includes the actual implementation of such measure, as appropriate.

[6] For purposes of subparagraph (a), wholesale rates set pursuant to a Party's law and regulations satisfy the standard of reasonableness.

suppliers provide at retail to end-users that are not suppliers of public telecommunications services; and

(b)   do not impose unreasonable or discriminatory conditions or limitations on the resale of such services.[7]

Unbundling of Network Elements

4.   (a)   Each Party shall provide its telecommunications regulatory body the authority to require major suppliers in its territory to offer access to network elements on an unbundled basis on terms, conditions, and at cost-oriented rates that are reasonable, non-discriminatory, and transparent for the supply of public telecommunications services.

       (b)   Each Party may determine the network elements required to be made available in its territory, and the suppliers that may obtain such elements, in accordance with its law and regulations.

Interconnection

5.   (a)   General Terms and Conditions

               Each Party shall ensure that major suppliers in its territory provide interconnection for the facilities and equipment of suppliers of public telecommunications services of another Party:

               (i)   at any technically feasible point in the major supplier's network;

               (ii)   under non-discriminatory terms, conditions (including technical standards and specifications), and rates;

               (iii)   of a quality no less favorable than that provided by such major suppliers for their own like services, for like services of non-affiliated service suppliers, or for their subsidiaries or other affiliates;

               (iv)   in a timely fashion, on terms, conditions (including technical standards and specifications), and, subject to Annex 13.4.5, cost-oriented rates that are transparent, reasonable, having regard to economic feasibility, and sufficiently unbundled so that the suppliers need not pay for network components or facilities that they do not require for the service to be provided; and

               (v)   on request, at points in addition to the network termination points offered to the majority of users, subject to charges that reflect the cost of construction of necessary additional facilities.

       (b)   Options for Interconnecting with Major Suppliers

---

[7] Where provided in its law or regulations, a Party may prohibit a reseller that obtains, at wholesale rates, a public telecommunications service available at retail to only a limited category of subscribers from offering the service to a different category of subscribers.

Each Party shall ensure that suppliers of public telecommunications services of another Party may interconnect their facilities and equipment with those of major suppliers in its territory pursuant to at least one of the following options:

(i)   a reference interconnection offer or another standard interconnection offer containing the rates, terms, and conditions that the major suppliers offer generally to suppliers of public telecommunications services; or

(ii)   the terms and conditions of an interconnection agreement in force or through negotiation of a new interconnection agreement.

(c)   Public Availability of Interconnection Offers

Each Party shall require major suppliers in its territory to make publicly available reference interconnection offers or other standard interconnection offers containing the rates, terms, and conditions that the major suppliers offer generally to suppliers of public telecommunications services.

(d)   Public Availability of the Procedures for Interconnection Negotiations Each Party shall make publicly available the applicable procedures for interconnection negotiations with major suppliers in its territory.

(e)   Public Availability of Interconnection Agreements Concluded with Major Suppliers

(i)   Each Party shall require major suppliers in its territory to file all interconnection agreements to which they are party with its telecommunications regulatory body or other relevant body.

(ii)   Each Party shall make publicly available interconnection agreements in force between major suppliers in its territory and other suppliers of public telecommunications services in its territory.

Provisioning and Pricing of Leased Circuits Services

6.   (a)   Each Party shall ensure that major suppliers in its territory provide enterprises of another Party leased circuits services that are public telecommunications services on terms, conditions, and at rates that are reasonable and nondiscriminatory.

(b)   In carrying out subparagraph (a), each Party shall provide its telecommunications regulatory body the authority to require major suppliers in its territory to offer leased circuits services that are public telecommunications services to enterprises of another Party at flat-rate, cost-oriented prices.

Co-location

7.   (a)   Subject to subparagraphs (b) and (c), each Party shall ensure that major suppliers in its territory provide to suppliers of public telecommunications services of another Party physical co-location of equipment necessary for interconnection on terms, conditions, and at cost-oriented rates that are reasonable, non-discriminatory, and transparent.

(b)   Where physical co-location is not practical for technical reasons or because of space limitations, each Party shall ensure that major suppliers in its territory:

    (i)   provide an alternative solution, or

    (ii)   facilitate virtual co-location in its territory, on terms, conditions, and at cost-oriented rates that are reasonable, nondiscriminatory, and transparent.

(c)   Each Party may specify in its law or regulations which premises are subject to subparagraphs (a) and (b).

Access to Rights-of-Way

8.   Subject to Annex 13.4.8, each Party shall ensure that major suppliers in its territory afford access to their poles, ducts, conduits, and rights-of-way to suppliers of public telecommunications services of another Party on terms, conditions, and at rates that are reasonable and non-discriminatory.

Article 13.5: Submarine Cable Systems

Each Party shall ensure reasonable and non-discriminatory treatment for access to submarine cable systems (including landing facilities) in its territory, where a supplier is authorized to operate a submarine cable system as a public telecommunications service.

Article 13.6: Conditions for the Supply of Information Services

1.   No Party may require an enterprise in its territory that it classifies[8] as a supplier of information services and that supplies such services over facilities that it does not own to:

(a)   supply such services to the public generally;

(b)   cost-justify its rates for such services;

(c)   file a tariff for such services;

(d)   interconnect its networks with any particular customer for the supply of such services; or

(e)   conform with any particular standard or technical regulation for interconnection other than for interconnection to a public telecommunications network.

2.   Notwithstanding paragraph 1, a Party may take the actions described in subparagraphs (a) through (e) to remedy a practice of a supplier of information services that the Party has found in a particular case to be anti-competitive under its law or regulations, or to otherwise promote competition or safeguard the interests of consumers.

---

[8] For purposes of applying this provision, each Party may, through its telecommunications regulatory body, classify which services in its territory are information services.

Article 13.7: Independent Regulatory Bodies[9] and Government-Owned Telecommunications Suppliers

1.   Each Party shall ensure that its telecommunications regulatory body is separate from, and not accountable to, any supplier of public telecommunications services. To this end, each Party shall ensure that its telecommunications regulatory body does not hold a financial interest or maintain an operating role in any such supplier.

2.   Each Party shall ensure that the decisions and procedures of its telecommunications regulatory body are impartial with respect to all interested persons. To this end, each Party shall ensure that any financial interest that it holds in a supplier of public telecommunications services does not influence the decisions and procedures of its telecommunications regulatory body.

3.   No Party may accord more favorable treatment to a supplier of public telecommunications services or to a supplier of information services than that accorded to a like supplier of another Party on the ground that the supplier receiving more favorable treatment is owned, wholly or in part, by the national government of the Party.

Article 13.8: Universal Service

Each Party shall administer any universal service obligation that it maintains in a transparent, non-discriminatory, and competitively neutral manner and shall ensure that its universal service obligation is not more burdensome than necessary for the kind of universal service that it has defined.

Article 13.9: Licenses and Other Authorizations

1.   Where a Party requires a supplier of public telecommunications services to have a license, concession, permit, registration, or other type of authorization, the Party shall make publicly available:

    (a)   all applicable licensing or authorization criteria and procedures it applies;

    (b)   the time it normally requires to reach a decision concerning an application for a license, concession, permit, registration, or other type of authorization; and

    (c)   the terms and conditions of all licenses or authorizations it has issued.

2.   Each Party shall ensure that, on request, an applicant receives the reasons for the denial of a license, concession, permit, registration, or other type of authorization.

Article 13.10: Allocation and Use of Scarce Resources

1.   Each Party shall administer its procedures for the allocation and use of scarce telecommunications resources, including frequencies, numbers, and rights-of-way, in an objective, timely, transparent, and non-discriminatory manner.

---

[9] Each Party shall endeavor to ensure that its telecommunications regulatory body has adequate resources to carry out its functions.

2.   Each Party shall make publicly available the current state of allocated frequency bands but shall not be required to provide detailed identification of frequencies allocated for specific government uses.

3.   For greater certainty, a Party's measures regarding the allocation and assignment of spectrum and regarding frequency management are not measures that are *per se* inconsistent with Article 11.4 (Market Access), which is applied to Chapter Ten (Investment) through Article 11.1.3 (Scope and Coverage). Accordingly, each Party retains the right to establish and apply its spectrum and frequency management policies, which may limit the number of suppliers of public telecommunications services, provided that it does so in a manner that is consistent with this Agreement. Each Party also retains the right to allocate frequency bands taking into account present and future needs.

Article 13.11: Enforcement

Each Party shall provide its competent authority with the authority to establish and enforce the Party's measures relating to the obligations set out in Articles 13.2 through 13.5. Such authority shall include the ability to impose effective sanctions, which may include financial penalties, injunctive relief (on an interim or final basis), or the modification, suspension, and revocation of licenses or other authorizations.

Article 13.12: Resolution of Domestic Telecommunications Disputes

Further to Articles 18.4 (Administrative Proceedings) and 18.5 (Review and Appeal), each Party shall ensure the following:

Recourse to Telecommunications Regulatory Bodies

(a)   (i)   Each Party shall ensure that enterprises of another Party may seek review by a telecommunications regulatory body or other relevant body to resolve disputes regarding the Party's measures relating to a matter set out in Articles 13.2 through 13.5.

(ii)   Each Party shall ensure that suppliers of public telecommunications services of another Party that have requested interconnection with a major supplier in the Party's territory may seek review, within a reasonable and publicly available period of time after the supplier requests interconnection, by a telecommunications regulatory body[10] to resolve disputes regarding the terms, conditions, and rates for interconnection with such major supplier.

Reconsideration

(b)   Each Party shall ensure that any enterprise that is aggrieved or whose interests are adversely affected by a determination or decision of the Party's telecommunications regulatory body may petition the body to reconsider that determination or decision. No Party may permit such a petition to constitute grounds for non-compliance with the determination or decision of the

---

[10] In the United States, this body may be a state regulatory authority.

telecommunications regulatory body unless an appropriate authority stays such determination or decision.

Judicial Review

(c)   Each Party shall ensure that any enterprise that is aggrieved or whose interests are adversely affected by a determination or decision of the Party's telecommunications regulatory body may obtain judicial review of such determination or decision by an independent judicial authority.

Article 13.13: Transparency

Further to Articles 18.2 (Publication) and 18.3 (Notification and Provision of Information), each Party shall ensure that:

(a)   rulemakings, including the basis for such rulemakings, of its telecommunications regulatory body and end-user tariffs filed with its telecommunications regulatory body are promptly published or otherwise made publicly available;

(b)   interested persons are provided with adequate advance public notice of, and the opportunity to comment on, any rulemaking that its telecommunications regulatory body proposes; and

(c)   its measures relating to public telecommunications services are made publicly available, including measures relating to:

    (i)   tariffs and other terms and conditions of service;

    (ii)   procedures relating to judicial and other adjudicatory proceedings;

    (iii)   specifications of technical interfaces;

    (iv)   bodies responsible for preparing, amending, and adopting standardsrelated measures affecting access and use;

    (v)   conditions for attaching terminal or other equipment to the public telecommunications network; and

    (vi)   notification, permit, registration, or licensing requirements, if any.

Article 13.14: Flexibility in the Choice of Technologies

No Party may prevent suppliers of public telecommunications services from having the flexibility to choose the technologies that they use to supply their services, including commercial mobile wireless services, subject to requirements necessary to satisfy legitimate public policy interests.

Article 13.15: Forbearance

The Parties recognize the importance of relying on market forces to achieve wide choices in the supply of telecommunications services. To this end, each Party may forbear from applying a regulation to a service that the Party classifies as a public telecommunications service, if its telecommunications regulatory body determines that:

(a)   enforcement of such regulation is not necessary to prevent unreasonable or discriminatory practices;

(b)   enforcement of such regulation is not necessary for the protection of consumers; and

(c)   forbearance is consistent with the public interest, including promoting and enhancing competition between suppliers of public telecommunications services.

Article 13.16: Relationship to Other Chapters

In the event of any inconsistency between this Chapter and another Chapter, this Chapter shall prevail to the extent of the inconsistency.

Article 13.17: Definitions

For purposes of this Chapter:

commercial mobile services means public telecommunications services supplied through mobile wireless means;

cost-oriented means based on cost, and may include a reasonable profit, and may involve different cost methodologies for different facilities or services;

dialing parity means the ability of an end-user to use an equal number of digits to access a like public telecommunications service, regardless of the public telecommunications service supplier chosen by such end-user;

end-user means a final consumer of or subscriber to a public telecommunications service, including a service supplier other than a supplier of public telecommunications services;

enterprise means an "enterprise" as defined in Article 2.1 (Definitions of General Application), and includes a branch of an enterprise;

essential facilities means facilities of a public telecommunications network or service that:

(a)   are exclusively or predominantly supplied by a single or limited number of suppliers; and

(b)   cannot feasibly be economically or technically substituted in order to supply a service;

information service means the offering of a capability for generating, acquiring, storing, transforming, processing, retrieving, utilizing, or making available information via telecommunications, and includes electronic publishing, but does not include any use of any such capability for the management, control, or operation of a telecommunications system or the management of a telecommunications service;

interconnection means linking with suppliers providing public telecommunications services in order to allow the users of one supplier to communicate with users of another supplier and to access services provided by another supplier;

leased circuits means telecommunications facilities between two or more designated points that are set aside for the dedicated use of or availability to a particular customer or other users of the customer's choosing;

major supplier means a supplier of public telecommunications services that has the ability to materially affect the terms of participation (having regard to price and supply) in the relevant market for public telecommunications services as a result of:

    (a)   control over essential facilities; or

    (b)   use of its position in the market;

network element means a facility or equipment used in supplying a public telecommunications service, including features, functions, and capabilities provided by means of such facility or equipment;

non-discriminatory means treatment no less favorable than that accorded to any other user of like public telecommunications services in like circumstances;

number portability means the ability of end-users of public telecommunications services to retain, at the same location, telephone numbers without impairment of quality, reliability, or convenience when switching between like suppliers of public telecommunications services;

physical co-location means physical access to and control over space in order to install, maintain, or repair equipment, at premises owned or controlled and used by a supplier to supply public telecommunications services;

public telecommunications service means any telecommunications service that a Party requires, explicitly or in effect, to be offered to the public generally. Such services may include, *inter alia*, telephone and data transmission typically involving customer-supplied information between two or more points without any end-to-end change in the form or content of the customer's information, but does not include information services;

reference interconnection offer means an interconnection offer extended by a major supplier and filed with or approved by a telecommunications regulatory body that is sufficiently detailed to enable a supplier of public telecommunications services that is willing to accept its rates, terms, and conditions to obtain interconnection without having to engage in negotiations with the major supplier;

telecommunications means the transmission and reception of signals by any electromagnetic means, including by photonic means;

telecommunications regulatory body means a national body responsible for the regulation of telecommunications; and

user means an end-user or a supplier of public telecommunications services.

Annex 13
Specific Commitments of Costa Rica on Telecommunications Services

I. Preamble

The Government of the Republic of Costa Rica:

acknowledging the unique nature of the Costa Rican social policy on telecommunications, and reaffirming its decision to ensure that the process of opening its telecommunications services sector must be based on its Constitution;

emphasizing that such process shall be to the benefit of the user and shall be based on the principles of graduality, selectivity, and regulation, and in strict conformity with the social objectives of universality and solidarity in the supply of telecommunications services; and

recognizing its commitment to strengthen and modernize the *Instituto Costarricense de Electricidad* (ICE) as a market participant in a competitive telecommunications marketplace while ensuring that the use of its infrastructure shall be remunerated and to develop a regulatory body to oversee market development;

undertakes through this Annex the following specific commitments on telecommunications services.

II. Modernization of ICE

Costa Rica shall enact a new legal framework to strengthen ICE, through its appropriate modernization, no later than December 31, 2004.

III. Selective and Gradual Market Opening Commitments

1.   Market Access Standstill

Costa Rica shall allow service providers of another Party to supply telecommunications services on terms and conditions that are no less favorable than those established by or granted pursuant to its legislation in force on January 27, 2003.

2.   Gradual and Selective Opening of Certain Telecommunications Services

(a)   As provided in Annex I, Costa Rica shall allow telecommunications services providers of another Party, on a non-discriminatory basis, to effectively compete to supply directly to the customer, through the technology of their choice, the following telecommunications services in its territory:[1]

(i) Private network services,[2] no later than January 1, 2006;

(ii) Internet services,[3] no later than January 1, 2006; and

(iii) mobile wireless services,[4] no later than January 1, 2007.

(b) Subparagraph (a) shall also apply to any other telecommunications service that Costa Rica may decide to allow in the future.

IV. Regulatory Principles[5]

The regulatory framework on telecommunications services that the Government of Costa Rica shall have in force as of January 1, 2006, shall conform, among others, to the following provisions:

1. Universal Service

Costa Rica has the right to define the kind of universal service obligations it wishes to maintain.

Such obligations will not be regarded as anti-competitive *per se*, provided they are administered in a transparent, non-discriminatory, and competitively neutral manner and are not more burdensome than necessary for the kind of universal service defined.

2. Independence of the Regulatory Authority

Costa Rica shall establish or maintain a regulatory authority for telecommunications services, which shall be separate from and not accountable to any supplier of telecommunications services. Costa Rica shall ensure that its telecommunications regulatory authority is authorized to impose effective sanctions to enforce domestic measures relating to the obligations set out in this Annex. This regulatory authority may include jurisdiction over spectrum management, universal service, tariffing, and licensing of new market entrants. The decisions and the procedures of the regulatory authority shall be impartial with respect to all market participants.

---

[1] If Costa Rica requires a license for the provision of a listed service, Costa Rica shall make licenses available within the timeframes specified in this subparagraph.

[2] **Private network services** (closed-user group services) mean networks provided for communications with no interconnection to the public switched telecommunications network at either end. Nothing in this Annex shall be construed to prevent Costa Rica from prohibiting persons operating private networks from using their networks to supply public telecommunications networks or services to third parties.

[3] Internet services shall include electronic mail, retrieval and processing of on-line information and databases and electronic data exchange services, and offering the ability to access the Internet.

[4] Mobile wireless services mean voice, data, and/or broadband services provided by radio electric means in specifically allocated bands, using mobile or fixed terminal equipment, using cellular, PCS (Personal Communications Service), satellite, or any other similar technology that may be developed in the future for these services.

[5] For greater certainty, this section does not create market access rights or obligations.

3.   Transparency

Costa Rica shall ensure that applicable procedures for interconnection to a major supplier and either its interconnection agreements or referenced interconnection offers are made publicly available. Costa Rica shall also make publicly available all licensing or authorization criteria and procedures required for telecommunications service suppliers, and the terms and conditions of all licenses or authorizations issued.

4.   Allocation and Use of Scarce Resources

Costa Rica shall ensure that procedures for the allocation and use of limited resources, including frequencies, numbers, and rights of way, are administered in an objective, timely, transparent, and non-discriminatory manner by a competent domestic authority.[6] The Republic of Costa Rica shall issue licenses for use of spectrum directly to the service providers, in accordance with article 121, item 14 of the *Constitución Política de la República de Costa Rica.*

5.   Regulated Interconnection

(a)   Costa Rica shall ensure that public telecommunications services suppliers of another Party are provided interconnection with a major supplier in a timely fashion, under non-discriminatory terms, conditions,[7] and cost-oriented rates that are transparent, reasonable, and having regard to economic feasibility.

(b)   Costa Rica shall also ensure that a service supplier requesting interconnection with a major supplier has recourse to an independent domestic body,[8] which may be the regulatory authority referred to in paragraph 2, to resolve disputes regarding appropriate terms, conditions, and rates for interconnection within a reasonable time.

6.   Access to and Use of the Network

(a)   Costa Rica shall ensure that enterprises of another Party have access to and use of any public telecommunications services, including leased circuits, offered in its territory or across its borders, on reasonable and non-discriminatory terms and conditions and are permitted to:

(i)   purchase or lease and attach terminal or other equipment that interfaces with a public telecommunications network;

(ii)   provide services to individual or multiple end-users over leased or owned circuits;

---

[6] The competent domestic authority shall be separate from and not accountable to any supplier of telecommunications services.

[7] For purposes of subparagraph (a), conditions include technical regulations and specifications, as well as the quality of interconnection.

[8] The independent domestic body shall be separate from and not accountable to any supplier of telecommunications services.

> (iii)   connect owned or leased circuits with public telecommunications networks and services in its territory, or across Costa Rica's borders or with circuits leased or owned by another person;
>
> (iv)   perform switching, signaling, processing, and conversion functions, and use operating protocols of their choice; and
>
> (v)   use public telecommunications services for the movement of informationcontained in databases or otherwise stored in machine-readable form in the territory of any Party.

(b)   Notwithstanding subparagraph (a), Costa Rica may take such measures as are necessary to ensure the security and confidentiality of messages or to protect the privacy of non-public personal data of subscribers to public telecommunications services, subject to the requirement that such measures are not applied in a manner that would constitute a means of arbitrary or unjustifiable discrimination or disguised restriction on trade in services.

(c)   Costa Rica shall also ensure that no condition is imposed on access to and use of public telecommunications networks or services, other than that necessary to safeguard the public service responsibilities of providers of public telecommunications networks or services, in particular their ability to make their networks or services available to the public generally, or protect the technical integrity of public telecommunications networks or services.

7.   <u>Provision of Information Services</u>

(a)   Costa Rica may not require an enterprise of another Party in its territory that it classifies[9] as a supplier of information services and that supplies such services over facilities that it does not own to:

> (i)   supply such services to the public generally;
>
> (ii)   cost-justify rates for such services;
>
> (iii)   file tariffs for such services;
>
> (iv)   interconnect its networks with any particular customer for the supply of such services; or
>
> (v)   conform to any particular standard or technical regulation for interconnection other than that for interconnection to a public telecommunications network.

(b)   Notwithstanding subparagraph (a), Costa Rica may take any action referred to in clauses (i) through (v) to remedy a practice of a supplier of information services that it has found in a particular case to be anti-competitive under its law or

---

[9] The telecommunications regulatory authority will have the competence within its territory to classify the services included in the information services category.

regulations, or to otherwise promote competition or safeguard the interests of consumers.

8.   Competition

Costa Rica shall maintain appropriate measures for the purpose of preventing suppliers who, alone or together, are a major supplier from engaging in anti-competitive practices, such as not making available, on a timely basis, to suppliers of public telecommunications services, technical information about essential facilities and commercially relevant information that is necessary for them to provide public telecommunications services.

9.   Submarine Cable Systems

Costa Rica shall ensure reasonable and non-discriminatory treatment for access to submarine cable systems (including landing facilities) in its territory, where a supplier is authorized to operate such submarine cable system as a public telecommunications service.

10.   Flexibility in the Choice of Technologies

Costa Rica may not prevent suppliers of public telecommunications services from having the flexibility to choose the technologies that they use to supply their services, subject to requirements necessary to satisfy legitimate public policy interests.

Annex 13.3
Rural Telephone Suppliers

1.   A state regulatory authority in the United States may exempt a rural local exchange carrier, as defined in section 251(f)(2) of the *Communications Act of 1934*, as amended, from the obligations contained in paragraphs 2 through 4 of Article 13.3 and from the obligations contained in Article 13.4.

2.   Article 13.4 does not apply to rural telephone companies in the United States, as defined in section 3(37) of the *Communications Act of 1934*, as amended, unless a state regulatory authority orders otherwise.

3.   El Salvador, Guatemala, Honduras, and Nicaragua may designate and exempt a rural telephone company in its territory from paragraphs 2 through 4 of Article 13.3 and from Article 13.4, provided that the rural telephone company supplies public telecommunications services to fewer than two percent of the subscriber lines installed in the Party's territory. The number of subscriber lines supplied by a rural telephone company includes all subscriber lines supplied by the company, and by its owners, subsidiaries, and affiliates.

4.   Nothing in this Annex shall be construed to preclude a Party from imposing the requirements set out in Article 13.4 on rural telephone companies.

Annex 13.4.5
Interconnection

1.   For any Party that does not have an existing commitment under the GATS to ensure that a major supplier in its territory provides interconnection at cost-oriented rates, the obligation under Article 13.4.5 to ensure the provision of cost-oriented interconnection shall become effective:

(a)   two years after the date of entry into force of this Agreement; or

(b)   January 1, 2007, whichever is earlier.

2.   During the transition period, each such Party shall ensure that major suppliers of public telecommunications services in its territory:

(a)   do not charge interconnection rates above the rates charged on December 31, 2003; and

(b)   proportionally reduce interconnection rates as necessary to ensure that a costoriented interconnection rate has been achieved by the end of the transition period.

Annex 13.4.8
Access to Rights-of-Way

Article 13.4.8 shall apply with respect to El Salvador beginning when its law provides that poles, ducts, conducts, and rights-of-way constitute essential resources.
[...]

Chapter Fifteen
Intellectual Property Rights

Article 15.1: General Provisions

1.   Each Party shall, at a minimum, give effect to this Chapter. A Party may, but shall not be obliged to, implement in its domestic law more extensive protection and enforcement of intellectual property rights than is required under this Chapter, provided that such protection and enforcement does not contravene this Chapter.

2.   Each Party shall ratify or accede to the following agreements by the date of entry into force of this Agreement:

(a)   the *WIPO Copyright Treaty* (1996); and

(b)   the *WIPO Performances and Phonograms Treaty* (1996).

3.   Each Party shall ratify or accede to the following agreements by January 1, 2006:

(a)   the *Patent Cooperation Treaty*, as revised and amended (1970); and

(b)   the *Budapest Treaty on the International Recognition of the Deposit of Microorganisms for the Purposes of Patent Procedure* (1980).

4.   Each Party shall ratify or accede to the following agreements by January 1, 2008:

(a)   the *Convention Relating to the Distribution of Programme-Carrying Signals Transmitted by Satellite* (1974); and

(b)   the *Trademark Law Treaty* (1994).

5.   (a)   Each Party shall ratify or accede to the *International Convention for the Protection of New Varieties of Plants* (1991) (UPOV Convention 1991).[1]Nicaragua shall do so by January 1, 2010. Costa Rica shall do so by June 1, 2007. All other Parties shall do so by January 1, 2006.[1]

(b)   Subparagraph (a) shall not apply to any Party that provides effective patent protection for plants by the date of entry into force of this Agreement. Such Parties shall make all reasonable efforts to ratify or accede to the UPOV Convention 1991.

6.   Each Party shall make all reasonable efforts to ratify or accede to the following agreements:

(a)   the Patent Law Treaty (2000);

(b)   the Hague Agreement Concerning the International Registration of Industrial Designs (1999); and

(c)   the Protocol Relating to the Madrid Agreement Concerning the International Registration of Marks (1989).

7.   Further to Article 1.3 (Relation to Other Agreements), the Parties affirm their existing rights and obligations under the TRIPS Agreement and intellectual property agreements concluded or administered under the auspices of the World Intellectual Property Organization (WIPO) and to which they are party.

8.   In respect of all categories of intellectual property covered in this Chapter, each Party shall accord to nationals[2] of the other Parties treatment no less favorable than it accords to its

---

[1] The Parties recognize that the UPOV Convention 1991 contains exceptions to the breeder's right, including for acts done privately and for non-commercial purposes, such as private and non-commercial acts of farmers. Further, the Parties recognize that the UPOV Convention 1991 provides for restrictions to the exercise of a breeder's right for reasons of public interest, provided that the Parties take all measures necessary to ensure that the breeder receives equitable remuneration. The Parties also understand that each Party may avail itself of these exceptions and restrictions. Finally, the Parties understand that there is no conflict between the UPOV Convention 1991 and a Party's ability to protect and conserve its genetic resources.

[2] For purposes of Articles 15.1.8, 15.1.9, 15.4.2, and 15.7.1, a national of a Party shall also mean, in respect of the relevant right, an entity located in that Party that would meet the criteria for eligibility for protection provided for in the agreements listed in Article 15.1.2 through 15.1.6 and the TRIPS Agreement.

own nationals with regard to the protection[3] and enjoyment of such intellectual property rights and any benefits derived from such rights.

9.   A Party may derogate from paragraph 8 in relation to its judicial and administrative procedures, including any procedure requiring a national of another Party to designate for service of process an address in its territory or to appoint an agent in its territory, provided that such derogation:

(a)   is necessary to secure compliance with laws and regulations that are not inconsistent with this Chapter; and

(b)   is not applied in a manner that would constitute a disguised restriction on trade.

10.   Paragraph 8 does not apply to procedures provided in multilateral agreements to which the Parties are party concluded under the auspices of WIPO in relation to the acquisition or maintenance of intellectual property rights.

11.   Except as it provides otherwise, this Chapter gives rise to obligations in respect of all subject matter existing on the date of entry into force of this Agreement that is protected on that date in the Party where protection is claimed, or that meets or comes subsequently to meet the criteria for protection under this Chapter.

12.   Except as otherwise provided in this Chapter, a Party shall not be required to restore protection to subject matter that on the date of entry into force of this Agreement has fallen into the public domain in the Party where the protection is claimed.

13.   This Chapter does not give rise to obligations in respect of acts that occurred before the date of entry into force of this Agreement.

14.   Each Party shall ensure that all laws, regulations, and procedures concerning the protection or enforcement of intellectual property rights shall be in writing and shall be published,[4] or where such publication is not practicable, made publicly available, in a national language in such a manner as to enable governments and right holders to become acquainted with them, with the object of making the protection and enforcement of intellectual property rights transparent.

15.   Nothing in this Chapter shall be construed to prevent a Party from adopting measures necessary to prevent anticompetitive practices that may result from the abuse of the intellectual property rights set out in this Chapter, provided that such measures are consistent with this Chapter.

16.   Recognizing the Parties' commitment to trade capacity building as reflected in the establishment of the Committee on Trade Capacity Building under Article 19.4 (Committee on Trade Capacity Building) and the importance of trade capacity building activities, the Parties

---

[3] For purposes of this paragraph, "protection" shall include matters affecting the availability, acquisition, scope, maintenance, and enforcement of intellectual property rights as well as matters affecting the use of intellectual property rights specifically covered by this Chapter. Further, for purposes of this paragraph, "protection" shall also include the prohibition on circumvention of effective technological measures set out in Article 15.5.7 and the rights and obligations concerning rights management information set out in Article 15.5.8.

[4] A Party may satisfy the requirement for publication by making the measure available to the public on the Internet.

shall cooperate through that Committee in the following initial capacity-building priority activities, on mutually agreed terms and conditions, and subject to the availability of appropriated funds:

(a)   educational and dissemination projects on the use of intellectual property as a research and innovation tool, as well as on the enforcement of intellectual property rights;

(b)   appropriate coordination, training, specialization courses, and exchange of information between the intellectual property offices and other institutions of the Parties; and

(c)   enhancing the knowledge, development, and implementation of the electronic systems used for the management of intellectual property.

Article 15.2: Trademarks

1.   Each Party shall provide that trademarks shall include collective, certification, and sound marks, and may include geographical indications and scent marks. A geographical indication is capable of constituting a mark to the extent that the geographical indication consists of any sign, or any combination of signs, capable of identifying a good or service as originating[5] in the territory of a Party, or a region or locality in that territory, where a given quality, reputation, or other characteristic of the good or service is essentially attributable to its geographical origin.

2.   In view of the obligations of Article 20 of the TRIPS Agreement, each Party shall ensure that measures mandating the use of the term customary in common language as the common name for a good or service ("common name") including, inter alia, requirements concerning the relative size, placement, or style of use of the trademark in relation to the common name, do not impair the use or effectiveness of trademarks used in relation to such goods.

3.   Each Party shall provide that the owner of a registered trademark shall have the exclusive right to prevent all third parties not having the owner's consent from using in the course of trade identical or similar signs, including geographical indications, for goods or services that are related to those goods or services in respect of which the owner's trademark is registered, where such use would result in a likelihood of confusion. In case of the use of an identical sign, including a geographical indication, for identical goods or services, a likelihood of confusion shall be presumed.

4.   Each Party may provide limited exceptions to the rights conferred by a trademark, such as fair use of descriptive terms, provided that such exceptions take account of the legitimate interest of the owner of the trademark and of third parties.

5.   Article 6bis of the Paris Convention for the Protection of Industrial Property (1967) (Paris Convention) shall apply, mutatis mutandis, to goods or services that are not identical or similar to those identified by a well-known trademark,[6] whether registered or not, provided that use of that trademark in relation to those goods or services would indicate a connection between

---

[5] For purposes of this Chapter, "originating" does not have the meaning ascribed to that term in Article 2.1 (Definitions of General Application).
[6] In determining whether a trademark is well known, the reputation of the trademark need not extend beyond the sector of the public that normally deals with the relevant goods or services.

those goods or services and the owner of the trademark, and provided that the interests of the owner of the trademark are likely to be damaged by such use.

6.   Each Party shall provide a system for the registration of trademarks, which shall include:

     (a)   providing to the applicant a communication in writing, which may be electronic, of the reasons for any refusal to register a trademark;

     (b)   an opportunity for the applicant to respond to communications from the trademark authorities, to contest an initial refusal, and to appeal judicially a final refusal to register;

     (c)   an opportunity for interested parties to petition to oppose a trademark application or to seek cancellation of a trademark after it has been registered; and

     (d)   a requirement that decisions in opposition or cancellation proceedings be reasoned and in writing.

7.   Each Party shall provide, to the maximum degree practical, a system for the electronic application, processing, registration, and maintenance of trademarks, and work to provide, to the maximum degree practical, a publicly available electronic database – including an on-line database – of trademark applications and registrations.

8.   (a)   Each Party shall provide that each registration or publication that concerns a trademark application or registration and that indicates goods or services shall indicate the goods or services by their common names, grouped according to the classes of the classification established by the Nice Agreement Concerning the International Classification of Goods and Services for the Purposes of the Registration of Marks (1979), as revised and amended (Nice Classification).

     (b)   Each Party shall provide that goods or services may not be considered as being similar to each other solely on the ground that, in any registration or publication, they appear in the same class of the Nice Classification. Conversely, each Party shall provide that goods or services may not be considered as being dissimilar from each other solely on the ground that, in any registration or publication, they appear in different classes of the Nice Classification.

9.   Each Party shall provide that initial registration and each renewal of registration of a trademark shall be for a term of no less than ten years.

10.   No Party may require recordal of trademark licenses to establish the validity of the license, to assert any rights in a trademark, or for other purposes.[7]

---

[7] A Party may establish a means to allow licensees to record licenses for the purpose of providing notice to the public as to the existence of the license. However, no Party may make notice to the public a requirement for asserting any rights under the license.

Article 15.3: Geographical Indications

Definition

1.   For purposes of this Article, geographical indications are indications that identify a good as originating in the territory of a Party, or a region or locality in that territory, where a given quality, reputation, or other characteristic of the good is essentially attributable to its geographical origin. Any sign or combination of signs, in any form whatsoever, shall be eligible to be a geographical indication.

Procedures with Respect to Geographical Indications

2.   Each Party shall provide the legal means to identify[8] and protect geographical indications of the other Parties that meet the criteria of paragraph 1. Each Party shall provide the means for persons of another Party to apply for protection or petition for recognition of geographical indications. Each Party shall accept applications and petitions from persons of another Party without the requirement for intercession by that Party on behalf of its persons.

3.   Each Party shall process applications or petitions, as the case may be, for geographical indications with a minimum of formalities.

4.   Each Party shall make its regulations governing filing of such applications or petitions, as the case may be, readily available to the public.

5.   Each Party shall ensure that applications or petitions, as the case may be, for geographical indications are published for opposition, and shall provide procedures for opposing geographical indications that are the subject of applications or petitions. Each Party shall also provide procedures to cancel any registration resulting from an application or a petition.

6.   Each Party shall ensure that measures governing the filing of applications or petitions, as the case may be, for geographical indications set out clearly the procedures for these actions. Each Party shall make available contact information sufficient to allow (a) the general public to obtain guidance concerning the procedures for filing applications or petitions and the processing of those applications or petitions in general; and (b) applicants, petitioners, or their representatives to ascertain the status of, and to obtain procedural guidance concerning, specific applications and petitions.

Relationship between Trademarks and Geographical Indications

7.   Each Party shall ensure that grounds for refusing protection or recognition of a geographical indication include the following:

(a)   the geographical indication is likely to be confusingly similar to a trademark that is the subject of a good-faith pending application or registration; and

---

[8] For purposes of this paragraph, legal means to identify means a system that permits applicants to provide information on the quality, reputation, or other characteristics of the asserted geographical indication.

(b)   the geographical indication is likely to be confusingly similar to a pre-existing trademark, the rights to which have been acquired in accordance with the Party's law.[9]

Article 15.4: Domain Names on the Internet

1.   In order to address trademark cyber-piracy, each Party shall require that the management of its country-code top-level domain (ccTLD) provides an appropriate procedure for the settlement of disputes based on the principles established in the Uniform Domain-Name Dispute-Resolution Policy.

2.   Each Party shall require that the management of its ccTLD provides on-line public access to a reliable and accurate database of contact information for domain-name registrants. In determining the appropriate contact information, the management of a Party's ccTLD may give due regard to the Party's laws protecting the privacy of its nationals.

Article 15.5: Obligations Pertaining to Copyright and Related Rights

1.   Each Party shall provide that authors, performers, and producers of phonograms[10] have the right[11] to authorize or prohibit all reproductions of their works, performances, or phonograms, in any manner or form, permanent or temporary (including temporary storage in electronic form).[12]

2.   Each Party shall provide to authors, performers, and producers of phonograms the right to authorize the making available to the public of the original and copies of their works, performances, and phonograms[13] through sale or other transfer of ownership.

3.   In order to ensure that no hierarchy is established between rights of authors, on the one hand, and rights of performers and producers of phonograms, on the other hand, each Party shall establish that in cases where authorization is needed from both the author of a work embodied in a phonogram and a performer or producer owning rights in the phonogram, the need for the authorization of the author does not cease to exist because the authorization of the performer or producer is also required. Likewise, each Party shall establish that in cases where authorization is needed from both the author of a work embodied in a phonogram and of a performer or producer owning rights in the phonogram, the need for the authorization of the performer or producer does not cease to exist because the authorization of the author is also required.

---

[9] For purposes of this paragraph, the Parties understand that each Party has already established grounds for refusing protection of a trademark under its law, including that (a) the trademark is likely to be confusingly similar to a geographical indication that is the subject of a registration; and (b) the trademark is likely to be confusingly similar to a pre-existing geographical indication, the rights to which have been acquired in accordance with the Party's law.

[10] References in this Chapter to "authors, performers, and producers of phonograms" include any successors in interest.

[11] With respect to copyrights and related rights in this Chapter, a right to authorize or prohibit or a right to authorize means an exclusive right.

[12] The Parties understand that the reproduction right as set out in this paragraph and in Article 9 of the Berne Convention for the Protection of Literary and Artistic Works (1971) (Berne Convention) and the exceptions permitted under the Berne Convention and Article 15.5.10(a) fully apply in the digital environment, in particular to the use of works in digital form.

[13] With respect to copyright and related rights in this Chapter, a "performance" refers to a performance fixed in a phonogram, unless otherwise specified.

4.   Each Party shall provide that, where the term of protection of a work (including a photographic work), performance, or phonogram is to be calculated:

(a)   on the basis of the life of a natural person, the term shall be not less than the life of the author and 70 years after the author's death; and

(b)   on a basis other than the life of a natural person, the term shall be:

(i)   not less than 70 years from the end of the calendar year of the first authorized publication of the work, performance, or phonogram, or

(ii)   failing such authorized publication within 50 years from the creation of the work, performance, or phonogram, not less than 70 years from the end of the calendar year of the creation of the work, performance, or phonogram.

5.   Each Party shall apply the provisions of Article 18 of the Berne Convention and Article 14.6 of the TRIPS Agreement, mutatis mutandis, to the subject matter, rights, and obligations provided for in this Article and Articles 15.6 and 15.7.

6.   Each Party shall provide that for copyright and related rights:

(a)   any person acquiring or holding any economic right in a work, performance, or phonogram may freely and separately transfer such right by contract; and

(b)   any person acquiring or holding any such economic right by virtue of a contract, including contracts of employment underlying the creation of works and performances, and production of phonograms, shall be able to exercise such right in that person's own name and enjoy fully the benefits derived from such right.

7.   (a)   In order to provide adequate legal protection and effective legal remedies against the circumvention of effective technological measures that authors, performers, and producers of phonograms use in connection with the exercise of their rights and that restrict unauthorized acts in respect of their works, performances, and phonograms, each Party shall provide that any person who:

(i)   circumvents without authority any effective technological measure that controls access to a protected work, performance, phonogram, or other subject matter; or

(ii)   manufactures, imports, distributes, offers to the public, provides, or otherwise traffics in devices, products, or components, or offers to the public or provides services, that:

(A)   are promoted, advertised, or marketed for the purpose of circumvention of any effective technological measure; or

(B)   have only a limited commercially significant purpose or use other than to circumvent any effective technological measure; or

(C)   are primarily designed, produced, or performed for the purpose of enabling or facilitating the circumvention of any effective technological measure,

shall be liable and subject to the remedies provided for in Article 15.11.14. Each Party shall provide for criminal procedures and penalties to be applied when any person, other than a nonprofit library, archive, educational institution, or public non-commercial broadcasting entity, is found to have engaged willfully and for purposes of commercial advantage or private financial gain in any of the foregoing activities.

(b)   In implementing subparagraph (a), no Party shall be obligated to require that the design of, or the design and selection of parts and components for, a consumer electronics, telecommunications, or computing product provide for a response to any particular technological measure, so long as the product does not otherwise violate any measures implementing subparagraph (a).

(c)   Each Party shall provide that a violation of a measure implementing this paragraph is a separate civil cause of action or criminal offense, independent of any infringement that might occur under the Party's law on copyright and related rights.

(d)   Each Party shall confine exceptions to any measures implementing the prohibition in subparagraph (a)(ii) on technology, products, services, or devices that circumvent effective technological measures that control access to, and, in the case of clause (i), that protect any of the exclusive rights of copyright or related rights in, a protected work, performance, or phonogram referred to in subparagraph (a)(ii), to the following activities, provided that they do not impair the adequacy of legal protection or the effectiveness of legal remedies against the circumvention of effective technological measures:

(i)   noninfringing reverse engineering activities with regard to a lawfully obtained copy of a computer program, carried out in good faith with respect to particular elements of that computer program that have not been readily available to the person engaged in those activities, for the sole purpose of achieving interoperability of an independently created computer program with other programs;

(ii)   noninfringing good faith activities, carried out by an appropriately qualified researcher who has lawfully obtained a copy, unfixed performance or display of a work, performance, or phonogram, and who has made a good faith effort to obtain authorization for such activities, to the extent necessary for the sole purpose of identifying and analyzing flaws and vulnerabilities of technologies for scrambling and descrambling of information;

(iii)   the inclusion of a component or part for the sole purpose of preventing the access of minors to inappropriate on-line content in a technology, product, service, or device that itself is not prohibited under the measures implementing subparagraph (a)(ii); and

(iv) noninfringing good faith activities that are authorized by the owner of a computer, computer system, or computer network for the sole purpose of testing, investigating, or correcting the security of that computer, computer system, or computer network.

(e) Each Party shall confine exceptions to any measures implementing the prohibition referred to in subparagraph (a)(i) to the activities listed in subparagraph (d) and the following activities, provided that they do not impair the adequacy of legal protection or the effectiveness of legal remedies against the circumvention of effective technological measures:

(i) access by a nonprofit library, archive, or educational institution to a work, performance, or phonogram, not otherwise available to it, for the sole purpose of making acquisition decisions;

(ii) noninfringing activities for the sole purpose of identifying and disabling a capability to carry out undisclosed collection or dissemination of personally identifying information reflecting the on-line activities of a natural person in a way that has no other effect on the ability of any person to gain access to any work; and

(iii) noninfringing uses of a work, performance, or phonogram, in a particular class of works, performances, or phonograms, when an actual or likely adverse impact on those noninfringing uses is demonstrated in a legislative or administrative proceeding by substantial evidence; provided that in order for any such exception to remain in effect for more than four years, a Party must conduct a review before the expiration of the four-year period and at intervals of at least every four years thereafter, pursuant to which it is demonstrated in such a proceeding by substantial evidence that there is a continuing actual or likely adverse impact on the particular noninfringing use.

(f) Each Party may provide exceptions to any measures implementing the prohibitions referred to in subparagraph (a) for lawfully authorized activities carried out by government employees, agents, or contractors for law enforcement, intelligence, essential security, or similar governmental purposes.

(g) Effective technological measure means any technology, device, or component that, in the normal course of its operation, controls access to a protected work, performance, phonogram, or other protected subject matter, or protects any copyright or any rights related to copyright.

8. In order to provide adequate legal protection and effective legal remedies to protect rights management information:

(a) Each Party shall provide that any person who, without authority, and knowing, or, with respect to civil remedies, having reasonable grounds to know, that it would induce, enable, facilitate, or conceal an infringement of any copyright or related right,

(i)   knowingly removes or alters any rights management information;

(ii)   distributes or imports for distribution rights management information knowing that the rights management information has been removed or altered without authority; or

(iii)   distributes, imports for distribution, broadcasts, communicates or makes available to the public copies of works, performances, or phonograms, knowing that rights management information has been removed or altered without authority,

shall be liable and subject to the remedies provided for in Article 15.11.14. Each Party shall provide for criminal procedures and penalties to be applied when any person, other than a nonprofit library, archive, educational institution, or public non-commercial broadcasting entity, is found to have engaged willfully and for purposes of commercial advantage or private financial gain in any of the foregoing activities.

(b)   Each Party shall confine exceptions to measures implementing subparagraph (a) to lawfully authorized activities carried out by government employees, agents, or contractors for law enforcement, intelligence, national defense, essential security, or similar governmental purposes.

(c)   Rights management information means:

(i)   information that identifies a work, performance, or phonogram, the author of the work, the performer of the performance, or the producer of the phonogram, or the owner of any right in the work, performance, or phonogram; or

(ii)   information about the terms and conditions of the use of the work, performance, or phonogram; or

(iii)   any numbers or codes that represent such information,

when any of these items is attached to a copy of the work, performance, or phonogram or appears in connection with the communication or making available of a work, performance, or phonogram to the public. Nothing in this paragraph shall obligate a Party to require the owner of any right in the work, performance, or phonogram to attach rights management information to copies of the work, performance, or phonogram, or to cause rights management information to appear in connection with a communication of the work, performance, or phonogram to the public.

9.   In order to confirm that all agencies at the central level of government use computer software only as authorized, each Party shall issue appropriate laws, orders, regulations, or decrees to actively regulate the acquisition and management of software for such use. These

measures may take the form of procedures such as preparing and maintaining inventories of software on agency computers and inventories of software licenses.

10. (a)   With respect to Articles 15.5, 15.6, and 15.7, each Party shall confine limitations or exceptions to exclusive rights to certain special cases that do not conflict with a normal exploitation of the work, performance, or phonogram, and do not unreasonably prejudice the legitimate interests of the right holder.

(b)   Notwithstanding subparagraph (a) and Article 15.7.3(b), no Party may permit the retransmission of television signals (whether terrestrial, cable, or satellite) on the Internet without the authorization of the right holder or right holders of the content of the signal and, if any, of the signal.

Article 15.6: Obligations Pertaining Specifically to Copyright

Without prejudice to Articles 11(1)(ii), 11bis(1)(i) and (ii), 11ter(1)(ii), 14(1)(ii), and 14bis(1) of the Berne Convention, each Party shall provide to authors the exclusive right to authorize or prohibit the communication to the public of their works, directly or indirectly, by wire or wireless means, including the making available to the public of their works in such a way that members of the public may access these works from a place and at a time individually chosen by them.

Article 15.7: Obligations Pertaining Specifically to Related Rights

1.   Each Party shall accord the rights provided for in this Chapter with respect to performers and producers of phonograms to the performers and producers of phonograms who are nationals of another Party and to performances or phonograms first published or fixed in the territory of a Party. A performance or phonogram shall be considered first published in the territory of a Party in which it is published within 30 days of its original publication.[14]

2.   Each Party shall provide to performers the right to authorize or prohibit:

(a)   the broadcasting and communication to the public of their unfixed performances except where the performance is already a broadcast performance; and

(b)   the fixation of their unfixed performances.

3. (a)   Each Party shall provide to performers and producers of phonograms the right to authorize or prohibit the broadcasting or any communication to the public of their performances or phonograms, by wire or wireless means, including the making available to the public of those performances and phonograms in such a way that members of the public may access them from a place and at a time individually chosen by them.

(b)   Notwithstanding subparagraph (a) and Article 15.5.10, the application of this right to traditional free over-the-air noninteractive broadcasting, and exceptions or limitations to this right for such broadcasting, shall be a matter of domestic law.

---

[14] For purposes of this Article, fixation includes the finalization of the master tape or its equivalent.

    (c)   Each Party may adopt limitations to this right in respect of other noninteractive transmissions in accordance with Article 15.5.10, provided that the limitations do not prejudice the right of the performer or producer of phonograms to obtain equitable remuneration.

4.   No Party may subject the enjoyment and exercise of the rights of performers and producers of phonograms provided for in this Chapter to any formality.

5.   For purposes of this Article and Article 15.5, the following definitions apply with respect to performers and producers of phonograms:

    (a)   performers means actors, singers, musicians, dancers, and other persons who act, sing, deliver, declaim, play in, interpret, or otherwise perform literary or artistic works or expressions of folklore;

    (b)   phonogram means the fixation of the sounds of a performance or of other sounds, or of a representation of sounds, other than in the form of a fixation incorporated in a cinematographic or other audiovisual work;

    (c)   fixation means the embodiment of sounds, or of the representations thereof, from which they can be perceived, reproduced, or communicated through a device;

    (d)   producer of a phonogram means the person, or the legal entity, who or which takes the initiative and has the responsibility for the first fixation of the sounds of a performance or other sounds, or the representations of sounds;

    (e)   publication of a performance or a phonogram means the offering of copies of the fixed performance or the phonogram to the public, with the consent of the right holder, and provided that copies are offered to the public in reasonable quantity;

    (f)   broadcasting means the transmission by wireless means or satellite to the public of sounds or sounds and images, or of the representations thereof, including wireless transmission of encrypted signals where the means for decrypting are provided to the public by the broadcasting organization or with its consent; and

    (g)   communication to the public of a performance or a phonogram means the transmission to the public by any medium, otherwise than by broadcasting, of sounds of a performance or the sounds or the representations of sounds fixed in a phonogram. For purposes of paragraph 3, "communication to the public" includes making the sounds or representations of sounds fixed in a phonogram audible to the public.

Article 15.8: Protection of Encrypted Program-Carrying Satellite Signals

1.   Each Party shall make it a criminal offense:

    (a)   to manufacture, assemble, modify, import, export, sell, lease, or otherwise distribute a tangible or intangible device or system, knowing or having reason to know that the device or system is primarily of assistance in decoding an encrypted program-carrying satellite signal without the authorization of the lawful distributor of such signal; and

(b)   willfully to receive and further distribute a program-carrying signal that originated as an encrypted satellite signal knowing that it has been decoded without the authorization of the lawful distributor of the signal.

2.   Each Party shall provide for civil remedies, including compensatory damages, for any person injured by any activity described in paragraph 1, including any person that holds an interest in the encrypted programming signal or its content.

Article 15.9: Patents

1.   Each Party shall make patents available for any invention, whether a product or a process, in all fields of technology, provided that the invention is new, involves an inventive step, and is capable of industrial application. For purposes of this Article, a Party may treat the terms "inventive step" and "capable of industrial application" as being synonymous with the terms "non-obvious" and "useful," respectively.

2.   Nothing in this Chapter shall be construed to prevent a Party from excluding inventions from patentability as set out in Articles 27.2 and 27.3 of the TRIPS Agreement. Notwithstanding the foregoing, any Party that does not provide patent protection for plants by the date of entry into force of this Agreement shall undertake all reasonable efforts to make such patent protection available. Any Party that provides patent protection for plants or animals on or after the date of entry into force of this Agreement shall maintain such protection.

3.   A Party may provide limited exceptions to the exclusive rights conferred by a patent, provided that such exceptions do not unreasonably conflict with a normal exploitation of the patent and do not unreasonably prejudice the legitimate interests of the patent owner, taking account of the legitimate interests of third parties.

4.   Without prejudice to Article 5.A(3) of the Paris Convention, each Party shall provide that a patent may be revoked or cancelled only on grounds that would have justified a refusal to grant the patent. However, a Party may also provide that fraud, misrepresentation, or inequitable conduct may be the basis for revoking, canceling, or holding a patent unenforceable.

5.   Consistent with paragraph 3, if a Party permits a third person to use the subject matter of a subsisting patent to generate information necessary to support an application for marketing approval of a pharmaceutical or agricultural chemical product, that Party shall provide that any product produced under such authority shall not be made, used, or sold in the territory of that Party other than for purposes related to generating information to meet requirements for approval to market the product once the patent expires, and if the Party permits exportation, the product shall only be exported outside the territory of that Party for purposes of meeting marketing approval requirements of that Party.

6.   (a)   Each Party, at the request of the patent owner, shall adjust the term of a patent to compensate for unreasonable delays that occur in granting the patent. For purposes of this paragraph, an unreasonable delay shall at least include a delay in the issuance of the patent of more than five years from the date of filing of the application in the territory of the Party, or three years after a request for

examination of the application has been made, whichever is later, provided that periods attributable to actions of the patent applicant need not be included in the determination of such delays.

(b)   With respect to any pharmaceutical product that is covered by a patent, each Party shall make available a restoration of the patent term to compensate the patent owner for unreasonable curtailment of the effective patent term resulting from the marketing approval process related to the first commercial marketing of the product in that Party.

7.   Each Party shall disregard information contained in public disclosures used to determine if an invention is novel or has an inventive step if the public disclosure (a) was made or authorized by, or derived from, the patent applicant, and (b) occurred within 12 months prior to the date of filing of the application in the territory of the Party.

8.   Each Party shall provide patent applicants with at least one opportunity to submit amendments, corrections, and observations in connection with their applications.

9.   Each Party shall provide that a disclosure of a claimed invention shall be considered to be sufficiently clear and complete if it provides information that allows the invention to be made and used by a person skilled in the art, without undue experimentation, as of the filing date.

10.   Each Party shall provide that a claimed invention is sufficiently supported by its disclosure if the disclosure reasonably conveys to a person skilled in the art that the applicant was in possession of the claimed invention as of the filing date.

11.   Each Party shall provide that a claimed invention is industrially applicable if it has a specific, substantial, and credible utility.

Article 15.10: Measures Related to Certain Regulated Products

1.   (a)   If a Party requires, as a condition of approving the marketing of a new pharmaceutical or agricultural chemical product, the submission of undisclosed data concerning safety or efficacy, the Party shall not permit third persons, without the consent of the person who provided the information, to market a product on the basis of (1) the information, or (2) the approval granted to the person who submitted the information for at least five years for pharmaceutical products and ten years for agricultural chemical products from the date of approval in the Party.[15]

(b)   If a Party permits, as a condition of approving the marketing of a new pharmaceutical or agricultural chemical product, third persons to submit evidence concerning the safety or efficacy of a product that was previously approved in another territory, such as evidence of prior marketing approval, the Party shall not permit third persons, without the consent of the person who previously obtained

---

[15] Where a Party, on the date it implemented the TRIPS Agreement, had in place a system for protecting pharmaceutical or agricultural chemical products not involving new chemical entities from unfair commercial use that conferred a period of protection shorter than that specified in paragraph 1, that Party may retain such system notwithstanding the obligations of paragraph 1.

such approval in the other territory, to obtain authorization or to market a product on the basis of (1) evidence of prior marketing approval in the other territory, or (2) information concerning safety or efficacy that was previously submitted to obtain marketing approval in the other territory, for at least five years for pharmaceutical products and ten years for agricultural chemical products from the date approval was granted in the Party's territory to the person who received approval in the other territory. In order to receive protection under this subparagraph, a Party may require that the person providing the information in the other territory seek approval in the territory of the Party within five years after obtaining marketing approval in the other territory.

(c)   For purposes of this paragraph, a new product is one that does not contain a chemical entity that has been previously approved in the territory of the Party.

(d)   For purposes of this paragraph, each Party shall protect such undisclosed information against disclosure except where necessary to protect the public, and no Party may consider information accessible within the public domain as undisclosed data. Notwithstanding the foregoing, if any undisclosed information concerning safety and efficacy submitted to a Party, or an entity acting on behalf of a Party, for purposes of obtaining marketing approval is disclosed by such entity, the Party is still required to protect such information from unfair commercial use in the manner set forth in this Article.

2.   Where a Party permits, as a condition of approving the marketing of a pharmaceutical product, persons, other than the person originally submitting safety or efficacy information, to rely on evidence or information concerning the safety and efficacy of a product that was previously approved, such as evidence of prior marketing approval in the territory of a Party or in another country, that Party:

(a)   shall implement measures in its marketing approval process to prevent such other persons from marketing a product covered by a patent claiming the previously approved product or its approved use during the term of that patent, unless by consent or acquiescence of the patent owner; and

(b)   shall provide that the patent owner shall be informed of the request and the identity of any such other person who requests approval to enter the market during the term of a patent identified as claiming the approved product or its approved use.

Article 15.11: Enforcement of Intellectual Property Rights

General Obligations

1.   Each Party understands that procedures and remedies required under this Article for enforcement of intellectual property rights are established in accordance with:

(a)   the principles of due process that each Party recognizes; and

(b)   the foundations of its own legal system.

2.   This Article does not create any obligation:

    (a)   to put in place a judicial system for the enforcement of intellectual property rights distinct from that for the enforcement of law in general; or

    (b)   with respect to the distribution of resources for the enforcement of intellectual property rights and the enforcement of law in general.

The Parties understand that the decisions that a Party makes on the distribution of enforcement resources shall not excuse that Party from complying with this Chapter.

3.   Each Party shall provide that final judicial decisions or administrative rulings of general applicability pertaining to the enforcement of intellectual property rights shall be in writing and shall state any relevant findings of fact and the reasoning or the legal basis on which the decisions and rulings are based. Each Party shall provide that such decisions or rulings shall be published,[16] or where such publication is not practicable, otherwise made publicly available, in a national language in such a manner as to enable governments and right holders to become acquainted with them.

4.   Each Party shall publicize information that it may collect on its efforts to provide effective enforcement of intellectual property rights in its civil, administrative, and criminal system, including any statistical information.

5.   In civil, administrative, and criminal proceedings involving copyright or related rights, each Party shall provide that:

    (a)   the person whose name is indicated as the author, producer, performer, or publisher of the work, performance, or phonogram in the usual manner, shall, in the absence of proof to the contrary, be presumed to be the designated right holder in such work, performance, or phonogram; and

    (b)   it shall be presumed, in the absence of proof to the contrary, that the copyright or related right subsists in such subject matter.

Civil and Administrative Procedures and Remedies

6.   Each Party shall make available to right holders[17] civil judicial procedures concerning the enforcement of any intellectual property right.

7.   Each Party shall provide that:

    (a)   in civil judicial proceedings concerning the enforcement of intellectual property rights, its judicial authorities shall have the authority to order the infringer to pay the right holder:

---

[16] A Party may satisfy the requirement for publication by making the document available to the public on the Internet.

[17] For the purpose of this Article, the term "right holder" shall include federations and associations as well as exclusive licensees and other duly authorized licensees, as appropriate, having the legal standing and authority to assert such rights. The term "licensee" shall include the licensee of any one or more of the exclusive intellectual property rights encompassed in a given intellectual property.

(i)   damages adequate to compensate for the injury the right holder has suffered as a result of the infringement; and

(ii)   at least in the case of copyright or related rights infringement and trademark counterfeiting, the profits of the infringer that are attributable to the infringement and are not taken into account in computing the amount of the damages referred to in clause (i); and

(b)   in determining damages for infringement of intellectual property rights, its judicial authorities shall consider, inter alia, the value of the infringed-upon good or service based on the suggested retail price or other legitimate measure of value that the right holder presents.

8.   In civil judicial proceedings, each Party shall, at least with respect to civil judicial proceedings concerning copyright or related rights infringement and trademark counterfeiting, establish or maintain pre-established damages as an alternative to actual damages. Such pre-established damages shall be set out in domestic law and determined by the judicial authorities in an amount sufficient to compensate the right holder for the harm caused by the infringement and constitute a deterrent to future infringements.

9.   Each Party shall provide that its judicial authorities, except in exceptional circumstances, shall have the authority to order, at the conclusion of civil judicial proceedings concerning copyright or related rights infringement and trademark counterfeiting, that the prevailing party shall be awarded payment of court costs or fees and reasonable attorney's fees by the losing party. Further, each Party shall provide that its judicial authorities, at least in exceptional circumstances, shall have the authority to order, at the conclusion of civil judicial proceedings concerning patent infringement, that the prevailing party be awarded payment of reasonable attorney's fees by the losing party.

10.   In civil judicial proceedings concerning copyright or related right infringement and trademark counterfeiting, each Party shall provide that its judicial authorities shall have the authority to order the seizure of suspected infringing goods, any related materials and implements, and, at least for trademark counterfeiting, documentary evidence relevant to the infringement.

11.   Each Party shall provide that:

(a)   its judicial authorities shall have the authority to order, at their discretion, the destruction of the goods that have been found to be pirated or counterfeit;

(b)   its judicial authorities shall have the authority to order that materials and implements that have been used in the manufacture or creation of such pirated or counterfeit goods be, without compensation of any sort, promptly destroyed or, in exceptional circumstances, without compensation of any sort, disposed of outside the channels of commerce in such a manner as to minimize the risks of further infringements. In considering requests for such destruction, the Party's judicial authorities may take into account, inter alia, the gravity of the infringement, as well as the interests of third parties holding ownership, possessory, contractual, or secured interests;

(c)   the charitable donation of counterfeit trademark goods and goods that infringe copyright and related rights shall not be ordered by the judicial authorities without the authorization of the right holder, except that counterfeit trademark goods may in appropriate cases be donated to charity for use outside the channels of commerce when the removal of the trademark eliminates the infringing characteristic of the good and the good is no longer identifiable with the removed trademark. In no case shall the simple removal of the trademark unlawfully affixed be sufficient to permit the release of goods into the channels of commerce.

12.   Each Party shall provide that in civil judicial proceedings concerning the enforcement of intellectual property rights, its judicial authorities shall have the authority to order the infringer to provide any information that the infringer possesses regarding any person involved in any aspect of the infringement and regarding the means of production or distribution channel for the infringing goods or services, including the identification of third persons that are involved in their production and distribution and their distribution channels, and to provide this information to the right holder. Each Party shall provide that its judicial authorities shall have the authority to impose sanctions, in appropriate cases, on a party to a proceeding that fails to abide by valid orders issued by such authorities.

13.   To the extent that any civil remedy can be ordered as a result of administrative procedures on the merits of a case, each Party shall provide that such procedures conform to principles equivalent in substance to those provided for in this Chapter.

14.   Each Party shall provide for civil remedies against the acts described in Article 15.5.7 and 15.5.8. Available civil remedies shall include at least:

(a)   provisional measures, including seizure of devices and products suspected of being involved in the prohibited activity;

(b)   actual damages (plus any profits attributable to the prohibited activity not taken into account in computing the actual damages) or pre-established damages as provided in paragraph 8;

(c)   payment to the prevailing right holder, at the conclusion of civil judicial proceedings, of court costs and fees and reasonable attorney's fees by the party engaged in the prohibited conduct; and

(d)   destruction of devices and products found to be involved in the prohibited activity, at the discretion of the judicial authorities, as provided in subparagraphs (a) and (b) of paragraph 11.

No Party may make damages available against a nonprofit library, archives, educational institution, or public broadcasting entity that sustains the burden of proving that it was not aware and had no reason to believe that its acts constituted a prohibited activity.

15.   In civil judicial proceedings concerning the enforcement of intellectual property rights, each Party shall provide that its judicial authorities shall have the authority to order a party to desist from an infringement, inter alia, to prevent the entry into the channels of commerce in their jurisdiction of imported goods that involve the infringement of an intellectual property right, immediately after customs clearance of such goods or to prevent their exportation.

16.   In the event that a Party's judicial or other authorities appoint technical or other experts in civil proceedings concerning the enforcement of intellectual property rights and require that the parties bear the costs of such experts, the Party should seek to ensure that such costs are closely related, inter alia, to the quantity and nature of work to be performed and do not unreasonably deter recourse to such proceedings.

Provisional Measures

17.   Each Party shall act on requests for relief inaudita altera parte and execute such requests expeditiously, in accordance with its rules of judicial procedure.

18.   Each Party shall provide that its judicial authorities shall have the authority to require the plaintiff to provide any reasonably available evidence in order to satisfy themselves with a sufficient degree of certainty that the plaintiff's right is being infringed or that such infringement is imminent, and to order the plaintiff to provide a reasonable security or equivalent assurance set at a level sufficient to protect the defendant and to prevent abuse, and so as not to unreasonably deter recourse to such procedures.

19.   In proceedings concerning the grant of provisional measures in relation to enforcement of a patent, each Party shall provide for a rebuttable presumption that the patent is valid.

Special Requirements Related to Border Measures

20.   Each Party shall provide that any right holder initiating procedures for its competent authorities to suspend the release of suspected counterfeit or confusingly similar trademark goods, or pirated copyright goods[18] into free circulation is required to provide adequate evidence to satisfy the competent authorities that, under the laws of the country of importation, there is prima facie an infringement of the right holder's intellectual property right and to supply sufficient information that may reasonably be expected to be within the right holder's knowledge to make the suspected goods reasonably recognizable by the competent authorities. The requirement to provide sufficient information shall not unreasonably deter recourse to these procedures.

21.   Each Party shall provide that its competent authorities shall have the authority to require a right holder initiating procedures for suspension to provide a reasonable security or equivalent assurance sufficient to protect the defendant and the competent authorities and to prevent abuse. Such security or equivalent assurance shall not unreasonably deter recourse to these procedures. Each Party shall provide that such security may take a form of an instrument issued by a financial services provider to hold the importer or owner of the imported merchandise harmless from any loss or damage resulting from any suspension of the release of goods in the event the competent authorities determine that the article is not an infringing good.

---

[18] For purposes of paragraphs 20 through 25:
counterfeit trademark goods means any goods, including packaging, bearing without authorization a trademark which is identical to the trademark validly registered in respect of such goods, or which cannot be distinguished in its essential aspects from such a trademark, and which thereby infringes the rights of the owner of the trademark in question under the law of the country of importation; and

pirated copyright goods means any goods which are copies made without the consent of the right holder or person duly authorized by the right holder in the country of production and which are made directly or indirectly from an article where the making of that copy would have constituted an infringement of a copyright or a related right under the law of the country of importation.

22.   Where its competent authorities have made a determination that goods are counterfeit or pirated, a Party shall grant its competent authorities the authority to inform the right holder of the names and addresses of the consignor, the importer, and the consignee, and of the quantity of the goods in question.

23.   Each Party shall provide that its competent authorities may initiate border measures ex officio, with respect to imported, exported, or in-transit merchandise suspected of infringing an intellectual property right, without the need for a formal complaint from a private party or right holder.

24.   Each Party shall provide that goods that have been determined to be pirated or counterfeit by its competent authorities shall be destroyed, pursuant as appropriate to judicial order, unless the right holder consents to an alternate disposition, except that counterfeit trademark goods may in appropriate cases be donated to charity for use outside the channels of commerce, when the removal of the trademark eliminates the infringing characteristic of the good and the good is no longer identifiable with the removed trademark. In regard to counterfeit trademark goods, the simple removal of the trademark unlawfully affixed shall not be sufficient to permit the release of the goods into the channels of commerce. In no event shall the competent authorities be authorized to permit the exportation of counterfeit or pirated goods or to permit such goods to be subject to other customs procedures, except in exceptional circumstances.

25.   Each Party shall provide that where an application fee or merchandise storage fee is assessed in connection with border measures to enforce an intellectual property right, the fee shall not be set at an amount that unreasonably deters recourse to such measures.

Criminal Procedures and Remedies

26.   (a)   Each Party shall provide for criminal procedures and penalties to be applied at least in cases of willful trademark counterfeiting or copyright or related rights piracy on a commercial scale. Willful copyright or related rights piracy on a commercial scale includes significant willful infringements of copyright or related rights, for purposes of commercial advantage or private financial gain, as well as willful infringements that have no direct or indirect motivation of financial gain, provided that there is more than a de minimis financial harm. Each Party shall treat willful importation or exportation of counterfeit or pirated goods as unlawful activities and provide for criminal penalties to the same extent as the trafficking or distribution of such goods in domestic commerce.[19]

        (b)   Specifically, each Party shall provide:

                (i)   remedies that include sentences of imprisonment or monetary fines, or both, sufficient to provide a deterrent to future acts of infringement. Each Party shall establish policies or guidelines that encourage penalties to be imposed by judicial authorities at levels sufficient to provide a deterrent to future infringements;

                (ii)   that its judicial authorities shall have the authority to order the seizure of suspected counterfeit or pirated goods, any related materials and

---

[19] A Party may comply with this subparagraph in relation to exportation through its measures concerning distribution or trafficking.

implements that have been used in the commission of the offense, any assets traceable to the infringing activity, and any documentary evidence relevant to the offense. Each Party shall provide that items that are subject to seizure pursuant to any such judicial order need not be individually identified so long as they fall within general categories specified in the order;

(iii)   that its judicial authorities shall have the authority to order, among other measures, (1) the forfeiture of any assets traceable to the infringing activity, (2) the forfeiture and destruction of all counterfeit or pirated goods, without compensation of any kind to the defendant, in order to prevent the re-entry of counterfeit and pirated goods into channels of commerce, and (3) with respect to willful copyright or related rights piracy, the forfeiture and destruction of materials and implements that have been used in the creation of the infringing goods; and

(iv)   that its authorities may, at least in cases of suspected trademark counterfeiting or copyright piracy, conduct investigations or exercise other enforcement measures ex officio, without the need for a formal complaint by a private party or right holder, at least for the purpose of preserving evidence or preventing the continuation of the infringing activity.

Limitations on Liability for Service Providers

27.   For the purpose of providing enforcement procedures that permit effective action against any act of infringement of copyright[20] covered under this Chapter, including expeditious remedies to prevent infringements, and criminal and civil remedies that constitute a deterrent to further infringements, each Party shall provide, consistent with the framework set out in this Article:

(a)   legal incentives for service providers to cooperate with copyright owners in deterring the unauthorized storage and transmission of copyrighted materials; and

(b)   limitations in its law regarding the scope of remedies available against service providers for copyright infringements that they do not control, initiate or direct, and that take place through systems or networks controlled or operated by them or on their behalf, as set out in this subparagraph.[21]

(i)   These limitations shall preclude monetary relief and provide reasonable restrictions on court-ordered relief to compel or restrain certain actions for the following functions and shall be confined to those functions:

(A)   transmitting, routing, or providing connections for material without modification of its content, or the intermediate and transient storage of such material in the course thereof;

(B)   caching carried out through an automatic process;

---

[20] For purposes of this paragraph, "copyright" shall also include related rights.
[21] The Parties understand that this subparagraph is without prejudice to the availability of defenses to copyright infringement that are of general applicability.

> > (C)   storage at the direction of a user of material residing on a system or network controlled or operated by or for the service provider; and
>
> > (D)   referring or linking users to an on-line location by using information location tools, including hyperlinks and directories.

> (ii)   These limitations shall apply only where the service provider does not initiate the chain of transmission of the material and does not select the material or its recipients (except to the extent that a function described in clause (i)(D) in itself entails some form of selection).

> (iii)   Qualification by a service provider for the limitations as to each function in clauses (i)(A) through (D) shall be considered separately from qualification for the limitations as to each other function, in accordance with the conditions for qualification set forth in clauses (iv) through (vii).

> (iv)   With respect to the function referred to in clause (i)(B), the limitations shall be conditioned on the service provider:

> > (A)   permitting access to cached material in significant part only to users of its system or network who have met conditions on user access to that material;
>
> > (B)   complying with rules concerning the refreshing, reloading, or other updating of the cached material when specified by the person making the material available on-line in accordance with a generally accepted industry standard data communications protocol for the system or network through which that person makes the material available;
>
> > (C)   not interfering with technology consistent with industry standards accepted in the Party's territory used at the originating site to obtain information about the use of the material, and not modifying its content in transmission to subsequent users; and
>
> > (D)   expeditiously removing or disabling access, on receipt of an effective notification of claimed infringement, to cached material that has been removed or access to which has been disabled at the originating site.

> (v)   With respect to functions referred to in clauses (i)(C) and (D), the limitations shall be conditioned on the service provider:

> > (A)   not receiving a financial benefit directly attributable to the infringing activity, in circumstances where it has the right and ability to control such activity;
>
> > (B)   expeditiously removing or disabling access to the material residing on its system or network on obtaining actual knowledge of the infringement or becoming aware of facts or circumstances from

which the infringement was apparent, such as through effective notifications of claimed infringement in accordance with clause (ix); and

(C)   publicly designating a representative to receive such notifications.

(vi)   Eligibility for the limitations in this subparagraph shall be conditioned on the service provider:

(A)   adopting and reasonably implementing a policy that provides for termination in appropriate circumstances of the accounts of repeat infringers; and

(B)   accommodating and not interfering with standard technical measures accepted in the Party's territory that protect and identify copyrighted material, that are developed through an open, voluntary process by a broad consensus of copyright owners and service providers, that are available on reasonable and nondiscriminatory terms, and that do not impose substantial costs on service providers or substantial burdens on their systems or networks.

(vii)   Eligibility for the limitations in this subparagraph may not be conditioned on the service provider monitoring its service, or affirmatively seeking facts indicating infringing activity, except to the extent consistent with such technical measures.

(viii)   If the service provider qualifies for the limitations with respect to the function referred to in clause (i)(A), court-ordered relief to compel or restrain certain actions shall be limited to terminating specified accounts, or to taking reasonable steps to block access to a specific, non-domestic on-line location. If the service provider qualifies for the limitations with respect to any other function in clause (i), court-ordered relief to compel or restrain certain actions shall be limited to removing or disabling access to the infringing material, terminating specified accounts, and other remedies that a court may find necessary provided that such other remedies are the least burdensome to the service provider among comparably effective forms of relief. Each Party shall provide that any such relief shall be issued with due regard for the relative burden to the service provider and harm to the copyright owner, the technical feasibility and effectiveness of the remedy and whether less burdensome, comparably effective enforcement methods are available. Except for orders ensuring the preservation of evidence, or other orders having no material adverse effect on the operation of the service provider's communications network, each Party shall provide that such relief shall be available only where the service provider has received notice and an opportunity to appear before the Party's judicial authority.

(ix)   For purposes of the notice and take down process for the functions referred to in clauses (i)(C) and (D), each Party shall establish appropriate procedures for effective notifications of claimed infringement, and effective counter-notifications by those whose material is removed or disabled through mistake or misidentification. At a minimum, each Party shall require that an effective notification of claimed infringement be a written communication, physically or electronically signed by a person who represents, under penalty of perjury or other criminal penalty, that he is an authorized representative of a right holder in the material that is claimed to have been infringed, and containing information that is reasonably sufficient to enable the service provider to identify and locate material that the complaining party claims in good faith to be infringing and to contact that complaining party. At a minimum, each Party shall require that an effective counter-notification contain the same information, mutatis mutandis, as a notification of claimed infringement, and contain a statement that the subscriber making the counter-notification consents to the jurisdiction of the courts of the Party. Each Party shall also provide for monetary remedies against any person who makes a knowing material misrepresentation in a notification or counter-notification that causes injury to any interested party as a result of a service provider relying on the misrepresentation.

(x) If the service provider removes or disables access to material in good faith based on claimed or apparent infringement, each Party shall provide that the service provider shall be exempted from liability for any resulting claims, provided that, in the case of material residing on its system or network, it takes reasonable steps promptly to notify the person making the material available on its system or network that it has done so and, if such person makes an effective counter-notification and is subject to jurisdiction in an infringement suit, to restore the material on-line unless the person giving the original effective notification seeks judicial relief within a reasonable time.

(xi) Each Party shall establish an administrative or judicial procedure enabling copyright owners who have given effective notification of claimed infringement to obtain expeditiously from a service provider information in its possession identifying the alleged infringer.

(xii) Service provider means:

(A) for purposes of the function referred to in clause (i)(A), a provider of transmission, routing, or connections for digital on-line communications without modification of their content between or among points specified by the user of material of the user's choosing; and

(B) for purposes of the functions referred to in clause (i)(B) through (D), a provider or operator of facilities for on-line services or network access.

Additional Procedures and Remedies

28.   Annex 15.11 applies between the Dominican Republic and the United States.

Article 15.12: Final Provisions

1.   Except as otherwise provided in paragraph 2 and Article 15.1, each Party shall give effect to this Chapter on the date of entry into force of this Agreement.

2.   As specified below, a Party may delay giving effect to certain provisions of this Chapter for no longer than the periods in this paragraph, beginning on the date of entry into force of the Agreement:

    (a)   in the case of Costa Rica:

        (i)   with respect to Articles 15.4.1 and 15.9.6, one year;
        (ii)   with respect to Article 15.8.1(b), 18 months;
        (iii)   with respect to Articles 15.3.7 and 15.5.8(a)(ii), two years;
        (iv)   with respect to Article 15.11.27, 30 months; and
        (v)   with respect to Articles 15.5.7(a)(ii), 15.5.7(e), 15.5.7(f), 15.11.8, and 15.11.14, three years;

    (b)   in the case of the Dominican Republic:

        (i)   with respect to Article 15.5.4, six months;
        (ii)   with respect to Articles 15.5.9 and 15.9.6, one year;
        (iii)   with respect to Article 15.2.1, 18 months;
        (iv)   with respect to Articles 15.3.7, and 15.11.27, two years; and
        (v)   with respect to Article 15.5.7(a)(ii), 15.5.7(e), and 15.5.7(f), three years.

    (c)   in the case of El Salvador:

        (i)   with respect to Article 15.11.27, one year;
        (ii)   with respect to Article 15.8.1(b), 18 months;
        (iii)   with respect to Article 15.11.23, two years;
        (iv)   with respect to Article 15.5.8(a)(ii), 30 months; and
        (v)   with respect to Articles 15.5.7(a)(ii), 15.5.7(e), 15.5.7(f), 15.11.8, and 15.11.14, three years;

    (d)   in the case of Guatemala:

        (i)   with respect to Article 15.5.4, six months;
        (ii)   with respect to Articles 15.5.9 and 15.9.6, one year;
        (iii)   with respect to Article 15.8, 18 months;
        (iv)   with respect to Articles 15.2.1, 15.3.7, 15.4, 15.5.8(a)(ii), 15.11.20, 15.11.21, 15.11.22, and 15.11.25, two years;
        (v)   with respect to Article 15.11.27, 30 months;
        (vi)   with respect to Articles 15.5.7(a)(ii), 15.5.7(e), 15.5.7(f), 15.11.8, 15.11.14, and 15.11.24, three years; and
        (vii)   with respect to Article 15.11.23, four years;

(e)   in the case of Honduras:

(i)   with respect to Articles 15.5.9 and 15.9.6, one year;
(ii)   with respect to Article 15.8, 18 months;
(iii)   with respect to Articles 15.2.1, 15.3.7, 15.4, 15.5.8(a)(ii), 15.11.20, 15.11.21, 15.11.22, and 15.11.25, two years;
(iv)   with respect to Article 15.11.27, 30 months;
(v)   with respect to Articles 15.5.7(a)(ii), 15.5.7(e), 15.5.7(f), 15.11.8, 15.11.14, and 15.11.24, three years; and
(vi)   with respect to Article 15.11.23, four years; and

(f)   in the case of Nicaragua:

(i)   with respect to Articles 15.5.9 and 15.9.6, one year;
(ii)   with respect to Article 15.8.1(b), 18 months;
(iii)   with respect to Articles 15.3.7, 15.4, 15.5.8(a)(ii), 15.11.20, 15.11.21, 15.11.22, and 15.11.25, two years;
(iv)   with respect to Articles 15.5.7(a)(ii), 15.5.7(e), 15.5.7(f), 15.11.8, 15.11.14, 15.11.24, and 15.11.27, three years; and
(v)   with respect to Article 15.11.23, four years.

Annex 15.11
Procedures and Remedies Concerning
Broadcast or Cable Transmissions or Retransmissions
in the Dominican Republic

1.   The Dominican Republic reaffirms its commitments under Chapter 15 to the application of administrative, civil, and criminal procedures and remedies in the case of broadcast or cable transmissions or retransmissions that are made without the authorization of the right holder or right holders of the content of the signal and, if any, of the signal.

2.   The Dominican Republic shall provide that procedures and remedies are set out in its law for the temporary suspension of concessions or operating licenses, or both, for broadcast or cable transmissions or retransmissions in cases where the Oficina Nacional de Derecho de Autor (ONDA) or its other competent authorities determine that transmissions or retransmissions that are the subject of the concession or operating license have been made without the permission of the right holder or right holders of the content of the signal and, if any, of the signal. Such procedures shall conform to the requirements of Article 15.11 applicable to administrative enforcement, and shall include:

(a)   an opportunity for right holders to make written requests to ONDA or other competent authorities for the temporary or permanent closure of establishments transmitting the unauthorized broadcast or cable transmissions (pursuant to Article 187 of the Ley sobre Derecho de Autor, No. 65-00, August 21, 2000, as implemented by Articles 116.4 and 116.5 of the Reglamento de Aplicación, No. 362-01, March 14, 2001), and for other sanctions available under its law, and to submit evidence in support of such requests;

(b)   a requirement that holders of such concessions or operating licenses cooperate with ONDA or other competent authorities so that investigations and inspections concerning such a request can take place without delay, including by providing access to all documents relating to the transmissions or retransmissions; and

(c)   a requirement that an administrative decision concerning such a request be rendered expeditiously and not later than 60 days after the date of the request. Such decisions shall be in writing and shall state the reasons on which they are based. Any closure shall become effective immediately following a decision requiring such closure. Temporary closure shall continue in effect for up to 30 days. Failure to cease transmission or retransmission following closure shall be considered a violation classified under Article 105(d) of the Ley General de Telecomunicaciones, No. 153-98, May 27, 1998, and shall be subject to all available sanctions authorized by that law.

The Dominican Republic shall further provide that ONDA or other competent authorities may initiate procedures for the temporary or permanent closure of establishments transmitting the unauthorized broadcast or cable transmissions and other sanctions available under national law ex officio, without the need for a written request from a private party or right holder.

3.   The Dominican Republic shall provide that ONDA and its other competent authorities shall have sufficient resources to carry out the actions described in paragraph 2, and hereby reaffirms its obligations under Article 15.11.2(b).

4.   INDOTEL shall exercise the powers conferred on it by the Ley General de Telecomunicaciones No. 153-98 to address copyright infringement in appropriate cases, consistent with the INDOTEL Resolution of January 30, 2004, sanctioning holders of cable transmission service authorizations who transmitted signals containing protected works or retransmitted signals issued by the entity originating the transmission without authorization. If the level of sanctions imposed in the INDOTEL Resolution of January 30, 2004 is not effective in eliminating the problem, then INDOTEL shall increase sanctions to an effective level.

5.   The Dominican Republic shall provide quarterly reporting of progress made in all judicial actions concerning television broadcasting piracy consistent with the understanding set out in an exchange of letters between the Dominican Republic and the United States on the date of signature of this Agreement.

[…]

*

AGREEMENT BETWEEN THE CARIBBEAN COMMUNITY (CARICOM), ACTING ON BEHALF OF THE GOVERNMENTS OF ANTIGUA AND BARBUDA, BARBADOS, BELIZE, DOMINICA, GRENADA, GUYANA, JAMAICA, ST. KITTS AND NEVIS, SAINT LUCIA, ST. VINCENT AND THE GRENADINES, SURINAME AND TRINIDAD AND TOBAGO AND THE GOVERNMENT OF THE REPUBLIC OF COSTA RICA[*]
[excerpts]

The Agreement Between the Caribbean Community (CARICOM), Acting on Behalf of the Governments of Antigua and Barbuda, Barbados, Belize, Dominica, Grenada, Guyana, Jamaica, St. Kitts and Nevis, Saint Lucia, St. Vincent and the Grenadines, Suriname and Trinidad and Tobago and the Government of the Republic of Costa Rica was signed on 9 March 2004.

[…]

Chapter IX: Services

Article IX.01 General Provisions

1.   The Parties recognise the increasing importance of trade in services in their economies. In their efforts to gradually develop and broaden their relations, the Parties shall cooperate in the WTO and plurilateral fora, with the aim of creating the most favourable conditions for achieving further liberalisation and additional mutual opening of markets for the trade in services.

2.   With a view to developing and deepening their relations under this Agreement, the Parties agree that within two (2) years of the date of entry into force of this Agreement, they will review developments related to trade in services and consider the need for further disciplines in this area.

3.   Upon request of a Party, the other Party shall provide information, on a timely basis, on measures that may have an impact on the trade in services.

Article IX.02 Services

1.   The Parties herein recognise the importance of their rights and obligations assumed in the General Agreement on Trade in Services (GATS).

2.   Each Party shall ensure that its competent authorities, within a reasonable time after the submission of an application for a license or certification by a national of the other Party:

---

[*] *Source*: The Organization of American States (2004). "Agreement Between the Caribbean Community (CARICOM), Acting on Behalf of the Governments of Antigua and Barbuda, Barbados, Belize, Dominica, Grenada, Guyana, Jamaica, St. Kitts and Nevis, Saint Lucia, St. Vincent and the Grenadines, Suriname and Trinidad and Tobago and the Government of the Republic of Costa Rica", available on the Internet (http://www.sice.oas.org/trade/crcrcom_e/crcrcomind_e.asp). [Note added by the editor.]

(a)   where the application is complete, make a determination on the application and inform the applicant of that determination; or

(b)   where the application is not complete, inform the applicant without undue delay of the status of the application and the additional information that is required under the Party's law.

3.   (a)   The Parties to this Agreement shall encourage bodies responsible for the regulation of professional services in their respective territories to:

      (i)   ensure that measures relating to the licensing or certification of nationals of the other Party are based on objective and transparent criteria, such as competence and the ability to provide a service; and

      (ii)   co-operate with the view to developing mutually acceptable standards and criteria for licensing and certification of professional service providers.

   (b)   The following elements may be examined with regard to the standards and criteria referred to in subparagraph (a)(ii):

      (i)   education - accreditation of schools or academic programs;

      (ii)   examinations - qualifying examinations for licensing, including alternative methods of assessment such as oral examinations and interviews;

      (iii)   experience - length and nature of experience required for licensing;

      (iv)   conduct and ethics - standards of professional conduct and the nature of disciplinary action for non-conformity with those standards;

      (v)   professional development and re-certification - continuing education and ongoing requirements to maintain professional certification;

      (vi)   scope of practice - extent of, or limitations on, permissible activities;

      (vii)   local knowledge - requirements for knowledge of such matters as local laws, regulations, language, geography or climate; and

      (viii)   consumer protection - alternatives to residency requirements, including bonding, professional liability insurance and client restitution funds, to provide for the protection of consumers.

   (c)   These bodies shall report on the result of their discussions related to the development of mutually acceptable standards mentioned in subparagraph (a)(ii) and, as appropriate, provide any recommendations to the Coordinators.

   (d)   With respect to the recognition of qualification and licensing requirements, the Parties note the existence of rights and obligations with respect to each other under Article VII (Recognition) of the GATS.

(e)   For the purpose of this paragraph, professional services means services, the provision of which requires specialised post-secondary education, or equivalent training or experience, and for which the right to practise is granted or restricted by a Party, but does not include services provided by trades-persons or vessel and aircraft crew members.

Chapter X: Investment

Article X.01 General Provisions

1.   The Parties recognise the increasing importance of investment in their economies. In their efforts to gradually develop and broaden their relations, the Parties shall cooperate in the WTO and plurilateral fora, with the aim of creating the most favourable conditions for achieving further liberalisation and additional mutual opening of markets for investment.

2.   With a view to developing and deepening their relations under this Agreement, the Parties agree that within two (2) years of the date of entry into force of this Agreement, they shall review developments related to investment, and consider the need for further disciplines in this area.

3.   Upon the request of a Party, the other Party shall provide information, on a timely basis, on measures that may have an impact on investment.

Article X.02 Definitions

For the purposes of this Chapter:

investors means, for either Party, the following subjects who have made investments in the territory of the other Party in accordance with the legislation of the latter and the provisions of this Chapter:

(a)   any natural person who is a national of one of the Parties; or

(b)   legal persons, including companies, business associations, corporations, branch offices and any other organization duly incorporated or constituted in accordance with the laws of that Party, which has its seat in the territory of that Party and carries on business in the territory of that Party whether or not it is for profit;

investment means any kind of asset, defined in accordance with the laws of the host country, which the investor of one Party invests in the territory of the other Party in accordance with the latter's laws and regulations, and includes, in particular, though not exclusively:

(a)   movable and immovable property and any other rights in rem such as mortgages, liens or pledges, and similar rights;

(b)   shares, stock, securities and debentures of companies or any other form of participation in a company;

     (c)   claims to money or to any performances having an economic value directly related to an investment;

     (d)   intellectual property rights, including copyright and related rights, trade marks, geographical indications, drawings, models and industrial designs, patents, layout-designs, distinctive signs and know-how;

     (e)   rights conferred by law or under contract, to undertake any economic and commercial activity, including any rights to search for, cultivate, extract or exploit natural resources.

Any change in the form of an investment does not affect its character as an investment; and

returns means all amounts yielded by an investment and in particular, though not exclusively, profits, interests, capital gains, dividends, royalties, fees or other current income.

Article X.03 Promotion and Admission

1.   Each Party shall encourage and create favorable conditions in its territory for investments of the other Party, and shall admit such investments in accordance with its laws and regulations.

2.   Once a Party has admitted an investment in its territory, it shall provide, in accordance with its laws and regulations, all necessary permits related to such investment.

Article X.04 Protection

1.   Investments of either Party shall at all times be accorded fair and equitable treatment, and shall enjoy full legal protection and security in accordance with international law.

2.   Neither of the Parties shall obstruct, in any manner, either through arbitrary or discriminatory measures, the enjoyment, use, management, conduct, operation and sale or other disposition thereof of such investments. Each Party shall comply with any obligation assumed regarding investments of the other Party.

3.   Returns from investments and in the event of their re-investment the returns therefrom shall enjoy the same protection as the investment.

Article X.05 National and Most Favored Nation Treatment

1.   In accordance with its laws and regulations, each Party shall accord to investments of the other Party in the former's territory, treatment no less favourable than that granted to investment of its own investors.

2.   Each Party shall accord to investments and returns of the other Party in the former's territory, treatment no less favourable than that granted to investments of investors of any non-Party.

3.   Each Party shall accord the treatment which is more favourable to the investment of the other Party, either national or most favored nation treatment.

4. Nothing in this Article shall be construed so as to oblige a Party to extend to investments of investors of the other Party advantages resulting from any existing or future association or participation in a free trade area, customs union, common market, economic and monetary union or any other similar institution of economic integration.

5. Nothing in this Article shall be construed so as to oblige a Party to extend to investments of investors of the other Party deductions, fiscal exemptions or any other similar advantages resulting from double taxation agreements or any other agreement regarding tax matters negotiated by one Party and any other non-Party.

Article X.06 Expropriation and Compensation

1. Investments of either Party in the territory of the other Party shall not be nationalized, expropriated or subjected to measures having an equivalent effect (hereinafter referred to as "expropriation"), except in cases when any of such measures have been adopted for the public good, in accordance with the due process of law, on a non-discriminatory basis and against prompt, adequate and effective compensation.

2. The compensation shall amount to the market value of the expropriated investment immediately before the expropriation or impending expropriation became public knowledge, whichever is earlier. It shall include interest from the date of dispossession of the expropriated property until the date of payment. Interest shall be based on the average deposit rate prevailing in the national banking system of the Party where the expropriation was made. Compensation shall be paid without undue delay, in convertible currency, and be effectively realizable and be freely transferable.

3. The investor affected shall have a right, under the law of the Party making the expropriation, to prompt review, by a judicial or other independent authority of that Party, of his or its case and of the valuation of his or its investment in accordance with the principles set out in this Article.

4. Nothing set out in this Article shall affect the ability of a government of a Party to negotiate with the other Party or any other non-Party, quantitative restrictions of its exports or its ability to assign export quotas negotiated through appropriate mechanisms and criteria. Consequently, any dispute in this regard will be resolved in accordance with the trade agreements applicable between the Parties. Thus, nothing in this Article shall be used as a basis for an investor to argue that the effects derived from the distribution or administration of a quota represent an indirect expropriation.

Article X.07 Compensation for Losses

Investors of one Party whose investments in the territory of the other Party suffer losses owing to war or other armed conflict, revolution, a state of national emergency, insurrection, riot or any other similar event, shall be accorded by the latter Party treatment, as regards restitution, indemnification, compensation or other settlement, no less favourable than that which the latter Party accords to investments of its own investors or investments of investors of any non-Party, whichever is more favourable to the investment of the investor of the former Party. All payments that may result shall be deemed freely transferable.

Article X.08 Transfers

1.	Each Party shall permit investors of the other Party, in accordance with its laws and regulations, the unrestricted transfer of payments related to their investments. Such transfers include, in particular, though not exclusively, the following:

>	(a)	initial capital and additional amounts needed to maintain, expand and develop the investment;

>	(b)	funds in repayment of loans made pursuant to Article X.02, subparagraph (c) under the definition 'investment ';

>	(c)	compensation referred to in Articles X.06 and X.07;

>	(d)	proceeds derived from the partial or total sale or liquidation of the investment;

>	(e)	proceeds derived from any compensation owed to an investor by virtue of a resolution of the dispute settlement procedures established by this Chapter;

>	(f)	returns;

>	(g)	the earnings of nationals of one Party who are allowed to work in connection with an investment in the territory of the other.

2.	Transfers referred to in this Article shall be effected in freely convertible currency at the applicable exchange rate on the date of the transfer without undue delay on a non-discriminatory basis. Transfers shall be considered to have been made "without undue delay" when they have been made within the period normally necessary for the completion of the transfer.

3.	Notwithstanding the provisions of paragraph 1 of this Article, each Party shall be entitled, under circumstances of exceptional or serious balance of payments difficulties, to limit transfers temporarily, on a fair and non-discriminatory basis, and in accordance with internationally accepted criteria. Limits on transfers adopted or maintained by a Party, as well as their elimination, under this paragraph shall be notified promptly to the other Party.

4.	When transfers are restricted by a Party due to balance of payments difficulties, the Party shall implement measures or a programme in accordance with the rules of the International Monetary Fund.

5.	Notwithstanding the above, a Party may prevent a transfer through the equitable and non-discriminatory application of its laws relating to:

>	(a)	bankruptcy, insolvency or the protection of the rights of creditors;

>	(b)	issuing, trading or dealing in securities;

>	(c)	criminal or administrative offenses;

>	(d)	failure to report transfers of currency or other monetary instruments; or

(e)   ensuring the satisfaction of judgments and awards in adjudicatory proceedings.

Article X.09 Application of Other Rules

If the laws of one of the Parties or any current or future obligation under International Law, provide more favourable conditions than those granted by this Chapter to investments of investors of the other Party, the most favourable provision shall apply.

Article X.10 Subrogation

If a Party or its designated agency, makes a payment under an indemnity against non-commercial risks given in respect of an investment in the territory of the other Party, the latter Party shall recognize the assignment, under the law of that country, of any right or claim from the investor to the former Party, or its designated agency, as well as the entitlement by virtue of subrogation, to exercise the rights and enforce the claims of that investor. This subrogation shall entitle the former Party, or its designated agency, to assert any such right or claim to the same extent as its predecessor.

Article X.11 Settlement of Investment Disputes Between One Party and Investors of the Other Party

1.   Any investment dispute which may arise between one Party and an investor of the other Party with respect to matters regulated by this Chapter, shall be notified in writing by the investor to the host Party. Such notification shall include in detail all relevant information. To the extent possible, the dispute shall be settled amicably between the parties.

2.   If a dispute has not been settled amicably within a period of six (6) months from the date of the notification referred in paragraph 1 above, it may be submitted, at the choice of the investor concerned, either to the competent Courts or Administrative Tribunals of the Party in whose territory the investment was made, or to international arbitration. Where the dispute is referred to international arbitration, the investor may submit the dispute to either:

(a)   the International Centre for the Settlement of Investment Disputes (ICSID), established by the "Convention on the Settlement of Investment Disputes between States and Nationals of other States" opened for signature at Washington D.C. on 18 March 1965, provided both Parties are signatories of the ICSID Convention; or

(b)   the Additional Facility Rules of ICSID, provided that one of the Parties, but not both, is a party to the ICSID Convention; or

(c)   an ad hoc arbitral tribunal established under the Arbitration Rules of the United Nations Commission on International Trade Law (UNCITRAL), where none of the Parties is a signatory of the ICSID Convention.

3.   Once the investor has submitted the dispute either to a competent Tribunal of the disputing Party or to an arbitral procedure, the selection of one or the other shall be final.

4.   The arbitral award shall be based on:

(a)   the provisions of this Chapter and any other binding agreements between the Parties;

(b)   the national laws of the Party where the investment was made, including the rules dealing with conflicts of laws; and

(c)   the rules and generally recognized principles of International Law.

5.   The arbitral awards shall be final and binding on both parties to the dispute. Each Party assumes the commitment to implement the awards in accordance with its national laws.

6.   The Parties shall abstain from addressing through diplomatic channels any matter submitted either to the domestic tribunals or to arbitration tribunals according to the terms of this Article, until such proceedings are concluded. Once the judicial proceedings or the international arbitration is concluded, a Party shall not make any diplomatic demand relating to the dispute, except where the disputing Party has not complied with the judicial or arbitral decision.

Chapter XI: Temporary Entry

Article XI.01 Temporary Entry

1.   The Parties recognise that there is a growing importance of investment and services related to trade in goods. In accordance with their applicable laws and regulations, they shall facilitate the temporary entry of:

(a)   nationals who are intra-company transferees (managers, executives, specialists) and business visitors;

(b)   nationals who are providing after-sales services directly related to the exportation of goods by an exporter of that same Party into the territory of the other Party;

(c)   spouses and children of nationals described in (a) above; and

(d)   legal residents in the territory of one of the Parties who are intra-company transferees (managers, executives, specialists) and have been continuously employed by the company at least one (1) year immediately preceding the date of application for entry, provided they comply with the immigration requirements of the other Party.

2.   With a view to developing and deepening their relations under this Chapter, the Parties agree that within two (2) years of the date of entry into force of this Agreement, they will review developments related to temporary entry and consider the need for further disciplines in this area.

3.   No later than six (6) months after the date of entry into force of this Agreement, Parties shall make available explanatory material regarding the requirements for temporary entry under this Article in such a manner as to enable citizens of the other Party to become acquainted with them.

4.   For the purposes of this Chapter:

after-sales services include those provided by persons installing, repairing and servicing, supervising installers, and setting up and testing commercial or industrial (including computer software) equipment, provided the services are being performed as part of an original or extended sales or lease agreement, warranty, or service contract. "Setting up" does not include hands-on installation generally performed by construction or building trades. After-sales services also include persons providing familiarisation or training sessions to potential users;

business visitors are short-term visitors who do not intend to enter the labour market of the Parties, but seek entry to engage in activities such as investigating business opportunities, buying, selling or marketing of goods or services, negotiating contracts, conferring with colleagues, attending conferences, trade fairs or trade missions;

national means a natural person who is a citizen of a Party; and

temporary entry means the right to enter and remain for the period authorised by the Parties in accordance with their laws and regulations.
[…]

Chapter XV: Government Procurement

Article XV.01: Government Procurement

1.   The Parties agree to promote greater liberalisation and greater transparency in their government procurement markets.

2.   Within a period of two (2) years of the date of entry into force of this Agreement, the Parties shall analyse the developments regarding paragraph 1 and shall consider adopting disciplines in this Chapter.

Chapter XVI: Exceptions

Article XVI.01 General Exceptions

For the purposes of Part Two (Trade in Goods), Article XX (General Exceptions) of the GATT 1994 and its interpretative notes, or any equivalent provision of a successor Agreement to which both Parties are party, are incorporated into and made part of this Agreement.

Article XVI.02 National Security

Pursuant to Article XXI (Security Exceptions) of the GATT 1994, nothing in this Agreement shall be construed:

(a)   to require any Party to furnish or allow access to any information the disclosure of which it determines to be contrary to its essential security interests;

(b)   to prevent any Party from taking any actions considered necessary for the protection of its essential security interests:

(i)   relating to the traffic in arms, ammunition and implements of war and to such traffic and transactions in other goods, materials, services and technology undertaken directly or indirectly for the purpose of supplying a military or other security establishment;

(ii)   adopted in time of war or other emergency in international relations; or

(iii)   relating to the implementation of national policies or international agreements regarding the non-proliferation of nuclear weapons or other nuclear explosive devices; or

(c)   to prevent any Party from taking action in pursuance of its obligations under the United Nations Charter for the Maintenance of International Peace and Security.

Article XVI.03 Taxation and Double Taxation

1.   Except as provided for in this Article, nothing in this Agreement shall apply to taxation measures.

2.   Nothing in this Agreement shall affect the rights and obligations of either Party under any tax convention. In the event of any inconsistency between this Agreement and any such conventions, those conventions shall prevail to the extent of the inconsistency.

3.   Notwithstanding paragraph 2:

(a)   Article III.03 (National Treatment) and such other provisions of this Agreement as are necessary to give effect to that Article, shall apply to taxation measures to the same extent as in Article III of the GATT 1994; and

(b)   Article III.15 (Export Taxes) shall apply to taxation measures.

4.   The Parties agree to conclude a bilateral double taxation agreement within a reasonable time after the date that this Agreement enters into force.

5.   The Parties agree that, upon conclusion of a bilateral double taxation Agreement, they will agree to an exchange of letters setting out the relationship between the double taxation Agreement and this Article.

Article XVI.04 Balance of Payments

1.   Nothing in this Agreement shall be construed to prevent a Party from adopting or maintaining measures that restrict transfers when the Party experiences serious balance of payments difficulties, or the threat thereof, and such restrictions are consistent with Chapter X (Investment) and this Article.

2.   Restrictions imposed on transfers related to trade in goods, shall not substantially impede those transfers from being made in a freely usable currency at a market rate of exchange and may not take the form of tariff surcharges or similar measures.

Article XVI.05 Exceptions to the Disclosure of Information

Nothing in this Agreement shall be construed to require any Party to furnish or allow access to information, the disclosure of which would impede law enforcement or would be contrary to the Party's laws protecting personal privacy or the financial affairs and accounts of individual customers of financial institutions.

[…]

*

FRAMEWORK AGREEMENT BETWEEN THE GOVERNMENT OF THE UNITED STATES OF AMERICA, THE GOVERNMENT OF THE REPUBLIC OF KAZAKHSTAN, THE GOVERNMENT OF THE KYRGYZ REPUBLIC, THE GOVERNMENT OF THE REPUBLIC OF TAJIKISTAN, THE GOVERNMENT OF TURKMENISTAN, AND THE GOVERNMENT OF THE REPUBLIC OF UZBEKISTAN CONCERNING THE DEVELOPMENT OF TRADE AND INVESTMENT RELATIONS[*]

The Framework Agreement Between the Government of the United States of America, the Government of the Republic of Kazakhstan, the Government of the Kyrgyz Republic, the Government of the Republic of Tajikistan, the Government of Turkmenistan, and the Government of the Republic of Uzbekistan Concerning the Development of Trade and Investment Relations was signed on 1 June 2004. It entered into force on the date of signature.

The Government of the United States of America, the Government of the Republic of Kazakhstan, the Government of the Kyrgyz Republic, the Government of the Republic of Tajikistan, the Government of Turkmenistan, and the Government of the Republic of Uzbekistan (individually a "Party" and collectively the "Parties"):

(1)   Desiring to enhance the bonds of friendship and spirit of cooperation between and amongst the countries;

(2)   Desiring to promote further the trade and investment existing between and amongst the countries;

(3)   Recognizing the importance of fostering an open and predictable environment for international trade and investment;

(4)   Recognizing that reduced barriers to trade in the region will increase and improve trade relations with and within the region and between the region and Afghanistan and hence will be conducive to regional stability;

(5)   Taking into account the membership of some of the Parties in the World Trade Organization (WTO) and the intention of other Parties to accede to the WTO and noting that this Agreement is without prejudice to the rights and obligations of the Parties, where applicable, under the Marrakesh Agreement Establishing the WTO and the agreements, understandings, and other instruments relating thereto or concluded under the auspices of the WTO;

---

[*] *Source*: The Government of the United States of America (2004). "Framework Agreement Between the Government of the United States of America, the Government of the Republic of Kazakhstan, the Government of the Kyrgyz Republic, the Government of the Republic of Tajikistan, the Government of Turkmenistan, and the Government of the Republic of Uzbekistan Concerning the Development of Trade and Investment Relations", available on the Internet (http://www.ustr.gov/assets/World_Regions/Europe_Mediterranean/Russia_the_NIS/asset_ upload_file683_4212.pdf). [Note added by the editor.]

(6)   Recognizing the benefits to each Party resulting from increased international trade and investment, and that trade-distorting investment measures and protectionist trade barriers would deprive the Parties of such benefits;

(7)   Recognizing the essential role of both domestic and foreign private investment in furthering growth, creating jobs, expanding trade, improving technology, and enhancing economic development;

(8)   Recognizing that foreign direct investment confers positive benefits on each Party;

(9)   Desiring to encourage and facilitate private sector and business contacts between and amongst the Parties;

(10)   Acknowledging the Agreement on Bilateral Trade Relations and the Bilateral Investment Treaty, both signed on May 19, 1992 between the Government of the United States of America and the Government of the Republic of Kazakhstan; the Agreement on Bilateral Trade Relations signed on May 8, 1992 and the Bilateral Investment Treaty signed on January 19, 1993 between the United States of America and the Government of the Kyrgyz Republic; the Agreement on Bilateral Trade Relations signed on July 1, 1993 between the Government of the United States of America and the Government of the Republic of Tajikistan; the Agreement on Bilateral Trade Relations signed on March 23, 1993 between the Government of the United States of America and the Government of Turkmenistan; the Agreement on Bilateral Trade Relations signed November 5, 1993, between the Government of the United States of America and the Government of Uzbekistan;

(11)   Noting that this Agreement is without prejudice to the rights and obligations of the Parties under the agreements cited in paragraph 10 of this preamble;

(12)   Recognizing the increased importance of services in the Central Asian economies and in relations between and amongst the Parties;

(13)   Taking into account the need to eliminate non-tariff barriers in order to facilitate greater access to the markets of the Parties and the mutual benefits thereof;

(14)   Recognizing the importance of providing adequate and effective protection and enforcement of intellectual property rights and of membership in and adherence to intellectual property rights conventions;

(15)   Recognizing the importance of providing adequate and effective protection and enforcement of worker rights in accordance with each Party's own labor laws and of improving the observance of internationally recognized core labor standards;

(16)   Desiring to ensure that trade and environmental policies are mutually supportive in the furtherance of sustainable development;

(17)   Desiring that this Framework Agreement reinforce the multilateral trading system by strengthening efforts of WTO members to complete successfully the Doha Development Agenda; and

(18)   Considering that it would be in the respective interests of the Parties to establish a mechanism between the Parties for encouraging the liberalization of trade and investment between and amongst them, including through the Central Asian Cooperation Organization.

To this end, the Parties agree as follows:

ARTICLE ONE

The Parties affirm their desire to promote an attractive investment climate and expand trade in products and services consistent with the terms of this Agreement. The Parties shall take appropriate measures to encourage and facilitate the exchange of goods and services and to secure favourable conditions for long-term development and diversification of trade between and amongst the Parties.

ARTICLE TWO

The Parties shall establish a United States-Central Asian Council on Trade and Investment ("the Council"), which shall be composed of representatives of the Parties. The side of each Central Asian republic will be chaired by the Deputy Prime Minister or Minister responsible for trade and investment issues; the Government of Kazakhstan has specified that the Ministry of Industry and Trade will be its lead agency. The U.S. side will be chaired by the Office of the U.S. Trade Representative ("USTR"). Officials of other government entities of the Parties may take part as needed. The Council will meet at least once a year and at such times and locations as agreed by the Parties.

ARTICLE THREE

The objectives of the Council are as follows:

1.   To monitor trade and investment relations, to identify opportunities for expanding trade and investment, and to identify issues relevant to trade or investment, such as intellectual property, labor, or environmental issues that may be appropriate for negotiation in an appropriate forum.

2.   To hold consultations on trade and investment matters not arising under the relevant Bilateral Investment Treaties of interest to the Parties.

3.   To identify and work toward the removal of impediments to trade and investment flows amongst the Parties and with Afghanistan.

4.   To seek the advice of the private sector, where appropriate, in their respective countries on matters related to the work of the Council.

ARTICLE FOUR

Any Party may raise for consultation any trade matter or any investment matter not arising under the relevant Bilateral Investment Treaty between or amongst the Parties. Requests for consultation shall be accompanied by a written explanation of the subject to be discussed and consultations shall be held within 30 days of receipt of the request, unless the requesting Party agrees to a later date. Each Party shall endeavor to provide for an opportunity for consultations before taking action that could affect adversely the trade or investment interests of the other Parties.

ARTICLE FIVE

This Agreement shall be without prejudice to the domestic law of the Parties or the rights and obligations of the Parties under any other agreement to which they are parties.

ARTICLE SIX

This Agreement shall enter into force on the date of its signature by the Parties.

ARTICLE SEVEN

This Agreement shall remain in force unless terminated by unanimous consent of the Parties. A Party may withdraw from the Agreement upon six months written notice to the other Parties.

IN WITNESS WHEREOF, the undersigned, being duly authorized by their respective governments, have signed this Agreement.

DONE at Washington D.C. this 1st day of June 2004, in the English and Russian languages, with both texts being equally authentic.

PART TWO
PROTOTYPE INSTRUMENTS

MODEL 2004
AGREEMENT BETWEEN CANADA AND _____ FOR THE PROMOTION AND PROTECTION OF INVESTMENTS*

Canada and _____, hereinafter referred to as the "Parties", Recognizing that the promotion and the protection of investments of investors of one Party in the territory of the other Party will be conducive to the stimulation of mutually beneficial business activity, to the development of economic cooperation between them and to the promotion of sustainable development,

Have agreed as follows:

Section A
Definitions

Article 1
Definitions

For the purpose of this Agreement:

administrative ruling of general application means an administrative ruling or interpretation that applies to all persons and fact situations that fall generally within its ambit and that establishes a norm of conduct, but does not include;

(a) a determination or ruling made in an administrative or quasi-judicial proceeding that applies to a particular person, good or service of the other Party in a specific case; or

(b) a ruling that adjudicates with respect to a particular act or practice.

Commission means the body established by the Parties under Article 51;

confidential information means business confidential information and information that is privileged or otherwise protected from disclosure;

covered investment means, with respect to a Party, an investment in its territory of an investor of the other Party existing on the date of entry into force of this Agreement, as well as investments made or acquired thereafter;

cultural industries means persons engaged in any of the following activities:

(i) the publication, distribution, or sale of books, magazines, periodicals or newspapers in print or machine readable form but not including the sole activity of printing or typesetting any of the foregoing;

---

* *Source*: The Government of Canada, Department of Foreign Affairs and International Trade (2004), available on the Internet (http://www.dfait-maeci.gc.ca/tna-nac/documents/2004-FIPA-model-en.pdf).

     (ii)   the production, distribution, sale or exhibition of film or video recordings;

     (iii)   the production, distribution, sale or exhibition of audio or video music recordings;

     (iv)   the publication, distribution, sale or exhibition of music in print or machine readable form; or

     (v)   radio communications in which the transmissions are intended for direct reception by the general public, and all radio, television or cable broadcasting undertakings and all satellite programming and broadcast network services.

days means calendar days, including weekends and holidays;

designate means to establish, designate or authorize, or to expand the scope of a monopoly to cover an additional good or service after the date of entry into force of the Agreement;

disputing investor means an investor that makes a claim under Section C;

disputing Party means a Party against which a claim is made under Section C;

disputing party means the disputing investor or the disputing Party;

enterprise means:

     (i)   any entity constituted or organized under applicable law, whether or not for profit, whether privately-owned or governmentally-owned, including any corporation, trust, partnership, sole proprietorship, joint venture or other association; and

     (ii)   a branch of any such entity;

enterprise of a Party means an enterprise constituted or organized under the law of a Party, and a branch located in the territory of a Party and carrying out business activities there;

equity or debt securities includes voting and non-voting shares, bonds, convertible debentures, stock options and warrants;

existing means in effect on the date of entry into force of this Agreement;

financial institution means any financial intermediary or other enterprise that is authorized to do business and regulated or supervised as a financial institution under the law of the Party in whose territory it is located;

financial service means a service of a financial nature, including insurance, and a service incidental or auxiliary to a service of a financial nature;

government monopoly means a monopoly that is owned, or controlled through ownership interests, by the federal government of a Party or by another such monopoly;

ICSID means the International Centre for Settlement of Investment Disputes;

ICSID Convention means the *Convention on the Settlement of Investment Disputes between States and Nationals of other States,* done at Washington, March 18, 1965;

intellectual property rights means copyright and related rights, trademark rights, rights in geographical indications, rights in industrial designs, patent rights, rights in layout designs of integrated circuits, rights in relation to protection of undisclosed information, and plant breeders' rights.

Inter-American Convention means the *Inter-American Convention on International Commercial Arbitration*, done at Panama, January 30, 1975;

investment means:

    (I)   an enterprise;

    (II)   an equity security of an enterprise;

    (III)   a debt security of an enterprise

        (i)   where the enterprise is an affiliate of the investor, or

        (ii)   where the original maturity of the debt security is at least three years, but does not include a debt security, regardless of original maturity, of a state enterprise;

    (IV)   a loan to an enterprise

        (i)   where the enterprise is an affiliate of the investor, or

        (ii)   where the original maturity of the loan is at least three years,

but does not include a loan, regardless of original maturity, to a state enterprise;

    (V)   (i)   notwithstanding subparagraph (III) and (IV) above, a loan to or debt security issued by a financial institution is an investment only where the loan or debt security is treated as regulatory capital by the Party in whose territory the financial institution is located, and

        (ii)   a loan granted by or debt security owned by a financial institution, other than a loan to or debt security of a financial institution referred to in (i), is not an investment;

for greater certainty:

        (iii)   a loan to, or debt security issued by, a Party or a state enterprise thereof is not an investment; and

        (iv)   a loan granted by or debt security owned by a cross-border financial service provider, other than a loan to or debt security issued by a financial institution, is an investment if such loan or debt security meets the criteria for investments set out elsewhere in this Article;

(VI)   an interest in an enterprise that entitles the owner to share in income or profits of the enterprise;

(VII)   an interest in an enterprise that entitles the owner to share in the assets of that enterprise on dissolution, other than a debt security or a loan excluded from subparagraphs (III) (IV) or (V);

(VIII) real estate or other property, tangible or intangible, acquired in the expectation or used for the purpose of economic benefit or other business purposes; and

(IX)   interests arising from the commitment of capital or other resources in the territory of a Party to economic activity in such territory, such as under

        (i)   contracts involving the presence of an investor's property in the territory of the Party, including turnkey or construction contracts, or concessions, or

        (ii)   contracts where remuneration depends substantially on the production, revenues or profits of an enterprise;

but investment does not mean,

(X)   claims to money that arise solely from

        (i)   commercial contracts for the sale of goods or services by a national or enterprise in the territory of a Party to an enterprise in the territory of the other Party, or

        (ii)   the extension of credit in connection with a commercial transaction, such as trade financing, other than a loan covered by subparagraphs (IV) or (V); and

(XI)   any other claims to money,

that do not involve the kinds of interests set out in subparagraphs (I) through (IX);

investment of an investor of a Party means an investment owned or controlled directly or indirectly by an investor of such Party;

investor of a Party means

in the case of Canada:

        (i)   Canada or a state enterprise of Canada, or

        (ii)   a national or an enterprise of Canada,

that seeks to make, is making or has made an investment;

in the case of _____:

_____;

that seeks to make, is making or has made an investment and that does not possess the citizenship of Canada.

investor of a non-Party means an investor other than an investor of a Party, that seeks to make, is making, or has made an investment;

measure includes any law, regulation, procedure, requirement, or practice;

monopoly means an entity, including a consortium or government agency, that in any relevant market in the territory of a Party is designated as the sole provider or purchaser of a good or service, but does not include an entity that has been granted an exclusive intellectual property right solely by reason of such grant;

national means a natural person who is a citizen or permanent resident of a Party;

New York Convention means the *United Nation Convention on the Recognition and Enforcement of Foreign Arbitral Awards*, done at New York, June 10, 1958;

person means a natural person or an enterprise;

person of a Party means a national, or an enterprise of a Party;

public entity means a central bank or monetary authority of a Party, or any financial institution owned or controlled by a Party;

Secretary-General means the Secretary-General of ICSID;

state enterprise means an enterprise that is owned or controlled through ownership interests by a Party;

sub-national government means:

in respect of Canada, provincial or local governments; and

in respect of_____.

tax convention means a convention for the avoidance of double taxation or other international taxation agreement or arrangement;

territory means

      (i)   in respect of Canada:

             (a)   the land territory of Canada, air space, internal waters and territorial sea of Canada;

             (b)   those areas, including the exclusive economic zone and the seabed and subsoil, over which Canada exercises, in accordance with international law, sovereign rights or jurisdiction for the purpose of exploration and exploitation of the natural resources; and

(c)   artificial islands, installations and structures in the exclusive economic zone or on the continental shelf over which Canada has jurisdiction as a coastal state.

(ii)   in respect of .

transfers include international payments;

Tribunal means an arbitration tribunal established under Article 27 (Submission of a Claim to Arbitration) or Article 32 (Consolidation);

UNCITRAL Arbitration Rules means the arbitration rules of the United Nations Commission on International Trade Law, approved by the United Nations General Assembly on December 15, 1976; and

WTO Agreement means the Agreement Establishing the World Trade Organization done at Marrakesh on April 15, 1994.

Section B
Substantive Obligations

Article 2
Scope

1.   This Agreement shall apply to measures adopted or maintained by a Party relating to:

(a)   investors of the other Party; and

(b)   covered investments.

Article 3
National Treatment

1.   Each Party shall accord to investors of the other Party treatment no less favourable than that it accords, in like circumstances, to its own investors with respect to the establishment, acquisition, expansion, management, conduct, operation and sale or other disposition of investments in its territory.

2.   Each Party shall accord to covered investments treatment no less favourable than that it accords, in like circumstances, to investments of its own investors with respect to the establishment, acquisition, expansion, management, conduct, operation and sale or other disposition of investments in its territory.

3.   The treatment accorded by a Party under paragraphs 1 and 2 means, with respect to a sub-national government, treatment no less favourable than the treatment accorded, in like

circumstances, by that sub-national government to investors, and to investments of investors, of the Party of which it forms a part.

Article 4[1]
Most-Favoured-Nation Treatment

1.   Each Party shall accord to investors of the other Party treatment no less favourable than that it accords, in like circumstances, to investors of a non-Party with respect to the establishment, acquisition, expansion, management, conduct, operation and sale or other disposition of investments in its territory.

2.   Each Party shall, accord to covered investments treatment no less favourable than that it accords, in like circumstances, to investments of investors of a non-Party with respect to the establishment, acquisition, expansion, management, conduct, operation and sale or other disposition of investments in its territory.

Article 5
Minimum Standard of Treatment

1.   Each Party shall accord to covered investments treatment in accordance with the customary international law minimum standard of treatment of aliens, including fair and equitable treatment and full protection and security.

2.   The concepts of "fair and equitable treatment" and "full protection and security" in paragraph 1 do not require treatment in addition to or beyond that which is required by the customary international law minimum standard of treatment of aliens.

3.   A determination that there has been a breach of another provision of this Agreement, or of a separate international agreement, does not establish that there has been a breach of this Article.

Article 6
Senior Management, Boards of Directors and Entry of Personnel

1.   A Party may not require that an enterprise of that Party, that is a covered investment, appoint to senior management positions individuals of any particular nationality.

2.   A Party may require that a majority of the board of directors, or any committee thereof, of an enterprise that is a covered investment be of a particular nationality, or resident in the territory of the Party, provided that the requirement does not materially impair the ability of the investor to exercise control over its investment.

3.   Subject to its laws, regulations and policies relating to the entry of aliens, each Party shall grant temporary entry to nationals of the other Party, employed by an investor of the other Party, who seeks to render services to an investment of that investor in the territory of the Party, in a capacity that is managerial or executive or requires specialized knowledge.

---

[1] For greater certainty, the treatment accorded by a Party under this Article means, with respect to a subnational government, treatment accorded, in like circumstances, by that sub-national government to investors, and to investments of investors, of a non-Party.

Article 7
Performance Requirements

1.   Neither Party may impose or enforce any of the following requirements, or enforce any commitment or undertaking, in connection with the establishment, acquisition, expansion, management, conduct or operation of an investment of an investor of a Party or a non-Party in its territory:

(a)   to export a given level or percentage of goods;

(b)   to achieve a given level or percentage of domestic content;

(c)   to purchase, use or accord a preference to goods produced or services provided in its territory, or to purchase goods or services from persons in its territory;

(d)   to relate in any way the volume or value of imports to the volume or value of exports or to the amount of foreign exchange inflows associated with such investment;

(e)   to restrict sales of goods or services in its territory that such investment produces or provides by relating such sales in any way to the volume or value of its exports or foreign exchange earnings;

(f)   to transfer technology, a production process or other proprietary knowledge to a person in its territory, except when the requirement is imposed or the commitment or undertaking is enforced by a court, administrative tribunal or competition authority, to remedy an alleged violation of competition laws or to act in a manner not inconsistent with other provisions of this Agreement; or

(g)   to supply exclusively from the territory of the Party the goods it produces or the services it provides to a specific regional market or to the world market.

2.   A measure that requires an investment to use a technology to meet generally applicable health, safety or environmental requirements shall not be construed to be inconsistent with paragraph 1(f). For greater certainty, Articles 3 and 4 apply to the measure.

3.   Neither Party may condition the receipt or continued receipt of an advantage, in connection with an investment in its territory of an investor of a Party or of a non-Party, on compliance with any of the following requirements:

(a)   to achieve a given level or percentage of domestic content;

(b)   to purchase, use or accord a preference to goods produced in its territory, or to purchase goods from producers in its territory;

(c)   to relate in any way the volume or value of imports to the volume or value of exports or to the amount of foreign exchange inflows associated with such investment; or

(d)   to restrict sales of goods or services in its territory that such investment produces or provides by relating such sales in any way to the volume or value of its exports or foreign exchange earnings.

4.   Nothing in paragraph 3 shall be construed to prevent a Party from conditioning the receipt or continued receipt of an advantage, in connection with an investment in its territory of an investor of a Party, on compliance with a requirement to locate production, provide a service, train or employ workers, construct or expand particular facilities, or carry out research and development, in its territory.

5.   Paragraphs 1 and 3 shall not apply to any requirement other than the requirements set out in those paragraphs.

6.   The provisions of:

(a)   Paragraphs (1) (a), (b) and (c), and (3) (a) and (b) shall not apply to qualification requirements for goods or services with respect to export promotion and foreign aid programs;

(b)   Paragraphs (1) (b), (c), (f) and (g), and (3) (a) and (b) shall not apply to procurement by a Party or a state enterprise; and

(c)   Paragraphs (3) (a) and (b) shall not apply to requirements imposed by an importing Party relating to the content of goods necessary to qualify for preferential tariffs or preferential quotas.

Article 8
Monopolies and State Enterprises

1.   Nothing in this Agreement shall be construed to prevent a Party from designating a monopoly, or from maintaining or establishing a state enterprise.

2.   Where a Party intends to designate a monopoly[2] and the designation may affect the interests of persons of the other Party, the Party shall, wherever possible, provide prior written notification to the other Party of the designation.

3.   Each Party shall ensure, through regulatory control, administrative supervision or the application of other measures, that any privately-owned monopoly that it designates and any government monopoly that it maintains or designates acts in a manner that is not inconsistent with the Party's obligations under this Agreement wherever such a monopoly exercises any regulatory, administrative or other governmental authority that the Party has delegated to it in connection with the monopoly good or service, such as the power to grant import or export licenses, approve commercial transactions or impose quotas, fees or other charges[3];

---

[2] Nothing in this Article shall be construed to prevent a monopoly from charging different prices in different geographic markets, where such differences are based on normal commercial considerations, such as taking account of supply and demand conditions in those markets.

[3] A "delegation" includes a legislative grant, and a government order, directive or other act transferring to the monopoly, or authorizing the exercise by the monopoly of, governmental authority.

4.   Each Party shall ensure, through regulatory control, administrative supervision or the application of other measures, that any state enterprise that it maintains or establishes acts in a manner that is not inconsistent with the Party's obligations under this Agreement wherever such enterprise exercises any regulatory, administrative or other governmental authority that the Party has delegated to it, such as the power to expropriate, grant licenses, approve commercial transactions or impose quotas, fees or other charges.

Article 9
Reservations and Exceptions

1.   Articles 3, 4, 6 and 7 shall not apply to:

    (a)   any existing non-conforming measure that is maintained by

        (i)   a Party at the national level, as set out in its Schedule to Annex I, or

        (ii)   a sub-national government;

    (b)   the continuation or prompt renewal of any non-conforming measure referred to in subparagraph (a);

    (c)   an amendment to any non-conforming measure referred to in subparagraph (a) to the extent that the amendment does not decrease the conformity of the measure, as it existed immediately before the amendment, with Articles 3, 4, 6 and 7.

2.   Articles 3, 4, 6 and 7 shall not apply to any measure that a Party adopts or maintains with respect to sectors, subsectors or activities, as set out in its schedule to Annex II.

3.   Article 4 shall not apply to treatment accorded by a Party pursuant to agreements, or with respect to sectors, set out in its schedule to Annex III.

4.   In respect of intellectual property rights, a Party may derogate from Articles 3 and 4 in a manner that is consistent with the WTO Agreement.

5.   The provisions of Articles 3, 4 and 6 of this Agreement shall not apply to:

    (a)   procurement by a Party or state enterprise;

    (b)   subsidies or grants provided by a Party or a state enterprise, including government-supported loans, guarantees and insurance;

6.   For greater certainty, Article 3 of this Agreement shall not apply to the granting by a Party to a financial institution of an exclusive right to provide activities or services forming part of a public retirement plan or statutory system of social security.

7.   The provisions of Article 4 of this Agreement shall not apply to financial services.

Article 10
General Exceptions

1.	Subject to the requirement that such measures are not applied in a manner that would constitute arbitrary or unjustifiable discrimination between investments or between investors, or a disguised restriction on international trade or investment, nothing in this Agreement shall be construed to prevent a Party from adopting or enforcing measures necessary:

(a)	to protect human, animal or plant life or health;

(b)	to ensure compliance with laws and regulations that are not inconsistent with the provisions of this Agreement; or

(c)	for the conservation of living or non-living exhaustible natural resources.

2.	Nothing in this Agreement shall be construed to prevent a Party from adopting or maintaining reasonable measures for prudential reasons, such as:

(a)	the protection of investors, depositors, financial market participants, policy-holders, policy-claimants, or persons to whom a fiduciary duty is owed by a financial institution;

(b)	the maintenance of the safety, soundness, integrity or financial responsibility of financial institutions; and

(c)	ensuring the integrity and stability of a Party's financial system.

3.	Nothing in this Agreement shall apply to non-discriminatory measures of general application taken by any public entity in pursuit of monetary and related credit policies or exchange rate policies. This paragraph shall not affect a Party's obligations under Article 7 (Performance Requirements) or Article 14 (Transfer of Funds);

4.	Nothing in this Agreement shall be construed:

(a)	to require any Party to furnish or allow access to any information the disclosure of which it determines to be contrary to its essential security interests;

(b)	to prevent any Party from taking any actions that it considers necessary for the protection of its essential security interests

(i)	relating to the traffic in arms, ammunition and implements of war and to such traffic and transactions in other goods, materials, services and technology undertaken directly or indirectly for the purpose of supplying a military or other security establishment,

(ii)	taken in time of war or other emergency in international relations, or

(iii)	relating to the implementation of national policies or international agreements respecting the non-proliferation of nuclear weapons or other nuclear explosive devices; or

(c)   to prevent any Party from taking action in pursuance of its obligations under the United Nations Charter for the maintenance of international peace and security.

5.   Nothing in this Agreement shall be construed to require a Party to furnish or allow access to information the disclosure of which would impede law enforcement or would be contrary to the Party's law protecting Cabinet confidences, personal privacy or the confidentiality of the financial affairs and accounts of individual customers of financial institutions.

6.   The provisions of this Agreement shall not apply to investments in cultural industries.

7.   Any measure adopted by a Party in conformity with a decision adopted, extended or modified by the World Trade Organization pursuant to Articles IX:3 or IX:4 of the WTO Agreement shall be deemed to be also in conformity with this Agreement. An investor purporting to act pursuant to Section C of this Agreement may not claim that such a conforming measure is in breach of this Agreement.

Article 11
Health, Safety and Environmental Measures

The Parties recognize that it is inappropriate to encourage investment by relaxing domestic health, safety or environmental measures. Accordingly, a Party should not waive or otherwise derogate from, or offer to waive or otherwise derogate from, such measures as an encouragement for the establishment, acquisition, expansion or retention in its territory of an investment of an investor. If a Party considers that the other Party has offered such an encouragement, it may request consultations with the other Party and the two Parties shall consult with a view to avoiding any such encouragement.

Article 12
Compensation for Losses

1.   Each Party shall accord to investors of another Party, and to covered investments, non-discriminatory treatment with respect to measures it adopts or maintains relating to losses suffered by investments in its territory owing to armed conflict, civil strife or a natural disaster.

2.   Paragraph (1) shall not apply to existing measures relating to subsidies or grants that would be inconsistent with Article 3 but for Article 9(5)(b).

Article 13[4]
Expropriation

1.   Neither Party shall nationalize or expropriate a covered investment either directly, or indirectly through measures having an effect equivalent to nationalization or expropriation (hereinafter referred to as "expropriation"), except for a public purpose, in accordance with due process of law, in a non-discriminatory manner and on prompt, adequate and effective compensation.

---

[4] For greater certainty, Article 13(1) shall be interpreted in accordance with Annex B.13(1) on the clarification of indirect expropriation.

2.   Such compensation shall be equivalent to the fair market value of the expropriated investment immediately before the expropriation took place ("date of expropriation"), and shall not reflect any change in value occurring because the intended expropriation had become known earlier. Valuation criteria shall include going concern value, asset value including declared tax value of tangible property, and other criteria, as appropriate, to determine fair market value.

3.   Compensation shall be paid without delay and shall be fully realizable and freely transferable. Compensation shall be payable in a freely convertible currency and shall include interest at a commercially reasonable rate for that currency from the date of expropriation until date of payment.

4.   The investor affected shall have a right, under the law of the Party making the expropriation, to prompt review, by a judicial or other independent authority of that Party, of its case and of the valuation of its investment in accordance with the principles set out in this Article.

5.   The provisions of this Article shall not apply to the issuance of compulsory licenses granted in relation to intellectual property rights, or to the revocation, limitation or creation of intellectual property rights, to the extent that such issuance, revocation, limitation or creation is consistent with the WTO Agreement.

Article 14
Transfer of Funds

1.   Each Party shall permit all transfers relating to a covered investment to be made freely, and without delay, into and out of its territory. Such transfers include:

   (a)   contributions to capital;

   (b)   profits, dividends, interest, capital gains, royalty payments, management fees, technical assistance and other fees, returns in kind and other amounts derived from the investment;

   (c)   proceeds from the sale of all or any part of the covered investment or from the partial or complete liquidation of the covered investment;

   (d)   payments made under a contract entered into by the investor, or the covered investment, including payments made pursuant to a loan agreement;

   (e)   payments made pursuant to Articles 12 and 13; and

   (f)   payments arising under Section C.

2.   Each Party shall permit transfers relating to a covered investment to be made in the convertible currency in which the capital was originally invested, or in any other convertible currency agreed by the investor and the Party concerned. Unless otherwise agreed by the investor, transfers shall be made at the rate of exchange applicable on the date of transfer.

3.   Notwithstanding paragraphs 1 and 2, a Party may prevent a transfer through the equitable, non-discriminatory and good faith application of its laws relating to:

     (a)   bankruptcy, insolvency or the protection of the rights of creditors;

     (b)   issuing, trading or dealing in securities;

     (c)   criminal or penal offences;

     (d)   reports of transfers of currency or other monetary instruments; or

     (e)   ensuring the satisfaction of judgments in adjudicatory proceedings.

4.   Neither Party may require its investors to transfer, or penalize its investors that fail to transfer, the income, earnings, profits or other amounts derived from, or attributable to investments in the territory of the other Party.

5.   Paragraph 4 shall not be construed to prevent a Party from imposing any measure through the equitable, non-discriminatory and good faith application of its laws relating to the matters set out in subparagraphs (a) through (e) of paragraph 3.

6.   Notwithstanding the provisions of paragraphs 1, 2 and 4, and without limiting the applicability of paragraph 5, a Party may prevent or limit transfers by a financial institution to, or for the benefit of, an affiliate of or person related to such institution, through the equitable, non-discriminatory and good faith application of measures relating to maintenance of the safety, soundness, integrity or financial responsibility of financial institutions.

7.   Notwithstanding paragraph 1, a Party may restrict transfers in kind in circumstances where it could otherwise restrict transfers under the WTO Agreement and as set out in paragraph 3.

Article 15
Subrogation

1.   If a Party or any agency thereof makes a payment to any of its investors under a guarantee or a contract of insurance it has entered into in respect of an investment, the other Party shall recognize the validity of the subrogation in favour of such Party or agency thereof to any right or title held by the investor.

2.   A Party or any agency thereof which is subrogated to the rights of an investor in accordance with paragraph 1 of this Article, shall be entitled in all circumstances to the same rights as those of the investor in respect of the investment. Such rights may be exercised by the Party or any agency thereof, or by the investor if the Party or any agency thereof so authorizes.

Article 16
Taxation Measures

1.   Except as set out in this Article, nothing in this Agreement shall apply to taxation measures. For further certainty, nothing in this Agreement shall affect the rights and obligations of the Parties under any tax convention. In the event of any inconsistency between the provisions of this Agreement and any such convention, the provisions of that convention shall apply to the extent of the inconsistency.

2.   Nothing in this Agreement shall be construed to require a Party to furnish or allow access to information the disclosure of which would be contrary to the Party's law protecting information concerning the taxation affairs of a taxpayer.

3.   A claim by an investor that a tax measure of a Party is in breach of an agreement between the central government authorities of a Party and the investor concerning an investment shall be considered a claim for breach of this Agreement unless the taxation authorities of the Parties, no later than six months after being notified by the investor of its intention to submit the claim to arbitration, jointly determine that the measure does not contravene such agreement. The investor shall refer the issue of whether a taxation measure does not contravene an agreement for a determination to the taxation authorities of the Parties at the same time that it gives notice under Article 24 (Notice of Intent to Submit a Claim to Arbitration).

4.   The provisions of Article 13 shall apply to taxation measures unless the taxation authorities of the Parties, no later than six months after being notified by an investor that the investor disputes a taxation measure, jointly determine that the measure in question is not an expropriation. The investor shall refer the issue of whether a taxation measure is an expropriation for a determination to the taxation authorities of the Parties at the same time that it gives notice under Article 24 (Notice of Intent to Submit a Claim to Arbitration).

5.   An investor may submit a claim relating to taxation measures covered by this Agreement to arbitration under Section C only if the taxation authorities of the Parties fail to reach the joint determinations specified in paragraph 3 and paragraph 4 of this Article within six months of being notified in accordance with the provisions of this Article.

6.   If, in connection with a claim by an investor of a Party or a dispute between the Parties, an issue arises as to whether a measure of a Party is a taxation measure, a Party may refer the issue to the taxation authorities of the Parties. The taxation authorities shall decide the issue, and their decision shall bind any Tribunal formed pursuant to Section C or arbitral panel formed pursuant to Section D, as the case may be, with jurisdiction over the claim or the dispute. A Tribunal or arbitral panel seized of a claim or a dispute in which the issue arises may not proceed pending receipt of the decision of the taxation authorities. If the taxation authorities have not decided the issue within six months of the referral, the Tribunal or arbitral panel shall decide the issue in place of the taxation authorities.

7.   The taxation authorities referred to in this Article shall be the following until notice in writing to the contrary is provided to the other Party:

(a)   for Canada: the Assistant Deputy Minister, Tax Policy, of the Department of Finance Canada;

(b)   for _____:

Article 17
Prudential Measures

1.   Where an investor submits a claim to arbitration under Section C, and the disputing Party invokes Articles Article 10(2) or 14(6), the Tribunal established pursuant to Article 22 (Claim by an Investor of a Party on its Own Behalf) or 23 (Claim by an Investor of a Party on Behalf of and Enterprise) shall, at the request of that Party, seek a report in writing from the Parties on the

issue of whether and to what extent the said paragraphs are a valid defence to the claim of the investor. The Tribunal may not proceed pending receipt of a report under this Article.

2.   Pursuant to a request received in accordance with paragraph (1), the Parties shall proceed in accordance with Section D to prepare a written report, either on the basis of agreement following consultations, or by means of an arbitral panel. The consultations shall be between the financial services authorities of the Parties. The report shall be transmitted to the Tribunal, and shall be binding on the Tribunal.

3.   Where, within 70 days of the referral by the Tribunal, no request for the establishment of a panel pursuant to paragraph (2) has been made, and no report has been received by the Tribunal, the Tribunal may proceed to decide the matter.

Article 18
Denial of Benefits

1.   A Party may deny the benefits of this Agreement to an investor of the other Party that is an enterprise of such Party and to investments of such investor if investors of a non-Party own or control the enterprise and the denying Party adopts or maintains measures with respect to the non-Party that prohibit transactions with the enterprise or that would be violated or circumvented if the benefits of this Agreement were accorded to the enterprises or to its investments.

2.   Subject to prior notification and consultation in accordance with Article 19, a Party may deny the benefits of this Agreement to an investor of the other Party that is an enterprise of such Party and to investments of such investors if investors of a non-Party own or control the enterprise and the enterprise has no substantial business activities in the territory of the Party under whose law it is constituted or organized.

Article 19
Transparency

1.   Each Party shall, to the extent possible, ensure that its laws, regulations, procedures, and administrative rulings of general application respecting any matter covered by this Agreement are promptly published or otherwise made available in such a manner as to enable interested persons and the other Party to become acquainted with them.

2.   To the extent possible, each Party shall:

   (a)   publish in advance any such measure that it proposes to adopt; and

   (b)   provide interested persons and the other Party a reasonable opportunity to comment on such proposed measures.

3.   Upon request by a Party, information shall be exchanged on the measures of the other Party that may have an impact on covered investments.

Annex B.13(1)
Expropriation

The Parties confirm their shared understanding that:

a)   Indirect expropriation results from a measure or series of measures of a Party that have an effect equivalent to direct expropriation without formal transfer of title or outright seizure;

b)   The determination of whether a measure or series of measures of a Party constitute an indirect expropriation requires a case-by-case, fact-based inquiry that considers, among other factors:

   i)   the economic impact of the measure or series of measures, although the sole fact that a measure or series of measures of a Party has an adverse effect on the economic value of an investment does not establish that an indirect expropriation has occurred;

   ii)   the extent to which the measure or series of measures interfere with distinct, reasonable investment-backed expectations; and

   iii)   the character of the measure or series of measures;

c)   Except in rare circumstances, such as when a measure or series of measures are so severe in the light of their purpose that they cannot be reasonably viewed as having been adopted and applied in good faith, non-discriminatory measures of a Party that are designed and applied to protect legitimate public welfare objectives, such as health, safety and the environment, do not constitute indirect expropriation.

Section C
Settlement of Disputes
between an Investor and the Host Party

Article 20
Purpose

Without prejudice to the rights and obligations of the Parties under Section D (State to State Dispute Settlement Procedures), this Section establishes a mechanism forthe settlement of investment disputes.

Article 21
Limitation of Claims with respect to financial institutions

With respect to:

   (a)   financial institutions of a Party; and

   (b)   investors of a Party, and investments of such investors, in financial institutions in the other Party's territory,

this Section applies only in respect of claims that the other Party has breached an obligation under Articles 11, 13, 14, or 18.

Article 22
Claim by an Investor of a Party on Its Own Behalf

1.   An investor of a Party may submit to arbitration under this Section a claim that the other Party has breached an obligation under Articles 2 to 5, 6(1), 6(2), 7, 8(3), 8(4) or 9 to 18, and that the investor has incurred loss or damage by reason of, or arising out of, that breach.

2.   An investor may not make a claim if more than three years have elapsed from the date on which the investor first acquired, or should have first acquired, knowledge of the alleged breach and knowledge that the investor has incurred loss or damage.

Article 23
Claim by an Investor of a Party on Behalf of an Enterprise

1.   An investor of a Party, on behalf of an enterprise of the other Party that is a juridical person that the investor owns or controls directly or indirectly, may submit to arbitration under this Section a claim that the other Party has breached an obligation under Articles 2 to 5, 6(1), 6(2), 7, 8(3), 8(4) or 9 to 18, and that the enterprise has incurred loss or damage by reason of, or arising out of, that breach.

2.   An investor may not make a claim on behalf of an enterprise described in paragraph 1 if more than three years have elapsed from the date on which the enterprise first acquired, or should have first acquired, knowledge of the alleged breach and knowledge that the enterprise has incurred loss or damage.

3.   Where an investor makes a claim under this Article and the investor or a noncontrolling investor in the enterprise makes a claim under Article 22 (Claim by an Investor of a Party on Its Own Behalf) arising out of the same events that gave rise to the claim under this Article, and two or more of the claims are submitted to arbitration under Article 27 (Submission of a Claim to Arbitration), the claims should be heard together by a Tribunal established under Article 32 (Consolidation), unless the Tribunal finds that the interests of a disputing party would be prejudiced thereby.

4.   An investment may not make a claim under this Section.

Article 24
Notice of Intent to Submit a Claim to Arbitration

1.   The disputing investor shall deliver to the disputing Party written notice of its intent to submit a claim to arbitration at least 90 days before the claim is submitted, which notice shall specify:

    (a)   the name and address of the disputing investor and, where a claim is made under Article 23 (Claim by an Investor of a Party on Behalf of an Enterprise), the name and address of the enterprise;

    (b)   the provisions of this Agreement alleged to have been breached and any other relevant provisions;

    (c)   the issues and the factual basis for the claim, including the measures at issue; and

(d)   the relief sought and the approximate amount of damages claimed.

2.   The disputing investor shall also deliver, with its Notice of Intent to Submit a Claim to Arbitration, evidence establishing that it is an investor of the other Party.

Article 25
Settlement of a Claim through Consultation

1.   Before a disputing investor may submit a claim to arbitration, the disputing parties shall first hold consultations in an attempt to settle a claim amicably.

2.   Consultations shall be held within 30 days of the submission of the notice of intent to submit a claim to arbitration, unless the disputing parties otherwise agree.

3. The place of consultation shall be the capital of the disputing Party, unless the disputing parties otherwise agree.

Article 26
Conditions Precedent to Submission of a Claim to Arbitration

1.   A disputing investor may submit a claim to arbitration under Article 22 (Claim by an Investor of a Party on Its Own Behalf) only if:

(a)   the investor consents to arbitration in accordance with the procedures set out in this Agreement;

(b)   at least six months have elapsed since the events giving rise to the claim;

(c)   not more than three years have elapsed from the date on which the investor first acquired, or should have first acquired, knowledge of the alleged breach and knowledge that the investor has incurred loss or damage thereby;

(d)   the investor has delivered the Notice of Intent required under Article 24 (Notice of Intent to Submit a Claim to Arbitration), in accordance with the requirements of that Article, at least 90 days prior to submitting the claim; and

(e)   the investor and, where the claim is for loss or damage to an interest in an enterprise of the other Party that is a juridical person that the investor owns or controls directly or indirectly, the enterprise waive their right to initiate or continue before any administrative tribunal or court under the law of any Party, or other dispute settlement procedures, any proceedings with respect to the measure of the disputing Party that is alleged to be a breach referred to in Article 22 (Claim by an Investor of a Party on Its Own Behalf), except for proceedings for injunctive, declaratory or other extraordinary relief, not involving the payment of damages, before an administrative tribunal or court under the law of the disputing Party.

2.   A disputing investor may submit a claim to arbitration under Article 23 (Claim by an Investor of a Party on Behalf of an Enterprise) only if:

(a)   both the investor and the enterprise consent to arbitration in accordance with the procedures set out in this Agreement;

(b)   at least six months have elapsed since the events giving rise to the claim;

(c)   not more than three years have elapsed from the date on which the enterprise first acquired, or should have first acquired, knowledge of the alleged breach and knowledge that the enterprise has incurred loss or damage thereby;

(d)   the investor has delivered the Notice of Intent required under Article 24 (Notice of Intent to Submit a Claim to Arbitration), in accordance with the requirements of that Article, at least 90 days prior to submitting the claim; and

(e)   both the investor and the enterprise waive their right to initiate or continue before any administrative tribunal or court under the law of any Party, or other dispute settlement procedures, any proceedings with respect to the measure of the disputing Party that is alleged to be a breach referred to in Article 23 (Claim by an Investor of a Party on Behalf of an Enterprise, except for proceedings for injunctive, declaratory or other extraordinary relief, not involving the payment of damages, before an administrative tribunal or court under the law of the disputing Party.

3.   A consent and waiver required by this Article shall be in the form provided for in Annex C.26, shall be delivered to the disputing Party and shall be included in the submission of a claim to arbitration.

4.   A waiver from the enterprise under paragraph 1(e) or 2(e) shall not be required only where a disputing Party has deprived a disputing investor of control of an enterprise.

5.   Failure to meet any of the conditions precedent provided for in paragraphs 1 through 3 shall nullify the consent of the Parties given in Article 28 (Consent to Arbitration).

Article 27
Submission of a Claim to Arbitration

1.   A disputing investor who meets the conditions precedent provided for in Article 26 (Conditions Precedent to Submission of a Claim to Arbitration) may submit the claim to arbitration under:

(a)   the ICSID Convention, provided that both the disputing Party and the Party of the disputing investor are parties to the Convention;

(b)   the Additional Facility Rules of ICSID, provided that either the disputing Party or the Party of the disputing investor, but not both, is a party to the ICSID Convention;

(c)   the UNCITRAL Arbitration Rules; or

(d)   any other body of rules approved by the Commission as available for arbitrations under this Section.

2.   The Commission shall have the power to make rules supplementing the applicable arbitral rules and may amend any rules of its own making. Such rules shall be binding on a Tribunal established under this Section, and on individual arbitrators serving on such Tribunals.

3.   The applicable arbitration rules shall govern the arbitration except to the extent modified by this Section, and supplemented by any rules adopted by the Commission under this Section.

Article 28
Consent to Arbitration

1.   Each Party consents to the submission of a claim to arbitration in accordance with the procedures set out in this Agreement.

2.   The consent given in paragraph 1 and the submission by a disputing investor of a claim to arbitration shall satisfy the requirement of:

(a)   Chapter II of the ICSID Convention (Jurisdiction of the Centre) and the Additional Facility Rules for written consent of the parties;

(b)   Article II of the New York Convention for an agreement in writing; and

[(c)   Article I of the Inter-American Convention for an agreement.]

Article 29
Arbitrators

1.   Except in respect of a Tribunal established under Article 32 (Consolidation), and unless the disputing parties agree otherwise, the Tribunal shall comprise three arbitrators, one arbitrator appointed by each of the disputing parties and the third, who shall be the presiding arbitrator, appointed by agreement of the disputing parties.

2.   Arbitrators shall:

(a)   have expertise or experience in public international law, international trade or international investment rules, or the resolution of disputes arising under international trade or international investment agreements;

(b)   be independent of, and not be affiliated with or take instructions from, either Party or disputing party; and

(c)   comply with any Code of Conduct for Dispute Settlement as agreed by the Commission.

3.   Where a disputing investor claims that a dispute involves measures adopted or maintained by a Party relating to financial institutions of the other Party, or investors of the other Party and investments of such investors, in financial institutions in a Party's territory, then (a) where the disputing parties are in agreement, the arbitrators shall, in addition to the criteria set out in paragraph 2, have expertise or experience in financial services law or practice, which may include the regulation of financial institutions; or

    (b)   where the disputing parties are not in agreement,

           (i)   each disputing party may select arbitrators who meet the qualifications set out in subparagraph (a), and

           (ii)   if the Party complained against invokes Articles 14(6) or 17, the chair of the panel shall meet the qualifications set out in subparagraph (a).

4.   The disputing parties should agree upon the arbitrators' remuneration. If the disputing parties do not agree on such remuneration before the constitution of the Tribunal, the prevailing ICSID rate for arbitrators shall apply.

5.   The Commission may establish rules relating to expenses incurred by the Tribunal.

Article 30
Constitution of a Tribunal When a Party Fails to Appoint an Arbitrator or the Disputing Parties Are Unable to Agree on a Presiding Arbitrator

1.   The Secretary-General shall serve as appointing authority for an arbitration under this Section.

2.   If a Tribunal, other than a Tribunal established under Article 32 (Consolidation), has not been constituted within 90 days from the date that a claim is submitted to arbitration, the Secretary-General, on the request of either disputing party, shall appoint, in his or her discretion, the arbitrator or arbitrators not yet appointed, except that the presiding arbitrator shall not be a national of either Party.

Article 31
Agreement to Appointment of Arbitrators

For purposes of Article 39 of the ICSID Convention and Article 7 of Schedule C to the ICSID Additional Facility Rules, and without prejudice to an objection to an arbitrator based on a ground other than citizenship or permanent residence:

    (a)   the disputing Party agrees to the appointment of each individual member of a Tribunal established under the ICSID Convention or the ICSID Additional Facility Rules;

    (b)   a disputing investor referred to in Article 22 (Claim by an Investor of a Party on Its Own Behalf) may submit a claim to arbitration, or continue a claim, under the ICSID Convention or the ICSID Additional Facility Rules, only on condition that the disputing investor agrees in writing to the appointment of each individual member of the Tribunal; and

    (c)   a disputing investor referred to in Article 23(1) (Claim by an Investor of a Party on Behalf of an Enterprise) may submit a claim to arbitration, or continue a claim, under the ICSID Convention or the ICSID Additional Facility Rules, only on condition that the disputing investor and the enterprise agree in writing to the appointment of each individual member of the Tribunal.

Article 32
Consolidation

1.   A Tribunal established under this Article shall be established under the UNCITRAL Arbitration Rules and shall conduct its proceedings in accordance with those Rules, except as modified by this Section.

2.   Where a Tribunal established under this Article is satisfied that claims submitted to arbitration under Article 27 (Submission of a Claim to Arbitration) have a question of law or fact in common, the Tribunal may, in the interests of fair and efficient resolution of the claims, and after hearing the disputing parties, by order:

   (a)   assume jurisdiction over, and hear and determine together, all or part of the claims; or

   (b)   assume jurisdiction over, and hear and determine one or more of the claims, the determination of which it believes would assist in the resolution of the others.

3.   A disputing party that seeks an order under paragraph 2 shall request the Secretary-General to establish a Tribunal and shall specify in the request:

   (a)   the name of the disputing Party or disputing investors against which the order is sought;

   (b)   the nature of the order sought; and

   (c)   the grounds on which the order is sought.

4.   The disputing party shall deliver to the disputing Party or disputing investors against which the order is sought a copy of the request.

5.   Within 60 days of receipt of the request, the Secretary-General shall establish a Tribunal comprising three arbitrators. The Secretary-General shall appoint the presiding arbitrator, from the ICSID Panel of Arbitrators, a presiding arbitrator who is not a national of any of the Parties. The Secretary-General shall appoint the two other members from the ICSID Panel of Arbitrators. To the extent arbitrators are not available from that Panel, appointments shall be at the discretion of the Secretary-General. One member shall be a national of the disputing Party and one member shall be a national of the Party of the disputing investors.

6.   Where a Tribunal has been established under this Article, a disputing investor that has submitted a claim to arbitration under Article 27 (Submission of a Claim to Arbitration) and that has not been named in a request made under paragraph 3 may make a written request to the Tribunal that it be included in an order made under paragraph 2, and shall specify in the request:

   (a)   the name and address of the disputing investor;

   (b)   the nature of the order sought; and

   (c)   the grounds on which the order is sought.

7.   A disputing investor referred to in paragraph 6 shall deliver a copy of its request to the disputing parties named in a request made under paragraph 3.

8.   A Tribunal established under Article 27 (Submission of a Claim to Arbitration) shall not have jurisdiction to decide a claim, or a part of a claim, over which a Tribunal established under this Article has assumed jurisdiction.

9.   On application of a disputing party, a Tribunal established under this Article, pending its decision under paragraph 2, may order that the proceedings of a Tribunal established under Article 27 (Submission of a Claim to Arbitration) be stayed, unless the latter Tribunal has already adjourned its proceedings.

Article 33
Notice to the Non-Disputing Party

A disputing Party shall deliver to the other Party a copy of the Notice of Intent to Submit a Claim to Arbitration and other documents, such as a Notice of Arbitration and Statement of Claim, no later than 30 days after the date that such documents have been delivered to the disputing Party.

Article 34
Documents

1.   The non-disputing Party shall be entitled, at its cost, to receive from the disputing Party a copy of:

    (a)   the evidence that has been tendered to the Tribunal;

    (b)   copies of all pleadings filed in the arbitration; and

    (c)   the written argument of the disputing parties.

2.   The Party receiving information pursuant to paragraph 1 shall treat the information as if it were a disputing Party.

Article 35
Participation by the Non-Disputing Party

1.   On written notice to the disputing parties, the non-disputing Party may make submissions to a Tribunal on a question of interpretation of this Agreement.

2.   The non-disputing Party shall have the right to attend any hearings held under this Section, whether or not it makes submissions to the Tribunal.

Article 36
Place of Arbitration

Unless the disputing parties agree otherwise, a Tribunal shall hold an arbitration in the territory of a Party that is a party to the New York Convention, selected in accordance with:

(a)   the ICSID Additional Facility Rules, if the arbitration is under those Rules or the ICSID Convention; or

(b)   the UNCITRAL Arbitration Rules, if the arbitration is under those Rules.

Article 37
Preliminary Objections to Jurisdiction or Admissibility

Where issues relating to jurisdiction or admissibility are raised as preliminary objections, a Tribunal shall, wherever possible, decide the matter before proceeding to the merits.

Article 38
Public Access to Hearings and Documents

1.   Hearings held under this Section shall be open to the public. To the extent necessary to ensure the protection of confidential information, including business confidential information, the Tribunal may hold portions of hearings *in camera*.

2.   The Tribunal shall establish procedures for the protection of confidential information and appropriate logistical arrangements for open hearings, in consultation with the disputing parties.

3.   All documents submitted to, or issued by, the Tribunal shall be publicly available, unless the disputing parties otherwise agree, subject to the deletion of confidential information.

4.   Notwithstanding paragraph 3, any Tribunal award under this Section shall be publicly available, subject to the deletion of confidential information.

5.   A disputing party may disclose to other persons in connection with the arbitral proceedings such unredacted documents as it considers necessary for the preparation of its case, but it shall ensure that those persons protect the confidential information in such documents.

6.   The Parties may share with officials of their respective federal and sub-national governments all relevant unredacted documents in the course of dispute settlement under this Agreement, but they shall ensure that those persons protect any confidential information in such documents.

7.   As provided under Article 10(4) and (5), the Tribunal shall not require a Party to furnish or allow access to information the disclosure of which would impede law enforcement or would be contrary to the Party's law protecting Cabinet confidences, personal privacy or the financial affairs and accounts of individual customers of financial institutions, or which it determines to be contrary to its essential security.

8.   To the extent that a Tribunal's confidentiality order designates information as confidential and a Party's law on access to information requires public access to that information, the Party's law on access to information shall prevail. However, a Party should endeavour to apply its law on access to information so as to protect information designated confidential by the Tribunal.

Article 39
Submissions by a Non-Disputing Party

1.   Any non-disputing party that is a person of a Party, or has a significant presence in the territory of a Party, that wishes to file a written submission with a Tribunal (the "applicant") shall apply for leave from the Tribunal to file such a submission, in accordance with Annex C.39. The applicant shall attach the submission to the application.

2.   The applicant shall serve the application for leave to file a non-disputing party submission and the submission on all disputing parties and the Tribunal.

3.   The Tribunal shall set an appropriate date for the disputing parties to comment on the application for leave to file a non-disputing party submission.

4.   In determining whether to grant leave to file a non-disputing party submission, the Tribunal shall consider, among other things, the extent to which:

   (a)   the non-disputing party submission would assist the Tribunal in the determination of a factual or legal issue related to the arbitration by bringing a perspective, particular knowledge or insight that is different from that of the disputing parties;

   (b)   the non-disputing party submission would address a matter within the scope of the dispute;

   (c)   the non-disputing party has a significant interest in the arbitration; and

   (d)   there is a public interest in the subject-matter of the arbitration.

5.   The Tribunal shall ensure that:

   (a)   any non-disputing party submission does not disrupt the proceedings; and

   (b)   neither disputing party is unduly burdened or unfairly prejudiced by such submissions.

6.   The Tribunal shall decide whether to grant leave to file a non-disputing party submission. If leave to file a non-disputing party submission is granted, the Tribunal shall set an appropriate date for the disputing parties to respond in writing to the nondisputing party submission. By that date, the non-disputing Party may, pursuant to Article 34 (Participation by the Non-Disputing Party), address any issues of interpretation of this Agreement presented in the non-disputing party submission.

7.   The Tribunal that grants leave to file a non-disputing party submission is not required to address the submission at any point in the arbitration, nor is the non-disputing party that files the submission entitled to make further submissions in the arbitration.

8.   Access to hearings and documents by non-disputing parties that file applications under these procedures shall be governed by the provisions pertaining to public access to hearings and documents under Article 38 (Public Access to Hearings and Documents).

Article 40
Governing Law

1.   A Tribunal established under this Section shall decide the issues in dispute in accordance with this Agreement and applicable rules of international law.

2.   An interpretation by the Commission of a provision of this Agreement shall be binding on a Tribunal established under this Section, and any award under this Section shall be consistent with such interpretation.

Article 41
Interpretation of Annexes

1.   Where a disputing Party asserts as a defence that the measure alleged to be a breach is within the scope of a reservation or exception set out in Annex I, Annex II or Annex III, on request of the disputing Party, the Tribunal shall request the interpretation of the Commission on the issue. The Commission, within 60 days of delivery of the request, shall submit in writing its interpretation to the Tribunal.

2.   Further to Article 40(2) (Governing Law), a Commission interpretation submitted under paragraph 1 shall be binding on the Tribunal. If the Commission fails to submit an interpretation within 60 days, the Tribunal shall decide the issue.

Article 42
Expert Reports

Without prejudice to the appointment of other kinds of experts where authorized by the applicable arbitration rules, a Tribunal, at the request of a disputing party or, unless the disputing parties disapprove, on its own initiative, may appoint one or more experts to report to it in writing on any factual issue concerning environmental, health, safety or other scientific matters raised by a disputing party in a proceeding, subject to such terms and conditions as the disputing parties may agree.

Article 43
Interim Measures of Protection

A Tribunal may order an interim measure of protection to preserve the rights of a disputing party, or to ensure that the Tribunal's jurisdiction is made fully effective, including an order to preserve evidence in the possession or control of a disputing party or to protect the Tribunal's jurisdiction. A Tribunal may not order attachment or enjoin the application of the measure alleged to constitute a breach referred to in Article 22 (Claim by an Investor of a Party on Its Own Behalf) or 23 (Claim by an Investor of a Party on Behalf of an Enterprise). For purposes of this paragraph, an order includes a recommendation.

Article 44
Final Award

1.   Where a Tribunal makes a final award against the disputing Party, the Tribunal may award, separately or in combination, only:

(a)   monetary damages and any applicable interest;

(b)   restitution of property, in which case the award shall provide that the disputing Party may pay monetary damages and any applicable interest in lieu of restitution.

The tribunal may also award costs in accordance with the applicable arbitration rules.

2.   Subject to paragraph 1, where a claim is made under Article 23(1) (Claim by an Investor of a Party on Behalf of an Enterprise):

(a)   an award of monetary damages and any applicable interest shall provide that the sum be paid to the enterprise;

(b)   an award of restitution of property shall provide that restitution be made to the enterprise; and

(c)   the award shall provide that it is made without prejudice to any right that any person may have in the relief under applicable domestic law.

3.   A Tribunal may not order a disputing Party to pay punitive damages.

Article 45
Finality and Enforcement of an Award

1.   An award made by a Tribunal shall have no binding force except between the disputing parties and in respect of that particular case.

2.   Subject to paragraph 3 and the applicable review procedure for an interim award, a disputing party shall abide by and comply with an award without delay.

3.   A disputing party may not seek enforcement of a final award until:

(a)   in the case of a final award made under the ICSID Convention

(i)   120 days have elapsed from the date the award was rendered and no disputing party has requested revision or annulment of the award, or

(ii)   revision or annulment proceedings have been completed; and

(b)   in the case of a final award under the ICSID Additional Facility Rules or the UNCITRAL Arbitration Rules

(i)   90 days have elapsed from the date the award was rendered and no disputing party has commenced a proceeding to revise, set aside or annul the award, or

(ii)   a court has dismissed or allowed an application to revise, set aside or annul the award and there is no further appeal.

4.   Each Party shall provide for the enforcement of an award in its territory.

5.   If the disputing Party fails to abide by or comply with a final award, the Commission, on delivery of a request by the Party of the disputing investor, shall establish an arbitral panel under Section D (State-to-State Dispute Settlement Procedures). The requesting Party may seek in such proceedings:

(a)   a determination that the failure to abide by or comply with the final award is inconsistent with the obligations of this Agreement; and

(b)   a recommendation that the disputing Party abide by or comply with the final award.

6.   A disputing investor may seek enforcement of an arbitration award under the ICSID Convention, [or] the New York Convention [or the Inter-American Convention] regardless of whether proceedings have been taken under paragraph 5.

7.   A claim that is submitted to arbitration under this Section shall be considered to arise out of a commercial relationship or transaction for purposes of Article I of the New York Convention [and Article I of the Inter-American Convention].

Article 46
General

Time when a Claim is Submitted to Arbitration

1.   A claim is submitted to arbitration under this Section when:

(a)   the request for arbitration under paragraph (1) of Article 36 of the ICSID Convention is received by the Secretary-General;

(b)   the notice of arbitration under Article 2 of Schedule C of the ICSID Additional Facility Rules is received by the Secretary-General; or

(c)   the notice of arbitration given under the UNCITRAL Arbitration Rules is received by the disputing Party.

Service of Documents

2.   Delivery of notice and other documents on a Party shall be made to the place named for that Party below.

For Canada _____

For _____

Receipts under Insurance or Guarantee Contracts

3.   In an arbitration under this Section, a disputing Party shall not assert, as a defence, counterclaim, right of setoff or otherwise, that the disputing investor has received or will receive, pursuant to an insurance or guarantee contract, indemnification or other compensation for all or part of its alleged damages.

Article 47
Exclusions

The dispute settlement provisions of this Section and of Section D (State-to-State Dispute Settlement Procedures) shall not apply to the matters referred to in Annex IV (Exclusions from Dispute Settlement).

Annex C.26
Standard Waiver and Consent
in Accordance with Article 26 of this Agreement

In the interest of facilitating the filing of waivers as required by Article 26 of this Agreement, and to facilitate the orderly conduct of the dispute resolution procedures set out in Section C, the following standard waiver forms shall be used, depending on the type of claim.

Claims filed under Article 22 (Claim by an investor of a Party on Its Own Behalf) must be accompanied by either Form 1, where the investor is a national of a Party, or Form 2, where the investor is a Party, a state enterprise thereof, or an enterprise of such Party.

Where the claim is based on loss or damage to an interest in an enterprise of the other Party that is a juridical person that the investor owns or controls directly or indirectly, either Form 1 or 2 must be accompanied by Form 3.

Claims made under Article 23 (Claim by an Investor of a Party on Behalf of an Enterprise) must be accompanied by either Form 1, where the investor is a national of a Party, or Form 2, where the investor is a Party, a state enterprise thereof, or an enterprise of such Party, and Form 4.

Form 1

Consent and waiver for an investor of a Party bringing a claim under Article 22 or Article 23 (where the investor is a national of a Party) of the Agreement between Canada and _____ for the Promotion and Protection of Investments of (date of entry-into-force):

I, (Name of investor), consent to arbitration in accordance with the procedures set out in this Agreement, and waive my right to initiate or continue before any administrative tribunal or court under the law of any Party to the Agreement, or other dispute settlement procedures, any proceedings with respect to the measure of (Name of disputing Party) that is alleged to be a breach referred to in Article 22 or Article 23, except for proceedings for injunctive, declaratory or other extraordinary relief, not involving the payment of damages, before an administrative tribunal or court under the law of (Name of disputing Party) .
(To be signed and dated)

Form 2

Consent and waiver for an investor of a Party bringing a claim under Article 22 or Article 23 (where the investor is a Party, a state enterprise thereof, or an enterprise of such Party) of the Agreement between Canada and _____ for the Promotion and Protection of Investments of (date of entry-into-force):

I, (Name of declarant), on behalf of (Name of investor), consent to arbitration in accordance with the procedures set out in this Agreement, and waive the right of (Name of investor) to initiate or continue before any administrative tribunal or court under the law of any Party to the Agreement, or other dispute settlement procedures, any proceedings with respect to the measure of (Name of disputing Party) that is alleged to be a breach referred to in Article 22 or Article 23, except for proceedings for injunctive, declaratory or other extraordinary relief, not involving the payment of damages before an administrative tribunal or court under the law of (Name of disputing Party) . I hereby solemnly declare that I am duly authorised to execute this consent and waiver on behalf of (Name of investor).

(To be signed and dated)

Form 3

Waiver of an enterprise that is the subject of a claim by an investor of a Party under Article 22 of the Agreement between Canada and _____ for the Promotion and Protection of Investments of (date of entry-into-force)**:**

I, (Name of declarant), waive the right of (Name of the enterprise) to initiate or continue before any administrative tribunal or court under the law of any Party to this Agreement, or other dispute settlement procedures, any proceedings with respect to the measure of (Name of disputing Party) that is alleged by (Name of investor) to be a breach referred to in Article 22, except for proceedings for injunctive, declaratory or other extraordinary relief, not involving the payment of damages, before an administrative tribunal or court under the law of (Name of disputing Party) . I hereby solemnly declare that I am duly authorised to execute this waiver on behalf of (Name of the enterprise).

(To be signed and dated)

Form 4

Consent and waiver of an enterprise that is the subject of a claim by an investor of a Party under Article 23 of the Agreement between Canada and _____ for the Promotion and Protection of Investments of (date of entry-into-force)**:**

I, (Name of declarant), on behalf of (Name of enterprise) , consent to arbitration in accordance with the procedures set out in this Agreement, and waive the right of (Name of enterprise) to initiate or continue before any administrative tribunal or court under the law of any Party to the Agreement, or other dispute settlement procedures, any proceedings with respect to the measure of (Name of disputing Party) that is alleged by (Name of investor) to be a breach referred to in Article 23, except for proceedings for injunctive, declaratory or other extraordinary relief, not involving the payment of damages before an administrative tribunal or court under the law of (Name of disputing Party) . I hereby solemnly declare that I am duly authorised to execute this consent and waiver on behalf of (Name of the enterprise).

(To be signed and dated)

Annex C.39
Submissions by Non-Disputing Parties

1.   The application for leave to file a non-disputing party submission shall:

(a)   be made in writing, dated and signed by the person filing the application, and include the address and other contact details of the applicant;

(b)   be no longer than 5 typed pages;

(c)   describe the applicant, including, where relevant, its membership and legal status (*e.g.*, company, trade association or other non-governmental organization), its general objectives, the nature of its activities, and any parent organization (including any organization that directly or indirectly controls the applicant);

(d)   disclose whether the applicant has any affiliation, direct or indirect, with any disputing party;

(e)   identify any government, person or organization that has provided any financial or other assistance in preparing the submission;

(f)   specify the nature of the interest that the applicant has in the arbitration;

(g)   identify the specific issues of fact or law in the arbitration that the applicant has addressed in its written submission;

(h)   explain, by reference to the factors specified in Article 39(4), why the Tribunal should accept the submission; and

(i)   be made in a language of the arbitration.

2.   The submission filed by a non-disputing party shall:

(a)   be dated and signed by the person filing the submission;

(b)   be concise, and in no case longer than 20 typed pages, including any appendices;

(c)   set out a precise statement supporting the applicant's position on the issues; and

(d)   only address matters within the scope of the dispute.

Section D
State-to-State Dispute Settlement Procedures

Article 48
Disputes between the Parties

1.   Either Party may request consultations on the interpretation or application of this Agreement. The other Party shall give sympathetic consideration to the request. Any dispute

between the Parties concerning the interpretation or application of this Agreement shall, whenever possible, be settled amicably through consultations.

2.   If a dispute cannot be settled through consultations, it shall, at the request of either Party, be submitted to an arbitral panel for decision.

3.   An arbitral panel shall be constituted for each dispute. Within two months after receipt through diplomatic channels of the request for arbitration, each Party shall appoint one member to the arbitral panel. The two members shall then select a national of a third State who, upon approval by the two Parties, shall be appointed Chairman of the arbitral panel. The Chairman shall be appointed within two months from the date of appointment of the other two members of the arbitral panel.

4.   If within the periods specified in paragraph (3) of this Article the necessary appointments have not been made, either Party may invite the President of the International Court of Justice to make the necessary appointments. If the President is a national of either Party or is otherwise prevented from discharging the said function, the Vice-President shall be invited to make the necessary appointments. If the Vice- President is a national of either Party or is prevented from discharging the said function, the Member of the International Court of Justice next in seniority, who is not a national of either Party, shall be invited to make the necessary appointments.

5.   Arbitrators shall:

(a)   have expertise or experience in public international law, international trade or international investment rules, or the resolution of disputes arising under international trade or international investment agreements;

(b)   be independent of, and not be affiliated with or take instructions from, either Party; and

(c)   comply with any Code of Conduct for Dispute Settlement as agreed by the Commission.

6.   Where a Party claims that a dispute involves measures relating to financial institutions, or to investors or investments of such investors in financial institutions, then

(a)   where the disputing Parties are in agreement, the arbitrators shall, in addition to the criteria set out in paragraph 5, have expertise or experience in financial services law or practice, which may include the regulation of financial institutions; or

(b)   where the disputing Parties are not in agreement,

(i)   each disputing Party may select arbitrators who meet the qualifications set out in subparagraph (a), and

(ii)   if the Party complained against invokes Articles 14(6) or 17, the chair of the panel shall meet the qualifications set out in subparagraph (a).

7. The arbitral panel shall determine its own procedure. The arbitral panel shall reach its decision by a majority of votes. Such decision shall be binding on both Parties.

Unless otherwise agreed, the decision of the arbitral panel shall be rendered within six months of the appointment of the Chairman in accordance with paragraphs (3) or (4) of this Article.

8. Each Party shall bear the costs of its own member of the panel and of its representation in the arbitral proceedings; the costs related to the Chairman and any remaining costs shall be borne equally by the Parties. The arbitral panel may, however, in its decision direct that a higher proportion of costs be borne by one of the two Parties, and this award shall be binding on both Parties.

9. The Parties shall, within 60 days of the decision of a panel, reach agreement on the manner in which to resolve their dispute. Such agreement shall normally implement the decision of the panel. If the Parties fail to reach agreement, the Party bringing thedispute shall be entitled to compensation or to suspend benefits of equivalent value to those awarded by the panel.

Section E

Final Provisions

Article 49
Consultations

A Party may request in writing consultation with the other Party regarding any actual or proposed measure or any other matter that it considers might affect the operation of this Agreement.

Article 50
Extent of Obligations

The Parties shall ensure that all necessary measures are taken in order to give effect to the provisions of this Agreement, including their observance, except as otherwise provided in this Agreement, by sub-national governments.

Article 51
Commission

1. The Parties hereby agree to establish a Commission, comprising cabinet-level representatives of the Parties or their designees.

2. The Commission shall:

    (a)   supervise the implementation of this Agreement;

    (b)   resolve disputes that may arise regarding its interpretation or application;

    (c)   consider any other matter that may affect the operation of this Agreement;

(d)   adopt a Code of Conduct for Arbitrators.

3.   The Commission may take such other action in the exercise of its functions as the Parties may agree, including amendment of the Code of Conduct for Arbitrators.

4.   The Commission shall establish its rules and procedures.

Article 52
Application and Entry into Force

1.   The Annexes hereto shall form integral parts hereof.

2.   Each Party shall notify the other in writing of the completion of the procedures required in its territory for the entry into force of this Agreement. This Agreement shall enter into force on the date of the latter of the two notifications.

3.   This Agreement shall remain in force unless either Party notifies the other Party in writing of its intention to terminate it. The termination of this Agreement shall become effective one year after notice of termination has been received by the other Party. In respect of investments or commitments to invest made prior to the date when the termination of this Agreement becomes effective, the provisions of Articles 1 to 51 inclusive, as well as paragraphs (1) and (2) of this Article, shall remain in force for a period of fifteen years.

ANNEX I
Reservations for Existing Measures and Liberalization Commitments

Schedule of Canada _____
Schedule of the other Party_____

ANNEX II
Reservations for Future Measures

Schedule of Canada _____
Schedule of the other Party _____

ANNEX III
Exceptions from Most-Favoured-Nation Treatment

1.   Article 4 shall not apply to treatment accorded under all bilateral or multilateral international agreements in force or signed prior to the date of entry into force of this Agreement.

2.   Article 4 shall not apply to treatment by a Party pursuant to any existing or future bilateral or multilateral agreement:

(a)   establishing, strengthening or expanding a free trade area or customs union;

(b)   relating to:

(i)   aviation;

    (ii) fisheries;

    (iii) maritime matters, including salvage.

3. For greater certainty, Article 4 shall not apply to any current or future foreign aid programme to promote economic development, whether under a bilateral agreement, or pursuant to a multilateral arrangement or agreement, such as the OECD Agreement on Export Credits.

<h3 style="text-align:center">Annex IV
Exclusions from Dispute Settlement</h3>

1. A decision by Canada following a review under the *Investment Canada Act*, with respect to whether or not to permit an acquisition that is subject to review, shall not be subject to the dispute settlement provisions under Sections C or D of this Agreement 2. Issues relating to the administration or enforcement of Canada's Competition Act, its regulations, policies and practices, or any successor legislation, policies and practices and any decision pursuant to the Competition Act made in any cases or patterns of cases by the Commissioner of Competition, Attorney General of Canada, the Competition Tribunal, the responsible Minister or the courts, shall not be subject to the dispute settlement provisions under Sections C or D of this Agreement.

<h3 style="text-align:center">Side letter
Code of Conduct (as agreed by the Commission)</h3>

<h2 style="text-align:center">INDEX</h2>

Section A - Definitions

Article 1: Definitions

Section B – Substantive Obligations

Article 2: Scope
Article 3: National Treatment
Article 4: Most-Favoured-Nation Treatment
Article 5: Minimum Standard of Treatment
Article 6: Senior Management, Boards of Directors and Entry of Personnel
Article 7: Performance Requirements
Article 8: Monopolies and State Enterprises
Article 9: Reservations and Exceptions
Article 10: General Exceptions
Article 11: Health, Safety and Environmental Measures
Article 12: Compensation for Losses
Article 13: Expropriation
Article 14: Transfer of Funds
Article 15: Subrogation
Article 16: Taxation Measures
Article 17: Prudential Measures
Article 18: Denial of Benefits

ANNEXES

ANNEX I: Reservations for Existing Measures and Liberalization Commitments

Schedule of Canada _____
Schedule of the other Party_____

ANNEX II: Reservations for Future Measures

Schedule of Canada _____
Schedule of the other Party _____

ANNEX III: Exceptions from Most-Favoured-Nation Treatment

ANNEX IV: Exclusions from Dispute Settlement

SIDE LETTER

Code of Conduct (as agreed by the Commission)

*

LIST OF PUBLICATIONS ON FDI AND TNCS, 1973-2004
(For more information, please visit www.unctad.org/en/pub on the web.)

I. TRENDS IN FDI AND THE ACTIVITIES OF TNCs

A.   World Investment Report

UNCTAD, *World Investment Report 2004. The Shift Towards Services* (New York and Geneva, 2004). 470 pages. Sales No. E.04.II.D.33.

UNCTAD, *World Investment Report 2004. The Shift Towards Services. Overview*. 54 pages (A, C, E, F, R, S). Document symbol: UNCTAD/WIR/2004 (Overview). Available free of charge.

UNCTAD, *World Investment Report 2003. FDI Policies for Development: National and International Perspectives* (New York and Geneva, 2003). 303 pages. Sales No. E.03.II.D.8.

UNCTAD, *World Investment Report 2003. FDI Policies for Development: National and International Perspectives. Overview*. 42 pages (A, C, E, F, R, S). Document symbol: UNCTAD/WIR/2003 (Overview). Available free of charge.

UNCTAD, *World Investment Report 2002: Transnational Corporations and Export Competitiveness* (New York and Geneva, 2002). 350 pages. Sales No. E.02.II.D.4.

UNCTAD, *World Investment Report 2002: Transnational Corporations and Export Competitiveness. Overview*. 66 pages (A, C, E, F, R, S). Document symbol: UNCTAD/WIR/2002 (Overview). Available free of charge.

UNCTAD, *World Investment Report 2001: Promoting Linkages* (New York and Geneva, 2001). 354 pages. Sales No. E.01.II.D.12.

UNCTAD, *World Investment Report 2001: Promoting Linkages. Overview*. 63 pages (A, C, E, F, R, S). Document symbol: UNCTAD/WIR/2001 (Overview). Available free of charge.

UNCTAD, *World Investment Report 2000: Cross-border Mergers and Acquisitions and Development* (New York and Geneva, 2000). 337 pages. Sales No. E.00.II.D.20.

UNCTAD, *World Investment Report 2000: Cross-border Mergers and Acquisitions and Development. Overview*. 65 pages (A, C, E, F, R, S). Document symbol: UNCTAD/WIR/2000 (Overview). Available free of charge.

UNCTAD, *World Investment Report 1999: Foreign Direct Investment and the Challenge of Development* (New York and Geneva, 1999). 541 pages. Sales No. E.99.II.D.3.

UNCTAD, *World Investment Report 1999: Foreign Direct Investment and the Challenge of Development. Overview*. 75 pages (A, C, E, F, R, S). Document symbol: UNCTAD/WIR/1999 (Overview). Available free of charge.

UNCTAD, *World Investment Report 1998: Trends and Determinants* (New York and Geneva, 1998). 463 pages. Sales No. E.98.II.D.5.

UNCTAD, *World Investment Report 1998: Trends and Determinants. Overview*. 72 pages (A, C, E, F, R, S). Document symbol: UNCTAD/WIR/1998 (Overview). Available free of charge.

UNCTAD, *World Investment Report 1997: Transnational Corporations, Market Structure and Competition Policy* (New York and Geneva, 1997). 416 pages. Sales No. E.97.II.D. 10.

UNCTAD, *World Investment Report 1997: Transnational Corporations, Market Structure and Competition Policy. Overview.* 76 pages (A, C, E, F, R, S). Document symbol: UNCTAD/ITE/IIT/5 (Overview). Available free of charge.

UNCTAD, *World Investment Report 1996: Investment, Trade and International Policy Arrangements* (New York and Geneva, 1996). 364 pages. Sales No. E.96.11.A. 14.

UNCTAD, *World Investment Report 1996: Investment, Trade and International Policy Arrangements. Overview.* 22 pages (A, C, E, F, R, S). Document symbol: UNCTAD/DTCI/32 (Overview). Available free of charge.

UNCTAD, *World Investment Report 1995: Transnational Corporations and Competitiveness* (New York and Geneva, 1995). 491 pages. Sales No. E.95.II.A.9.

UNCTAD, *World Investment Report 1995: Transnational Corporations and Competitiveness. Overview.* 68 pages (A, C, E, F, R, S). Document symbol: UNCTAD/DTCI/26 (Overview). Available free of charge.

UNCTAD, *World Investment Report 1994: Transnational Corporations, Employment and the Workplace* (New York and Geneva, 1994). 482 pages. Sales No.E.94.11.A.14.

UNCTAD, *World Investment Report 1994: Transnational Corporations, Employment and the Workplace. An Executive Summary.* 34 pages (C, E, also available in Japanese). Document symbol: UNCTAD/DTCI/10 (Overview). Available free of charge.

UNCTAD, *World Investment Report 1993: Transnational Corporations and Integrated International Production* (New York and Geneva, 1993). 290 pages. Sales No. E.93.II.A.14.

UNCTAD, *World Investment Report 1993: Transnational Corporations and Integrated International Production. An Executive Summary.* 31 pages (C, E). Document symbol: ST/CTC/159 (Executive Summary). Available free of charge.

DESD/TCMD, *World Investment Report 1992: Transnational Corporations as Engines of Growth* (New York, 1992). 356 pages. Sales No. E.92.II.A.24.

DESD/TCMD, *World Investment Report 1992: Transnational Corporations as Engines of Growth: An Executive Summary.* 26 pages. Document symbol: ST/CTC/143 (Executive Summary). Available free of charge.

UNCTC, *World Investment Report 1991: The Triad in Foreign Direct Investment* (New York, 1991). 108 pages. Sales No. E.9 1.II.A. 12. $25.

B.   Other Studies

UNCTAD, *FDI in Landlocked Developing Countries at a Glance* (Geneva, 2003). Document symbol: UNCTAD/ITE/IIA/2003/5. Available free of charge.

UNCTAD, *Foreign Direct Investment in the World and Poland: Trends, Determinants and Economic Impact.* (Warsaw, 2002). ISBN 83-918182-0-9.

UNCTAD, *FDI in Least Developed Countries at a glance: 2002* (Geneva, 2002). Document symbol: UNCTAD/ITE/IIA/6. 150 pages. Available free of charge.

UNCTAD, *Tax incentives and FDI: A Global Survey* (Geneva, 2001). Sales No. E.01.II.D.5.

UNCTAD, *FDI in Least Developed Countries at a glance: 2001* (Geneva, 2001). Document symbol: UNCTAD/ITE/IIA/3. 150 pages. Available free of charge.

UNCTAD, Invest in France Mission, DATAR and Arthur Andersen, *International Investment: Towards the Year 2002* (Paris, 1998). 167 pages (E,F). Sales No. GV.E.98.0.15. $29.

UNCTAD, Invest in France Mission, DATAR and Arthur Andersen, *International Investment: Towards the Year 2001* (Paris, 1997). 81 pages. Sales No. GV.E.97.0.5. $35.

UNCTAD, *Sharing Asia's Dynamism: Asian Direct Investment in the European Union* (Geneva, 1997). 143 pages. Sales No. E.97.II.D. 1. $26.

UNCTAD and the European Commission, *Investing in Asia's Dynamism: European Union Direct Investment in Asia* (A joint publication with the Office for Official Publications of the European Communities, Luxembourg, 1996). 124 pages. ISBN 92-827-7675-1. ECU 14.

UNCTAD, *Foreign Direct Investment in Africa*. Current Studies, Series A, No. 28 (Geneva, 1996). 115 pages (E, F). Sales No. E.95.II.A.6. $20.

John H. Dunning and Khalil A. Hamdani (eds.), *The New Globalism and Developing Countries* (United Nations University Press, on behalf of UNCTAD, DITE, 1996). 336 pages (E). ISBN 92-808-0944-X. $25.

Karl P. Sauvant, Persephone Economou and Fiorina Mugione (eds.), *Companies without Borders: Transnational Corporations in the 1990s* (Published by International Thomson Business Press, for and on behalf of UNCTAD DITE, 1996). 224 pages. ISBN 0-415-12526-X. E47.50.

UNCTAD, *Transnational Corporations and World Development* (Published by International Thomson Business Press, for and on behalf of UNCTAD DITE, 1996). 656 pages. ISBN 0-415-08560-8 (hardback), 0-415-08561-6 (paperback). £65.00 (hardback), £20.99 (paperback).

UNCTC, *TNCs in South Africa: List of Companies with Investments and Disinvestments, 1990* (New York, 1991). 282 pages. Sales No. E.91.II.A.9. $22.

UNCTC, *Transnational Corporations in World Development: Trends and Prospects* (New York, 1988). 630 pages (A, C, E, F, R, S). Sales No. E.88.II.A.7. Out of print. Available on microfiche. Paper copy from microfiche: $650.

UNCTC, *Transnational Corporations in World Development: Trends and Prospects. Executive Summary* (New York, 1988). 63 pages. Sales No. E.88.II.A.15. Out of print. Available on microfiche.

UNCTC, *Foreign Direct Investment in Latin America: Recent Trends, Prospects and Policy Issues.* Current Studies, Series A, No. 3. (New York, 1986). 28 pages. Sales No. E.86.II.A. 14. Out of print. Available on microfiche. Paper copy from microfiche: $40.

UNCTC, *Trends and Issues in Foreign Direct Investment and Related Flows:* **A Technical Paper** (New York, 1985). 96 pages. Sales No. E.85.II.A.15. Out of print. Available on microfiche. Paper copy from microfiche: $110.

UNCTC, *Transnational Corporations in World Development: Third Survey* (New York, 1983). (Also published by Grahain and Trotman, London, 1985). 386 pages (A, C, E, F, R, S). Sales No. E.83.II.A. 14 and Corrigendum. Out of print. Available on microfiche. Paper copy from microfiche: $400.

UNCTC, *Salient Features and Trends in Foreign Direct Investment* (New York, 1983). 71 pages (A, C, E, F, R, S). Sales No. E.83.II.A.8. Out of print. Available on microfiche. Paper copy from microfiche: $82.

UNCTC, *Transnational Corporations in World Development: A Re-examination* (New York, 1978). 346 pages (E, F, S). Sales No. E.78.1I.A.5. Out of print. Available on microfiche. Paper copy from microfiche: $360.

United Nations Department of Economic and Social Affairs, *Multinational Corporations in World Development* (New York, 1973). (Also published by Praeger, New York, 1974, 200 pages). 196 pages (E, F, R, S). Sales No. E.73.II.A. 11. Out of print. Available on microfiche. Paper copy from microfiche: $204.

United Nations Department of Economic and Social Affairs, *Summary of the Hearings Before the Group of Eminent Persons to Study the Impact of Multinational Corporations on Development and on International Relations* (New York, 1974). 455 pages. Sales No. E.74.II.A.9. Out of print. Available on microfiche. Paper copy from microfiche: $450.

United Nations Department of Economic and Social Affairs, *The Impact of Multinational Corporations on Development and on International Relations* (New York, 1974). 162 pages (E, F, R, S). Sales No. E.74.II.A.5. Out of print. Available on microfiche. Paper copy from microfiche: $160.

The United Nations Library on Transnational Corporations. (The original, hardback version was published by Routledge, for and on behalf of UNCTAD, 1994). Twenty volumes, in five boxed sets of four volumes per set, ISBN 0-415-08559-4, £1,750 (£350 per set), can be ordered in the U.S.A. and Canada from Routledge, Inc., 29 West 35th Street, New York, NY 1000 1, U. S.A. (U.S.A. Tel.: ++ 1212 244 6412 and Fax: ++ 1212 268 9964; Canada Tel.: ++ 1 800 248 4724). In the U.K., by contacting: Routledge Customer Services Department, FREEPOST, ITPS, Cheriton House, North Way, Andover, Hants SP 10 5BR, U.K. (Tel.: ++44 1264 342811/342939; Fax: ++44 1264 364418).

Volume 1: Dunning, John H. (ed.). *The Theory of Transnational Corporations*. 464 pages. Also available in paperback version (published by International Thomson Business Press, for and on behalf of UNCTAD DITE). ISBN 0-415-14106-0. £20.99.

Volume 2: Jones, Geoffrey (ed.). *Transnational Corporations: A Historical Perspective.* 464 pages.

Volume 3: Lall, Sanjaya (ed.). *Transnational Corporations and Economic Development*. 448 pages. Also available in paperback version (published by International Thomson Business Press, for and on behalf of UNCTAD DITE). ISBN 0-415-14110-9. $29.95.

Volume 4: Lecraw, Donald J. and Allen J. Morrison (eds.). *Transnational Corporations and Business Strategy*. 416 pages. Also available in paperback version (published by International Thomson Business Press, for and on behalf of UNCTAD DITE). ISBN 0-415-14109-5. $29.95.

Volume 5: Stonehill, Arthur I. and Michael H. Moffet (eds.). *International Financial Management*. 400 pages. Also available in paperback version (published by International Thomson Business Press, for and on behalf of UNCTAD DITE). ISBN 0-415-14107-9.; £19.95.

Volume 6: Hedlund, Gunnar (ed.). *Organization of Transnational Corporations*. 400 pages. Also available in paperback version (published by International Thomson Business Press, for and on behalf of UNCTAD DITE). ISBN 0-415-14108-7. $29.95.

Volume 7: Moran, Theodore H. (ed.). *Governments and Transnational Corporations*. 352 pages.

Volume 8: Gray, H. Peter (ed.). *Transnational Corporations and International Trade and Payments*. 320 pages.

Volume 9: Robson, Peter (ed.). *Transnational Corporations and Regional Economic Integration*. 331 pages.

Volume 10: McKern, Bruce (ed.). *Transnational Corporations and the Exploitation of Natural Resources*. 397 pages.

Volume 11: Chudnovsky, Daniel (ed.). *Transnational Corporations and Industrialization.* 425 pages.

Volume 12: Sauvant, Karl P. and Padma Mallampally (eds.). *Transnational Corporations in Services.* 437 pages.

Volume 13: Buckley, Peter J. (ed.). *Cooperative Forms of Transnational Corporation Activity*. 419 pages.

Volume 14: Plasschaert, Sylvain (ed.). *Transnational Corporations: Transfer Pricing and Taxation*. 330 pages.

Volume 15: Frischtak, Claudio and Richard Newfarmer (eds.). *Transnational Corporations: Market Structure and Industrial Performanc*e. 383 pages.

Volume 16: Enderwick, Peter (ed.). *Transnational Corporations and Human Resources*. 429 pages.

Volume 17: Cantwell, John (ed.). *Transnational Corporations and Innovatory Activities*. 447 pages.

Volume 18: Chen, Edward (ed.). *Transnational Corporations and Technology Transfer to Developing Countries*. 486 pages.

Volume 19: Rubin, Seymour and Don Wallace, Jr. (eds.). *Transnational Corporations and National Law*. 322 pages.

Volume 20: Fatouros, Arghyrios (ed.). *Transnational Corporations. The International Legal Framework*. 545 pages.

II. DEVELOPMENT ISSUES AND FDI

Transnational Corporations. A refereed journal published three times a year. (Supersedes the *CTC Reporter* as of February 1992). Annual subscription (3 issues): $45. Single issue: $20.

UNCTAD, *Investment and Technology Policies for Competitiveness: Review of Successful Country Experiences* (Geneva, 2003). Document symbol: UNCTAD/ITE/ICP/2003/2.

UNCTAD, *The Development Dimension of FDI: Policy and Rule-Making Perspectives* (Geneva, 2003). Sales No. E.03.II.D.22. $35.

UNCTAD, *FDI and Performance Requirements: New Evidence from Selected Countries* (Geneva, 2003). Sales No. E.03.II.D.32. 318 pages. $ 35.

UNCTAD, *Measures of the Transnationalization of Economic Activity* (New York and Geneva, 2001). Document symbol: UNCTAD/ITE/IIA/1. Sales No. E.01.II.D.2.

UNCTAD, *FDI Determinants and TNC Strategies: The Case of Brazil* (Geneva, 2000). Sales No. E.00:II.D.2.

UNCTAD, *The Competitiveness Challenge: Transnational Corporations and Industrial Restructuring in Developing Countries* (Geneva, 2000). Sales No. E.00.II.D.35.

UNCTAD, *Foreign Direct Investment in Africa: Performance and Potential* (Geneva, 1999). Document symbol: UNCTAD/ITE/IIT/Misc.15. Available free of charge.

UNCTAD, *The Financial Crisis in Asia and Foreign Direct Investment An Assessment* (Geneva, 1998). 110 pages. Sales No. GV.E.98.0.29. $20.

UNCTAD, *Handbook on Foreign Direct Investment by Small and Medium-sized Enterprises: Lessons from Asia* (New York and Geneva, 1998). 202 pages. Sales No. E.98.II.D.4. $48.

UNCTAD, *Handbook on Foreign Direct Investment by Small and Medium-sized Enterprises: Lessons from Asia. Executive Summary and Report on the Kunming Conference.* 70 pages. Document symbol: UNCTAD/ITE/IIT/6 (Summary). Available free of charge.

UNCTAD, *Survey of Best Practices in Investment Promotion* (New York and Geneva, 1997). 81 pages. Sales No. E.97.II.D.11. $35.

UNCTAD, *Incentives and Foreign Direct Investment* (New York and Geneva, 1996). Current Studies, Series A, No. 30. 98 pages. Sales No. E.96.II.A.6. $25.

UNCTC, *Foreign Direct Investment in the People's Republic of China* (New York, 1988). 110 pages. Sales No. E.88.II.A.3. Out of print. Available on microfiche. Paper copy from microfiche: $122.

UNCTAD, *Foreign Direct Investment, Trade, Aid and Migration* Current Studies, Series A, No. 29. (A joint publication with the International Organization for Migration, Geneva, 1996). 90 pages. Sales No. E.96M.A.8. $25.

UNCTAD, *Explaining and Forecasting Regional Flows of Foreign Direct Investment* (New York, 1993). Current Studies, Series A, No. 26. 58 pages. Sales No. E.94.II.A.5. $25.

UNCTAD, *Small and Medium-sized Transnational Corporations: Role, Impact and Policy Implications* (New York and Geneva, 1993). 242 pages. Sales No. E.93.II.A. 15. $35.

UNCTAD, *Small and Medium-sized Transnational Corporations: Executive Summary and Report of the Osaka Conference* (Geneva, 1994). 60 pages. Available free of charge.

DESD/TCMD, *From the Common Market to EC 92: Regional Economic Integration in the European Community and Transnational Corporations* (New York, 1993). 134 pages. Sales No. E.93.11.A.2. $25.

DESD/TCMD, *Debt-Equity Swaps and Development* (New York, 1993). 150 pages. Sales No. E.93.11.A.7. $35.

DESD/TCMD, *Transnational Corporations from Developing Countries: Impact on Their Home Countries* (New York, 1993). 116 pages. Sales No. E.93.11.A.8. $15.

DESD/TCMD, *Foreign Investment and Trade Linkages in Developing Countries* (New York, 1993). 108 pages. Sales No. E.93.II.A. 12. Out of print.

UNCTC, *Foreign Direct Investment and Industrial Restructuring in Mexico*. Current Studies, Series A, No. 18. (New York, 1992). 114 pages. Sales No. E.92.11.A.9. $12.50.

UNCTC, *The Determinants of Foreign Direct Investment: A Survey of the Evidence* (New York, 1992). 84 pages. Sales No. E.92.11.A.2. $12.50.

UNCTC and UNCTAD, *The Impact of Trade-Related Investment Measures on Trade and Development* (Geneva and New York, 1991). 104 pages. Sales No. E.91 II.A. 19. $17.50.

UNCTC, *The Challenge of Free Economic Zones in Central and Eastern Europe: International Perspective* (New York, 1991). 442 pages. Sales No. E.90.11.A.27. $75.

UNCTC, *The Role of Free Economic Zones in the USSR and Eastern Europe*. Current Studies, Series A, No. 14. (New York, 1990). 84 pages. Sales No. E.90.11.A.5. $10.

UNCTC, *Foreign Direct Investment, Debt and Home Country Policies*. Current Studies, Series A, No. 20. (New York, 1990). 50 pages. Sales No. E.90.II.A. 16. $12.50.

UNCTC, *News Issues in the Uruguay Round of Multilateral Trade Negotiations*. Current Studies, Series A, No. 19. (New York, 1990). 52 pages. Sales No. E.90.II.A. 15. $12.50.

UNCTC, *Regional Economic Integration and Transnational Corporations in the 1990s: Europe 1992, North America, and Developing Countries*. Current Studies, Series A, No. 15. (New York, 1990). 52 pages. Sales No. E.90.II.A. 14. $12.50.

UNCTC, *Transnational Corporations and International Economic Relations: Recent Developments and Selected Issues*. Current Studies, Series A, No. 11. (New York, 1989). 50 pages. Sales No. E.89.11.A.15. Out of print. Available on microfiche. Paper copy from microfiche: $60.

UNCTC, *The Process of Transnationalization and Transnational Mergers*. **Current Studies**, Series A, No. 8. (New York, 1989). 91 pages. Sales No. E.89.11.A.4. Out of print. Available on microfiche. Paper copy from microfiche: $106.

UNCTC and ILO, *Economic and Social Effects of Multinational Enterprises in Export Processing Zones* (Geneva, International Labour Office, 1988). 169 pages. ISBN: 92-2106194-9. S1727.50.

UNCTC, *Measures Strengthening the Negotiating Capacity of Governments in Their Relations with Transnational Corporations: Regional Integration cum/versus Corporate Integration. A Technical Paper* (New York, 1982). 63 pages. Sales No. E..82.II.A.6. Out of print. Available on microfiche. Paper copy from microfiche: $71.

III. SECTORAL STUDIES

A.   TNCs in the Manufacturing and Extractive Sectors

UNCTC, *New Approaches to Best-Practice Manufacturing: The Role of Transnational Corporations and Implications for Developing Countries*. Current Studies, Series A, No. 12. (New York, 1990). 76 pages. Sales No. E.90.II.A. 13. $20.

Blomström, Magnus, *Transnational Corporations and Manufacturing Exports from Developing Countries* (New York, 1990). 124 pages. Sales No. E.90.II.A.21. $25.

UNCTC, *Transnational Corporations in the Plastics Industry* (New York, 1990). 167 pages. Sales No. 90.II.A. 1. $20.

Hoffman, Kurt and Raphael Kaplinsky, *Driving Force: The Global Restructuring of Technology, Labour and Investment in the Automobile and Components Industries.*. (Boulder: Westview and UNCTC, 1988). 385 pages. ISBN: 0-8133-7502-9. $32.50.

UNCTC, *Transnational Corporations in Biotechnology* (New York, 1988). 130 pages. Sales No. E.88.II.A.4. $17.

UNCTC, *Transnational Corporations and Non-fuel Primary Commodities in Developing Countries* (New York, 1987). 89 pages. Sales No. E.87.II.A. 17. Out of print. Available on microfiche. Paper copy from microfiche: $98.

UNCTC and ESCAP Joint Unit, *Transnational Corporations and the Electronics Industries ofASEAN Economies*. Current Studies, Series A, No. 5. (New York, 1987). 55 pages. Sales No. E.87.II.A. 13. $7.50.

UNCTC, *Transnational Corporations in the Man-made Fibre, Textile and Clothing Industries* (New York, 1987). 154 pages. Sales No. E.87.II.A. 11. $19.

UNCTC, *Transnational Corporations in the International Semiconductor Industry* (New York, 1986). 471 pages. Sales No. E.86.II.A. 1. $41.

UNCTC, *Transnational Corporations in the Pharmaceutical Industry of Developing Countries* (New York, 1984). 223 pages. Sales No. E. 84.II.A. 10. Out of print. Available on microfiche. Paper copy from microfiche: $238.

UNCTC, *Transnational Corporations in the International Auto Industry* (New York, 1983). 223 pages. Sales No. E.83.II.A.6. Out of print. Available on microfiche. Paper copy from microfiche: $242.

UNCTC, *Transnational Corporations in the Agricultural Machinery and Equipment Industry* (New York, 1983). 134 pages. Sales No. E.83.II.A.4. Out of print. Available on microfiche. Paper copy from microfiche: $148.

UNCTC, *Transnational Corporations in the Power Equipment Industry* (New York, 1982). 95 pages (E, F, S). Sales No.E.82.II.A.1 1. Out of print. Available on microfiche. Paper copy from microfiche: $108.

UNCTC, *Transnational Corporations in the Fertilizer Industry* (New York, 1982). 69 pages (E, F, S). Sales No. E.82.H.A.10. Out of print. Available on microfiche. Paper copy from microfiche: $80.

UNCTC, *Transnational Corporations in Food and Beverage Processing* (New York, 1981). 242 pages. Sales No. E.8 I.II.A. 12. Out of print. Available on microfiche. Paper copy from microfiche: $26 1.

UNCTC, *Transnational Corporations in the Bauxite and Aluminium Industry* (New York, 1981). 88 pages (E, F, S). Sales No. E.8 1.II.A.5. Out of print. Available on microfiche. Paper copy from microfiche: $104.

UNCTC, *Transnational Corporation Linkages in Developing Countries: The Case of Backward Linkages via Subcontracting* (New York, 1981). 75 pages. Sales No. E.8 1.II.A.4. Out of print. Available on microfiche. Paper copy from microfiche:

UNCTC, *Transnational Corporations in the Copper Industry* (New York, 1981). 80 pages (E, F, S). Sales No. E.81.II.A.3. Out of print. Available on microfiche. Paper copy from microfiche: $92.

UNCTC, *Transnational Corporations and the Pharmaceutical Industry* (New York, 1979). 163 pages. Sales No. E.79.II.A.3. Out of print. Available on microfiche. Paper copy from microfiche: $160.

B.   TNCs in the Services Sector and Transborder Data Flows

UNCTAD, *Tradability of Consulting Services and Its Implications for Developing Countries* (New York and Geneva, 2002).189 pages. UNCTAD/ITE/IPC/Misc.8.

UNCTAD and the World Bank, *Liberalizing International Transactions in Services: A Handbook* (New York and Geneva, 1994). 182 pages. Sales No. E.94.II.A. 11. $45.

UNCTAD, *Tradability of Banking Services: Impact and Implications*. Current Studies, Series A, No. 27. (Geneva, 1994). 242 pages. Sales No. E.94.II.A. 12. $50.

UNCTAD, *Management Consulting: A Survey of the Industry and Its Largest Firms* (New York, 1993). 100 pages. Sales No. E.93.II.A. 17. $25.

UNCTAD, *International Tradability in Insurance Services*. Current Studies, Series A, No. 25. (New York, 1993). 54 pages. Sales No. E.93.II.A. 11. $20.

UNCTAD, *The Transnationalization of Service Industries: An Empirical Analysis of the Determinants of Foreign Direct Investment by Transnational Service Corporations*. Current Studies, Series A, No. 23. (New York, 1993). 62 pages. Sales No. E.93.II.A.3. $15.

UNCTC, *Transnational Banks and the External Indebtedness of Developing Countries: Impact of Regulatory Changes*. Current Studies, Series A, No. 22. (New York, 1992). 48 pages. Sales No. E.92.11.A.10. Out of print. Available on microfiche. Paper copy from microfiche: $60.

UNCTC, *Transnational Banks and the International Debt Crisis* (New York, 1991). 148 pages. Sales No. E.90.II.A. 19. $22.50.

UNCTC, *Transborder Data Flows and Mexico* (New York, 1991). 194 pages. Sales No. E.90.II.A.17. $27.50.

UNCTC and World Bank, *The Uruguay Round., Services in the World Economy* (Washington and New York, 1990). 220 pages. ISBN: 0-8213-1374-6.

UNCTC, *New Issues in the Uruguay Round of Multilateral Trade Negotiations*. Current Studies, Series A, No. 19. (New York, 1990). 52 pages. Sales No. E.90.II.A. 15. $12.50.

UNCTC, *Transnational Corporations, Services and the Uruguay Round* (New York, 1990). 252 pages. Sales No. E.90.II.A. 11. $28.50.

UNCTC, *Services and Development: The Role of Foreign Direct Investment and Trade* (New York, 1989). 187 pages. Sales No. E.89.II.A. 17. Out of print. Available on microfiche. Paper copy from microfiche: $200.

(Also published in Spanish as *Servicios y el Desarrollo: El Papel de la Inversion y el Commercio*, by Junta del Acuerdo de Cartagena (Lima, 1990). 206 pages.)

UNCTC, *Transnational Service Corporations and Developing Countries: Impact and Policy Issues.* Current Studies, Series A, No. 10. (New York, 1989). 50 pages. Sales No. E.89.II.A. 14. Out of print. Available on microfiche. Paper copy from microfiche: $60.

UNCTC, *Transnational Corporations in the Construction and Design Engineering Industry* (New York, 1989). 60 pages. Sales No. E.89.II.A.6. Out of print. Available on microfiche. Paper copy from microfiche: $74.

Dunning, John H., *Transnational Corporations and the Growth of Services: Some Conceptual and Theoretical Issues.* Current Studies, Series A, No. 9. (New York, 1989). 80 pages. Sales No. E.89.II.A.5. Out of print. Available on microfiche. Paper copy from microfiche: $92.

UNCTC, *Foreign Direct Investment and Transnational Corporations in Services* (New York, 1989). 229 pages. Sales No. E.89.II.A. 1. Out of print. Available on microfiche. Paper copy from microfiche: $240.

UNCTC, *Data Goods and Data Services in the Socialist Countries of Eastern Europe* (New York, 1988). 103 pages. Sales No. E.88.II.A.20. Out of print. Available on microfiche. Paper copy from microfiche: $114.

UNCTC, *Foreign Direct Investment, the Service Sector and International Banking.* Current Studies, Series A, No. 7. (New York, 1987). (Also published by Graham and Trotman, Londori, 1988). 71 pages. Sales No. E.87.II.A. 15. $9.

UNCTC, *Transborder Data Flows: Transnational Corporations and Remote-Sensing Data* (New York, 1984). 74 pages. Sales No. E.84.II.A.11 and Corrigendum. (book reads: E.84.II.A.8). Outofprint. Available on microfiche. Paper copy from microfiche: $82.

UNCTC, *Transborder Data Flows and Poland. Polish Case Study. A Technical Paper* (New York, 1984). (Also published by North-Holland, Amsterdam, 1984). 75 pages. Sales No. E.84.11.A.8. Out of print. Available on microfiche. Paper copy from microfiche: $86.

UNCTC, *Transborder Data Flows and Brazil* (New York, 1983). (Also published by NorthHolland, Amsterdam, 1984). 418 pages. Sales No. E.83.II.A.3. Out of print. Available on microfiche. Paper copy from microfiche: $400.

UNCTC, *Transborder Data Flows: Access to the International On-line Data-base Market* (New York, 1983). (Also published by North-Holland, Amsterdam, 1984.) 140 pages. Sales No. E.83.II.A. 1. Out of print. Available on microfiche. Paper copy from microfiche: S 154.

UNCTC, *Transnational Corporations in International Tourism* (New York, 1982). 113 pages. Sales No. E.82.II.A.9. Out of print. Available on microfiche. Paper copy from microfiche: $123.

UNCTC, *Transnational Corporations and Transborder Data Flows: A Technical Paper* (New York, 1982). 149 pages. Sales No. E.82.II.A.4. Out of print. Available on microfiche. Paper copy from microfiche: $159.

UNCTC, *Transnational Banks: Operations, Strategies and Their Effects in Developing Countries* (New York, 1981). 140 pages. Sales No. E.8 1.II.A.7. Out of print. Available on microfiche. Paper copy from microfiche: $15 1.

UNCTC, *Transnational Reinsurance Operations: A Technical Paper* (New York, 1980). 51 pages. Sales No. E.80.II.A.10. Out of print. Available on microfiche. Paper copy from microfiche: $59.

UNCTC, *Transnational Corporations in Advertising. A Technical Paper* (New York, 1979). 54 pages (E, F, S). Sales No. E.79.II.A.2. Out of print. Available on microfiche. Paper copy from microfiche: $62.

IV. TNCs, TECHNOLOGY TRANSFER AND INTELLECTUAL PROPERTY RIGHTS

UNCTAD, *Transfer of Technology for Successful Integration into the Global Economy* (New York and Geneva, 2003). Sales No. E.03.II.D.31. 206 pages.

UNCTAD, *Compendium of International Arrangements on Transfer of Technology* (Geneva, 2001). Sales No. E.01.II.D.28.

UNCTAD, *The TRIPS Agreement and Developing Countries* (Geneva, 1997). 64 pages. Sales No. E.96.II.13. 10. $22.

UNCTAD, *Fostering Technological Dynamism: Evolution of Thought and Technological Development Process and Competitiveness: A Literature Review* (Geneva, 1995). 183 pages. Sales No. E.95.II.D.21. $35.

UNCTAD, *Intellectual Property Rights and Foreign Direct Investment*. Current Studies, Series A, No. 24. (New York, 1993). 108 pages. Sales No. E.93.II.A. 10. $20.

UNCTC, *Foreign Direct Investment and Technology Transfer in India* (New York, 1992). 150 pages. Sales No. E.92.II.A.3. $20.

UNCTC, *Transnational Corporations and the Transfer of New and Emerging Technologies to Developing Countries* (New York, 1990). 141 pages. Sales No. E.90.II.A.20. $27.50.

UNCTC, *Transnational Corporations and the Transfer of New Management Practices to Developing Countries* (New York, 1993). ST/CTC/153.

UNCTC, *New Approaches to Best-Practice Manufacturing: The Role of Transnational Corporations and Implications for Developing Countries*. Current Studies, Series A, No. 12. (New York, 1990). 76 pages. Sales No. E.90.II.A. 13. $12.50.

UNCTC and ESCAP Joint Unit, *Technology Acquisition under Alternative Arrangements with Transnational Corporations: Selected Industrial Case Studies in Thailand*. Current Studies,

Series A, No. 6. (New York, 1987). 55 pages. Sales No. E. 87.II.A. 14. Out of print. Available on microfiche. Paper copy from microfiche: $64.

UNCTC, *Transnational Corporations and Technology Transfer: Effects and Policy Issues* (New York, 1987). 77 pages. Sales No. E.87.II.A.4. Out of print. Available on microfiche. Paper copy from microfiche: $90.

UNCTC, *Measures Strengthening the Negotiating Capacity of Governments in Their Relations with Transnational Corporations: Technology Transfer through Transnational Corporations. A Technical Paper* (New York, 1979). 37 pages. Sales No. E.79.II.A.6. Out of print. Available on microfiche. Paper copy from microfiche: $43.

United Nations Department of Economic and Social Affairs, *Acquisition of Technology from Multinational Corporations by Developing Countries* (New York, 1974). 50 pages. Sales No. E.74.II.A.7. Out of print. Available on microfiche. Paper copy from microfiche: $57.

V. POLITICAL, SOCIAL AND ENVIRONMENTAL IMPACTS OF TNCs

UNCTAD, *The Social Responsibility of Transnational Corporations*. Document symbol: UNCTAD/ITE/IIT/Misc.21. Available free of charge.

UNCTAD, *Self-regulation of Environmental Management: An Analysis of Guidelines Set by World Industry for Their Member Firms* (Geneva, 1996). 165 pages. Sales No. E.96.II.A.5. $35.

UNCTC, *Environmental Management in Transnational Corporations: Report on the Benchmark Corporate Environment Survey* (Geneva, 1993). 265 pages. Sales No. E.94.II.A.2.

UNCTAD, *Environmental Management in Transnational Corporations: Report on the Benchmark Corporate Environment Survey* (Geneva, 1994). 278 pages. Sales No. E.94.II.A.2. 529.95.

DESD/TCMD, *Climate Change and Transnational Corporations: Analysis and Trends* (New York, 1992). 110 pages. Sales No. E.92.II.A.7. $16.50.

UNCTC, *Transnational Corporations and Industrial Hazards Disclosure* (New York, 1991). 86 pages. Sales No. E.91.II.A.18. $17.50.

UNCTC and DIESA, *Consolidated, List of Products Whose Consumption and/or Sale Have Been Banned, Withdrawn, Severely Restricted or not Approved by Governments*, Fourth ed. (New York, 1991). 769 pages. Sales No. E.91.1V.4. Out of print. Available on microfiche. Paper copy ftom microfiche: $800.

UNCTC, *Transnational Corporations in South Africa: Second United Nations Public Hearings, 1989*:

Vol. I *Report of the Panel of Eminent Persons, Background Documentation* (New York, 1990). 162 pages. Sales No. E.90.II.A.6. $19.

Vol. II *Statements and Submissions* (New York, 1990). 210 pages. Document symbol: ST/CTC/102. Sales No.E.90.II.A.12. $21.

UNCTC and DESA, *Consolidated List of Products Whose Consumption and/or Sale Have Been Banned, Withdrawn, Severely Restricted or Not Approved by Government,* Second issue. Prepared jointly by the Food and Agriculture Organization of the United Nations, the World Health Organization, the International Labour Organization, the United Nations Centre on Transnational Corporations and other relevant intergovernmental organizations (New York, 1987). 655 pages. Sales No. E.87.1V. I. Out of print.

UNCTC, *Transnational Corporations in South Africa and Namibia*: United Nations Public Hearings, 1986:

Vol. I **Reports of the Panel of Eminent Persons and of the Secretary-General** (New York, 1986). 242 pages. Document symbol: ST/CTC/68 (Vol. I). Sales No. E.86.II.A.6. Out of print. Available on microfiche. Paper copy from microfiche: $240.

Vol. II **Verbatim Records** (New York, 1986). 282 pages. Document symbol: ST/CTC/68 (Vol. II). Sales No. E.86.II.A.7. Out of print. Available on microfiche. Paper copy from microfiche: $300.

Vol. III **Statements and Submissions** (New York, 1987). 518 pages. Document symbol: ST/CTC/68 (Vol. III). Sales No. E.86.1I.A.8. Out of print. Available on microfiche. Paper copy from microfiche: $530.

Vol. IV **Policy Instruments and Statements** (New York, 1987). 444 pages. Document symbol: ST/CTC/68 (Vol. IV). Sales No. E.86.II.A.9. Out of print. Available on microfiche. Paper copy from microfiche: $474.

UNCTC, *Activities of Transnational Corporations in South Africa and Namibia and the Responsibilities of Home Countries with Respect to Their Operations in This Area* (New York, 1986). 59 pages (E, F, S). Sales No. E.85.II.A. 16. Out of print. Available on microfiche. Paper copy from microfiche: $66.

UNCTC, *Environmental Aspects of the Activities of Transnational Corporations: A Survey* (New York, 1985). 114 pages (E, F, S). Sales No. E.85.II.A. 11. Out of print. Available on microfiche. Paper copy from microfiche: $126.

UNCTC and ILO, *Women Workers in Multinational Enterprises in Developing Countries: A Contribution to the United Nations Decade for Women*. A joint publication by the United Nations Centre on Transnational Corporations and the International Labour Office (Geneva, International Labour Office, 1985). 119 pages (E, F, S). ISBN: 92-2-100532-1. SF15.

UNCTC and DIESA, *Listé récapitulative desproduits dont la consommation ou la vente ont été interdites ou rigoureusement réglementées, ou qui ont été retirées du marché ou n'ont pas été approuvés par les gouvernements. Première édition révisée* (New York, 1985). (E, F, S). Sales No. F.85.IV.8. Out of print. Available on microfiche. Paper copy from microfiche: $370.

UNCTC, *Policies and Practices of Transnational Corporations Regarding Their Activities in South Africa and Namibia* (New York, 1984). 55 pages (E, F, S). Sales No. E.84.1I.A.5. Out of print. Available on microfiche. Paper copy from microfiche: $55.

UNCTC, *Transnational Corporations in Southern Africa: Update on Financial Activities and Employment Practices* (New York, 1982). 44 pages. Sales No. E.82.II.A. 12. Out of print. Available on microfiche. Paper copy from microfiche: $62.

UNCTC, *Activities of Transnational Corporations in Southern Africa: Impact on Financial and Social Structures* (New York, 1978). 80 pages. Sales No. E.78.II.A.6. Out of print. Available on microfiche. Paper copy from microfiche: $85.

VI. INTERNATIONAL ARRANGEMENTS AND AGREEMENTS

A.   Series on Issues in International Investment Agreements (IIAs)

UNCTAD, *Glossary of Key Concepts Used in IIAs*. UNCTAD Series on Issues in International Investment Agreements (New York and Geneva, 2003)

UNCTAD, *Incentives* UNCTAD Series on Issues in International Investment Agreements (New York and Geneva, 2003). Sales No. E.04.II.D.6. $15.

UNCTAD, *Transparency*. UNCTAD Series on Issues in International Investment Agreements (New York and Geneva, 2003). Sales No. E.03.II.D.7. $15.

UNCTAD, *Dispute Settlement: Investor-State*. UNCTAD Series on Issues in International Investment Agreements (New York and Geneva, 2003). 128 pages. Sales No. E.03.II.D.5. $15.

UNCTAD, *Dispute Settlement: State-State*. UNCTAD Series on Issues in International Investment Agreements (New York and Geneva, 2003). 109 pages. Sales No. E.03.II.D.6 $16.

UNCTAD, *Transfer of Technology*. UNCTAD Series on Issues on International Investment Agreements (New York and Geneva, 2001). 135 pages. Sales No. E.01.II.D.33. $16.

UNCTAD, *Illicit Payments*. UNCTAD Series on Issues on IInternational Investment Agreements (New York and Geneva, 2001). 112 pages. Sales No. E.01.II.D.20. $13.

UNCTAD, *Home Country Measures*. UNCTAD Series on Issues on International Investment Agreements (New York and Geneva, 2001). 95 pages. Sales No. E.01.II.D.19. $12.

UNCTAD, *Host Country Operational Measures*. UNCTAD Series on Issues on International Investment Agreements (New York and Geneva, 2001). 105 pages. Sales No. E.01.II.D.18. $18.

UNCTAD, *Social Responsibility*. UNCTAD Series on Issues on International Investment Agreements (New York and Geneva, 2001). 87 pages. Sales No. E.01.II.D.4.$15.

UNCTAD, *Environment*. UNCTAD Series on Issues on International Investment Agreements (New York and Geneva 2001). 106 pages. Sales No. E.01.II.D.3. $15.

UNCTAD, *Transfer of Funds*. UNCTAD Series on Issues on International Investment Agreements (New York and Geneva 2000). 79 pages. Sales No. E.00.II.D.38. $10.

UNCTAD, *Flexibility for Development*. UNCTAD Series on Issues on International Investment Agreements (New York and Geneva 2000). 185 pages. Sales No. E.00.II.D.6. $15.

UNCTAD, *Employment*. UNCTAD Series on Issues on International Investment Agreements (New York and Geneva, 2000). 64 pages. Sales No. E.00.II.D.15. $12.

UNCTAD, *Taxation*. UNCTAD Series on Issues on International Investment Agreements (New York and Geneva, 2000). 111 pages. Sales No. E.00.II.D.5. $15.

UNCTAD, *Taking of Property*. UNCTAD Series on Issues on International Investment Agreements (New York and Geneva, 2000). 78 pages. Sales No. E.00.II.D.4. $12.

UNCTAD, *Trends in International investment Agreements: An Overview.* UNCTAD Series on Issues on International Investment Agreements (New York and Geneva, 1999). 133 pages. Sales No. E.99.II.D.23. $12.

UNCTAD, *Lessons from the MAI.* UNCTAD Series on Issues on International Investment Agreements (New York and Geneva 1999). 52 pages. Sales No. E.99.II.D.26. $10.

UNCTAD, *National Treatment.* UNCTAD Series on Issues in International Investment Agreements (New York and Geneva, 1999). 88 pages. Sales No. E.99.II.D. 16. $12.

UNCTAD, *Fair and Equitable Treatment.* UNCTAD Series on Issues in International Investment Agreements (New York and Geneva, 1999). 80 pages. Sales No. E.99.II.D.15. $12.

UNCTAD, *Investment-Related Trade Measures.* UNCTAD Series on Issues in International Investment Agreements (New York and Geneva, 1999). 64 pages. Sales No. E.99.II.D.12.$12.

UNCTAD, *Most-Favoured-Nation Treatment.* UNCTAD Series on Issues in International Investment Agreements (New York and Geneva, 1999). 72 pages. Sales No. E.99.II.D.11. $12.

UNCTAD, *Admission and Establishment.* UNCTAD Series on Issues in International Investment Agreements (New York and Geneva, 1999). 72 pages. Sales No. E.99.II.D.10. $12.

UNCTAD, *Scope and Definition.* UNCTAD Series on Issues in International Investment Agreements (New York and Geneva, 1999). 96 pages. Sales No. E.99.II.D.9. $12.

UNCTAD, *Transfer Pricing.* UNCTAD Series on Issues in International Investment Agreements (New York and Geneva, 1999). 72 pages. Sales No. E.99.II.D.8. $12.

UNCTAD, *Foreign Direct Investment and Development.* UNCTAD Series on Issues in International Investment Agreements (New York and Geneva, 1999). 88 pages. Sales No. E.98.1I.D.15A12.

B.   Other studies

UNCTAD's Work Programme on International Investment Agreements: **From UNCTAD IX to UNCTAD X**. Document symbol: UNCTAD/ITE/IIT/Misc.26. Available free of charge.

UNCTAD, Progress Report. Work undertaken within UNCTAD's work programme on International Investment Agreements between the 10th Conference of UNCTAD 10th Conference of UNCTAD, Bangkok, February 2000, and July 2002 (New York and Geneva, 2002). UNCTAD/ITE/Misc.58. Available free of charge.

UNCTAD, *Bilateral Investment Treaties in the Mid-1990s* (New York and Geneva, 1998). 322 pages. Sales No. E.98.II.D.8. $46.

UNCTAD, *Bilateral Investment Treaties: 1959-1999* (Geneva and New York, 2000) Sales No. E.92.II.A.16. $22.

UNCTAD, *International Investment Instruments: A Compendium* (New York and Geneva, 1996 to 2003). 12 volumes. Vol. I: Sales No. E.96.A.II.A.9. Vol. II: Sales No. E.96.II.A.10. Vol. III: Sales No. E.96.II.A.11. Vol. IV: Sales No. E.00.II.D.13. Vol. V: Sales No. E.00.II.A.14. Vol. VI: Sales No. E.01.II.D.34. Vol. VII: Sales No. E.02.II.D.14. Vol. VIII: Sales No. E.02.II.D.15. Vol. IX: Sales No. E.02.II.D.16. Vol. X: Sales No. E.02.II.D.21. Vol. XI: Sales No. E.04.II.D.9. Vol. XII: Sales No. E.04.II.D.10. $60.

UNCTC and ICC, ***Bilateral Investment Treaties***. A joint publication by the United Nations Centre on Transnational Corporations and the International Chamber of Commerce (New York, 1992). 46 pages. Sales No. E.92.II.A. 16. $22.

UNCTC, ***The New Code Environment***. Current Studies, Series A, No. 16. (New York, 1990). 54 pages. Sales No. E.90.II.A.7. Out of print. Available on microfiche. Paper copy from microfiche: $68.

UNCTC, ***Key Concepts in International Investment Arrangements and Their Relevance to Negotiations on International Transactions in Services***. Current Studies, Series A, No. 13. (New York, 1990). 66 pages. Sales No. E.90.II.A.3. $9.

UNCTC, ***Bilateral Investment Treaties*** (New York, 1988). (Also published by Graham and Trotman, London/Dordrecht/Boston, 1988). 188 pages. Sales No. E.88.II.A. 1. $20.

UNCTC, ***The United Nations Code of Conduct on Transnational Corporations***. Current Studies, Series A, No. 4. (New York, 1986). 80 pages. Sales No. E.86.II.A. 15. Out of print. Available on microfiche. Paper copy from microfiche: $88.

Vagts, Detlev F., ***The Question of a Reference to International Obligations in the United Nations Code of Conduct on Transnational Corporations: A Different View***. Current Studies,

Series A, No. 2. (New York, 1986). 17 pages. Sales No. E.86.II.A.11. Out of print. Available on microfiche. Paper copy from microfiche: $24.

Robinson, Patrick, ***The Question of a Reference to International Law in the United Nations Code of Conduct on Transnational Corporations***. Current Studies, Series A, No.1. (New York, 1986). 22 pages. Sales No. E.86.II.A.5. $4.

UNCTC, ***Transnational Corporations: Material Relevant to the Formulation of a Code of Conduct*** (New York, 1977). 114 pages (E, F, S). UN Document Symbol: EX. 10/ 10 and Corr. 1. $7.

UNCTC, ***Transnational Corporations: Issues Involved in the Formulation of a Code of Conduct*** (New York, 1976). 41 pages (E, F, R, S). Sales No. E.77.II.A.5. Out of print. Available on microfiche. Paper copy from microfiche: $41.

VII. NATIONAL POLICIES, LAWS, REGULATIONS AND CONTRACTS RELATING TO TNCs

A.   Investment Policy Reviews

UNCTAD, ***Investment Policy Review of Algeria*** (Geneva, 2004). 110 pages. UNCTAD/ITE/IPC/2003/9.

UNCTAD, ***Investment Policy Review of Sri Lanka*** (Geneva, 2003). 89 pages. UNCTAD/ITE/IPC/2003/8

UNCTAD, ***Investment Policy Review of Lesotho*** (Geneva, 2003). 105 pages. Sales No. E.03.II.D.18.

UNCTAD, ***Investment Policy Review of Nepal.*** (Geneva, 2003). 89 pages. Sales No.E.03.II.D.17.

UNCTAD, ***Investment Policy Review of Ghana*** (Geneva, 2002). 103 pages. Sales No. E.02.II.D.20.

UNCTAD, ***Investment Policy Review of Botswana*** (Geneva, 2003). 107 pages. Sales No. E.03.II.D.1.

UNCTAD, *Investment Policy Review of Tanzania* (Geneva, 2002). 109 pages. Sales No. E.02.II.D.6. $ 20.

UNCTAD, *Investment and Innovation Policy Review of Ethiopia* (Geneva, 2001). 130 pages. Sales No. E.01.II.D.5.

UNCTAD, *Investment Policy Review of Ecuador*. (Geneva, 2001). 136 pages. Sales No. E.01.II.D.31. $25. Also available in Spanish.

UNCTAD, *Investment Policy Review of Mauritius* (Geneva, 2000). 92 pages. Sales No. E.00.II.D.11.

UNCTAD, *Investment Policy Review of Peru* (Geneva, 2000). 109 pages. Sales No. E.00.II.D.7.

UNCTAD, *Investment Policy Review of Uganda* (Geneva, 1999). 71 pages. Sales No. E.99.II.D.24.

UNCTAD, *Investment Policy Review of Uzbekistan* (Geneva, 1999). 65 pages. Document number: UNCTAD/ITE/IIP/Misc.13.

UNCTAD, *Investment Policy Review of Egypt* (Geneva, 1999). 119 pages. Sales No. E.99.II.D.20. $19.

B.   Investment Guides

UNCTAD and ICC, *An Investment Guide to Mauritania* (Geneva, 2004). Document symbol: UNCTAD/IIA/2004/4. Free of charge.

UNCTAD and ICC, *An Investment Guide to Cambodia* (Geneva, 2003). 89 pages. Document symbol: UNCTAD/IIA/2003/6. Free of charge.

UNCTAD and ICC, *An Investment Guide to Nepal* (Geneva, 2003). 97 pages. Document symbol: UNCTAD/IIA/2003/2. Free of charge.

UNCTAD and ICC, *An Investment Guide to Mozambique* (Geneva, 2002). 109 pages. Document symbol: UNCTAD/IIA/4. Free of charge.

UNCTAD and ICC, *An Investment Guide to Uganda* (Geneva, 2001). 76 pages. Document symbol: UNCTAD/ITE/IIT/Misc.30. Publication updated in 2004. New document symbol UNCTAD/ITE/IIA/2004/3. Free of charge.

UNCTAD and ICC, *An Investment Guide to Mali* (Geneva, 2001). 105 pages. Document symbol: UNCTAD/ITE/IIT/Misc.24. Publication updated in 2004. New document symbol UNCTAD/ITE/IIA/2004/1. Free of charge.

UNCTAD and ICC, *An Investment Guide to Ethiopia* (Geneva, 2000). 68 pages. Document symbol: UNCTAD/ITE/IIT/Misc.19. Publication updated in 2004. New document symbol UNCTAD/ITE/IIA/2004/2. Free of charge.

UNCTAD and ICC, *An Investment Guide to Bangladesh* (Geneva, 2000). 66 pages. Document symbol: UNCTAD/ITE/IIT/Misc.29. Free of charge.

C.   Contracts and Agreements

UNCTC and Moody's Investors Service, *Directory of the World's Largest Service Companies: Series I* (New York, 1991). 834 pages. ISSN 10 14-8507. $95.

(To order and other information, please write to: Moody's Investors Service, 99 Church St., New York, N.Y. 10003, USA.)

UNCTC, *International Hotel Chain Management Agreements: A Primer for Hotel Owners in Developing Countries*. Advisory Studies, Series B, No. 5. (New York, 1990). 60 pages. Sales No. E.90.II.A.8. $9.

UNCTC, *International Debt Restructuring: Substantive Issues and Techniques*. Advisory Studies, Series B, No. 4. (New York, 1989). 91 pages. Sales No. E.89.II.A.10. $ 10.

UNCTC, *Joint Ventures as a Form of International Economic Co-operation. Background documents of the High-Level Seminar organized by the United Nations Centre on Transnational Corporations in co-operation with the State Foreign Economic Commission, and the State Committee on Science and Technology of the Union of Soviet Socialist Republics, Moscow, 10 March 1988* (New York, 1988). (Also published by Taylor & Francis, New York, 1989). 205 pages (E, R). Sales No. E.88.II.A.12. Out of print. Available on microfiche. Paper copy from microfiche: $270.

UNCTC, *Licence Agreements in Developing Countries* (New York, 1987). 108 pages. Sales No. E.87.II.A.21. Out of print. Available on microfiche. Paper copy from microfiche: $118.

UNCTC/ESCAP Joint Unit, *Technology Acquisition under Alternative Arrangements with Transnational Corporations: Selected Industrial Case Studies in Thailand*. Current Studies, Series A, No. 6. (New York, 1987). 55 pages. Sales No. E.87.II.A. 14. Out of print. Available on microfiche. Paper copy from microfiche: $64.

UNCTC, *Financial and Fiscal Aspects of Petroleum Exploitation*. Advisory Studies, Series B, No. 3. (New York, 1987). 39 pages. Sales No. E.87.II.A.10. $6.

UNCTC, *Arrangements Between Joint Venture Partners in Developing Countries*. Advisory Studies, Series B, No. 2. (New York, 1987). 43 pages. Sales No. E.87.II.A.5. $6.

UNCTC, *Natural Gas Clauses in Petroleum Arrangements*. Advisory Studies, Series B, No. 1. (New York, 1987). 54 pages. Sales No. E.87.II.A.3. $8.

UNCTC, *Analysis of Engineering and Technical Assistance Consultancy Contracts* (New York, 1986). 517 pages. Sales No. E.86.II.A.4. Out of print. Available on microfiche. Paper copy from microfiche: $530.

UNCTC, *Analysis of Equipment Leasing Contracts* (New York, 1984). 138 pages. Sales No. E.84.II.A.4. Out of print. Available on microfiche. Paper copy from microfiche: $148.

UNCTC, *Measures Strengthening the Negotiating Capacity of Governments in Their Relations with Transnational Corporations. Joint Ventures Among Firms in Latin America: A Technical Paper* (New York, 1983). 97 pages. Sales No. E.83.II.A.19. Out of print. Available on microfiche. Paper copy from microfiche: $ 100.

UNCTC, *Issues in Negotiating International Loan Agreements with Transnational Banks* (New York, 1983). 103 pages. Sales No. E. 83.II.A. 18. Out of print. Available on microfiche. Paper copy from microfiche: $110. ~

UNCTC, *Transnational Corporations and Contractual Relations in the World Uranium Industry: A Technical Paper* (New York, 1983). 167 pages. Sales No. E.83.II.A. 17. Out of print. Available on microfiche. Paper copy from microfiche: $179.

UNCTC, *Features and Issues in Turnkey Contracts in Developing Countries: A Technical Paper* (New York, 1983). 156 pages. Sales No. E.83.II.A.13. Out of print. Available on microfiche. Paper copy from microfiche: $160.

UNCTC, *Main Features and Trends in Petroleum and Mining Agreements* (New York, 1983). 129 pages. Sales No. E.83.II.A.9. Out of print. Available on microfiche. Paper copy from microfiche: $140.

UNCTC, *Alternative Arrangements for Petroleum Development* (New York, 1982). 70 pages. Sales No. E.82.II.A.22. Out of print. Available on microfiche. Paper copy from microfiche: $82.

UNCTC, *Management Contracts in Developing Countries: An Analysis of Their Substantive Provisions* (New York, 1983). 139 pages (E, F, S). Sales No. E.82.II.A.21. Out of print. Available on microfiche. Paper copy from microfiche: $150.

D.   Other Studies

UNCTAD, *Investment Regimes in the Arab World: Issues and Policies*. (Geneva, 2000). Sales No. E/F.00.II.D.32. $39.

UNCTC, *Debt Equity Conversions: A Guide for Decision-makers* (New York, 1991). 149 pages. Sales No. E.90.II.A.22. $27.50.

UNCTAD, *Comparative Analysis of Petroleum Exploration Contracts* (New York and Geneva, 1995). Advisory Studies, Series B, No. 21. 80 pages. Sales No. E. 96.11.A.7. $35.

UNCTAD, *Administration of Fiscal Regimes for Petroleum Exploration and Development* (New York and Geneva, 1995). Advisory Studies, Series B, No. 20. Sales No. E.95.II.A.8. $28.

DESD/TCMD, *Formulation and Implementation of Foreign Investment Policies: Selected Key Issues*. Advisory Studies, Series B, No. 10. (New York, 1992). 84 pages. Sales No. E.92.II.A.21. $12.

UNCTC, *Government Policies and Foreign Direct Investment*. Current Studies, Series A, No. 17. (New York, 1991). 66 pages. Sales No. E.91.II.A.20. $12.50.

UNCTC, *National Legislation and Regulations Relating to Transnational Corporations*:

Vol. VIII	(Geneva, 1994), 263 pages. Sales No. E.94.1I.A. 18. $60.
Vol. VII	(New York, 1989). 320 pages. Sales No. E.89.II.A.9. Out of print. Available on microfiche. Paper copy from microfiche: $328.
Vol. VI	(New York, 1988). (Also published by Graham and Trotman, London/Dordrecht/Boston, 1988). 322 pages (E, F, S). Sales No. E.87.H.A.6. Out of print. Available on microfiche. Paper copy from microfiche: $330.
Vol. V	(New York, 1986). 246 pages (E, F, S). Sales No. E.86.II.A.3. Out of print. Available on microfiche. Paper copy from microfiche: $250.
Vol. IV	(New York, 1986). 241 pages (E, F, S). Sales No. E.85.II.A. 14. Out of print. Available on microfiche. Paper copy from microfiche: $250.

Vol. III	(New York, 1983). 345 pages (E, F, S). Sales No. E.83.II.A. 15. Out of print. Available on microfiche. Paper copy from microfiche: $360.
Vol. II	(New York, 1983). 338 pages (E, F, S). Sales No. E.83.II.A.7. Out of print. Available on microfiche. Paper copy from microfiche: $340.
Vol. I	(Part Two) (New York, 1980). 114 pages (E, F, S). Sales No. E.80.II.A.5 and corrigendum. Out of print. Available on microfiche. Paper copy from microfiche: $120.
Vol. I	(Part One) (New York, 1978). 302 pages (E, F, S). Sales No. E.78.II.A.3 and corrigendum. Out of print. Available on microfiche. Paper copy from microfiche: $300.

UNCTC, *International Income Taxation and Developing Countries* (New York, 1988). 103 pages. Sales No. E.88.II.A.6. Out of print. Available on microfiche. Paper copy from microfiche: $120.

UNCTC, *The Impact of Multinational Corporations on Development and on International Relations. Technical Paper*: **Taxation** (New York, 1974). 111 pages. Sales No. E.74.II.A.6. Out of print. Available on microfiche. Paper copy from microfiche: $110.

VIII. INTERNATIONAL STANDARDS OF ACCOUNTING AND REPORTING

UNCTAD, *International Accounting and Reporting Issu*es:

2003 Review (Geneva, 2003). UNCTAD/ITE/TEB/2003/4.

2002 Review (Geneva, 2002). UNCTAD/ITE/TEB/2003/9.

2001 Review (Geneva, 2001). 66 pages. Sales No. E.03.II.E.3

1999 Review (Geneva, 1999). 155 pages. Sales No. E.99.II.D.27.

1998 Review (Geneva, 1998). 463 pages. Sales No. E.98.II.D.5. $50.

1996 Review (Geneva, 1997). 175 pages. Sales No. E.97.II.D. 12. $50.

1995 Review (Geneva, 1995). 155 pages. Sales No. E.95.II.A. 11. $47.50.

1994 Review. (Geneva, 1995). 94 pages. Sales No. E.95.II.A.3. $27.50.

1993 Review. (Geneva, 1994). 245 pages. Sales No. E.94.II.A. 16. $25.

1992 Review (Geneva, 1993). 328 pages. Sales No. E.93.II.A.6. $25.

1991 Review (New York, 1992). 243 pages (E, F, S). Sales No. E.92.II.A.8. $25.

1990 Review (New York, 1991). 236 pages (E, F, S). Sales No. E.90.II.A.3. $9.

1989 Review (New York, 1990). 152 pages (E, F, S). Sales No. E.90.II.A.4. $17.

1988 Review (New York, 1989). 95 pages (E, F, S). Sales No. E.89.1I.A.3.

Out of print. Available on microfiche. Paper copy from microfiche: $165.

1987 Review (New York, 1988). (Also published by Graham and Trotman, London/Dordrecht/Boston, 1988). 135 pages. Sales No. E.88.II.A.8. Out of print. Available on microfiche. Paper copy from microfiche: $152.

1986 Review (New York, 1986). 158 pages. Sales No. E.86.II.A.16. Out of print. Available on microfiche. Paper copy from microfiche: $162.

1985 Review (New York, 1985). 141 pages (E, F, S). Sales No. E.85.II.A. 13. Out of print. Available on microfiche. Paper copy from microfiche: $152.

1984 Review (New York, 1985). 122 pages (E, F, S). Sales No. E.85.II.A.2. Out of print. Available on microfiche. Paper copy from microfiche: $138.

These annual publications report of sessions of the Intergovernmental Working Group of Experts on International Standards of Accounting and Reporting (ISAR).

UNCTAD, *A Manual for the Preparers and Users of ECO-efficiency Indicators* (New York and Geneva, 2004). Sales No. E.04.II.D.13

UNCTAD, *Selected Issues in Corporate Governance: Regional and Country Experiences* (New York and Geneva, 2003). Sales No. E.03.II.D.26

UNCTAD, *Accounting and Financial Reporting for Environmental Costs and Liabilities* (New York and Geneva, 1998).184 pages (A, C, E, F, R, S). Sales No. A/C/E/F/WS.98.II.D. 14. $19.

UNCTAD, *Financial Disclosure by Banks: Proceedings of an UNCTAD Forum* (New York and Geneva, 1998). 84 pages. Sales No. E.98.II.D. 13. $13.

UNCTAD, *Responsibilities and Liabilities of Accountants and Auditors: Proceedings of a Forum* (Geneva, 1995). Sales No. E.95.II.A. 10.

UNCTAD, *Accounting for Sustainable Forestry Management: A Case Study* (New York and Geneva, 1994). 46 pages. Sales No. E.94.II.A. 17. $22.

UNCTAD, *Conclusions on Accounting and Reporting by Transnational Corporations* (New York and Geneva, 1994). 47 pages. Sales No. E.94.II.A.9. $12.

UNCTAD, *Accounting, Valuation and Privatization* (New York and Geneva, 1994). 190 pages. Sales No. E.94.II.A.3. $25.

UNCTC, *Accounting for East-West Joint Ventures* (New York, 1992). 282 pages. Sales No. E.92.II.A. 13. $25.

DES13/TCMD, *Environmental Accounting: Current Issues, Abstracts and Bibliography*. Advisory Studies, Series B, No. 9. (New York, 1992). 86 pages. Sales No. E.92.II.A.23. $15.

UNCTC, *Accountancy Development in Africa: Challenge of the 1990s* (New York, 1991). 200 pages (E, F). Sales No. E.91.II.A.2. $25.

UNCTC, *Joint Venture Accounting in the USSR: Direction for Change*. Advisory Studies, Series B, No. 7. (New York, 1990). 46 pages. Sales No. E.90.II.A.26. $11.

UNCTC, *Curricula for Accounting Education for East- West Joint Ventures in Centrally Planned Economies.* Advisory Studies, Series B, No. 6. (New York, 1990). 86 pages. Sales No. E.90.II.A.2. $10.

UNCTC, *Objectives and Concepts Underlying Financial Statements* (New York, 1989). 32 pages (A, C, E, F, R, S). Sales No. E.89.II.A.18. $8.

UNCTC, *Conclusions on Accounting and Reporting by Transnational Corporations: The Intergovernmental Working Group of Experts on International Standards of Accounting and Reporting* (New York, 1988). 58 pages (A, C, E, F, R, S). Sales No. E.88.II.A.18. $7.50.

UNCTC, *International Standards of Accounting and Reporting: Report of the Ad Hoc Intergovernmental Working Group of Experts on International Standards of Accounting and Reporting* (New York, 1984). 55 pages (C, E, F, R, S). Sales No. E.84.II.A.2. Out of print. Available on microfiche. Paper copy from microfiche: $63.

UNCTC, *Towards International Standardization of Corporate Accounting and Reporting* (New York, 1982). 104 pages (E, F, R, S). Sales No. E.82.II.A.3. Out of print. Available on microfiche. Paper copy from microfiche: $25.

UNCTC, *International Standards of Accounting and Reporting for Transnational Corporations: Report of the Secretary- General, and Report of the Group of Experts on International Standards of Accounting and Reporting* (New York, 1977). 79 pages (E, F, R, S). Sales No. E.77.II.A.17. Out of print. Available on microfiche. Paper copy from microfiche: $80.

UNCTC, *International Standards of Accounting and Reporting for Transnational Corporations: Technical Papers* (New York, 1977). 96 pages (E, F, S). Sales No. E.77.II.A. 15. Out of print. Available on microfiche. Paper copy from microfiche: $ 100.

IX. DATA AND INFORMATION SOURCES

UNCTAD, *World Investment Directory.*

Volume VIII: Latin America and the Caribbean (New York and Geneva, 2004). Sales No. E.03.II.D.12. $25.

Volume VIII: Central and Eastern Europe (New York and Geneva, 2003). Sales No. E.03.II.D.12. $25.

Volume VII: Asia and the Pacific (New York and Geneva, 2000). 356 pages. Sales No. E.00.II.D.11. $80.

Volume VI: West Asia (New York and Geneva, 1997). 138 pages. Sales No. E.97.II.A.2. $35.

Volume V: Africa (New York and Geneva, 1997). 462 pages. Sales No. E.97.II.A.1. $75.

Volume IV: Latin America and the Caribbean (New York, 1994). 478 pages. Sales No. E.94.II.A.10. $65.

Volume III: Developed Countries (New York, 1993). 532 pages. Sales No. E.93.II.A.9. $75.

Volume II: Central and Eastern Europe (New York, 1992) 432 pages. Sales No. E.93.II.A.1. $65.

Volume I: Asia and the Pacific (New York, 1992). 3 56 pages. Sales No. E.92.II.A.11. Out of print. Available on microfiche. Paper copy from microfiche: $370.

The *World Investment Directory* contains time-series data on FDI, as well as corporate data on the largest foreign affiliates and legal information for the countries of each region. A number of volumes also contain analytical overviews and detailed technical introductions.

UNCTAD, *Investment Promotion Agencies: Directory of Members of the World Association of Investment Promotion Agencies 1999,* Fifth Edition (Geneva, 1999). An annual publication containing contact addresses of heads of investment promotion agencies and institutions worldwide. Available free of charge.

DESD/TCMD, *Transnational Corporations: A Selective Bibliography, 1991-1992* (New York, 1993). 736 pages (E, F). Sales No. E1F.93.II.A. 16. $75.

DESD)/TCMD, *The East- West Business Directory 1991-1992* (New York, 1992). 567 pages. Sales No. E.92.II.A.20. $65.

UNCTC, *Transnational Business Information: A Manual of Needs and Sources* (New York, 1991). 228 pages (E, F, S). Sales No. E.91.II.A. 13. $45.

The manual discusses the needs of developing countries for information in all phases of their relations with TNCs and identifies sources that can help to meet those needs.

UNCTC, *University Curriculum on Transnational Corporations*:

Vol. I	*Economic Development* (New York, 1991). 186 pages. Sales No. E.91.II.A.5. $20.
Vol. II	*International Business* (New York, 1991).154 pages. Sales No. E.9 I.H.A.6. $20.
Vol. III	*International Law* (New York, 1991). 180 pages. Sales No. E.91.II.A.7. $20.

(The set: Document Symbol: ST/CTC/62. Sales No. E.91.II.A.8. $50.)

UNCTC, T*ransnational Corporations: A Selective Bibliography, 1988-1990 Les Sociétés Transnationales: Bibliographie Sélective, 1988-1990* (New York, 1991). 617 pages (E, F). Sales No. E/R9 1.II.A.10. $75.

UNCTC, *Workshop Papers of UNCM, Annotated Bibliography with Indexes, 1978-91* (New York, 1991). 153 pages. Free of charge.

UNCTC, *Documents of the Joint Units of UNCTC and the Regional Commissions, 1975-1991* (New York, 1991). 33 pages. Free of charge.

UNCTC, *Transnational Corporations in South Africa and Namibia: A Selective Bibliography* (New York, 1989). 98 pages. Sales No. E.89.II.A. 13. Out of print. Available on microfiche. Paper copy from microfiche: $ 100.

UNCTC, *Transnational Corporations: A Selective Bibliography, 1983-1987. Les Sociétés Transnationales: Bibliographie Sélective, 1983-1987*:

Main List by Category, Author Index, Title Index1Liste Principale par Catigorie, Index des Auteurs, Index des Titres. Volume I (New York, 1988). 442 pages. Sales No. E.88.H.A.9. Out of print. Available on microfiche. Paper copy from microfiche: $450.

Subject Index/Index des Matiéres. Volume II (New York, 1988). 458 pages (E, F). Sales No. E/F.88.II.A.10. Two-volume set. Out of print. Available on microfiche. Paper copy from microfiche: $170.

UNCTC, ***UNCTC Bibliography 1974-1987*** (New York, 1988). 83 pages. Sales No. E.87.H.A.23. Out of print. Available on microfiche. Paper copy from microfiche: $90.

UNCTC, ***Publication Reviews: 1975-1987*** (New York, 1988). 101 pages. Free of charge.

UNCTC, ***List of Company Directories and Summary of Their Contents/List d'Annuaires de Sociétés et Résumé de Leurs Données,*** *Second ed.* (New York, 1983). 160 pages (E, F). Sales No. E/E83.II.A. 10. Out of print. Available on microfiche. Paper copy from microfiche: $170.

UNCTC, ***Users Guide to the Info~tion System on Transnational Corporations: A Technical Paper*** (New York, 1980). 30 pages (E, F, R, S). Sales No. E.80.II.A.6. Out of print. Available on microfiche. Paper copy from microfiche: $35.

UNCTC, ***International Directory of Data Bases Relating to Companies*** (New York, 1979). 246 pages. Sales No. E.79.II.A. 1. Out of print. Available on microfiche. Paper copy from microfiche: $260.

UNCTC, ***Bibliography on Transnational Corporations*** (New York, 1979). 426 pages (E, F). Sales No. E/E78.II.A.4. Out of print. Available on microfiche. Paper copy from microfiche: $430.

UNCTC, ***Survey of Research on Transnational Corporations*** (New York, 1977). 534 pages. Sales No. E.77.II.A.16. Out of print. Available on microfiche. Paper copy from microfiche: $530.

UNCTC, ***List of Company Directories and Summary of Their Contents*** (New York, 1977). 60 pages. Sales No. E.77.11.A.8. Out of print. Available on microfiche. Paper copy from microfiche: $62.

UNCTC, ***Establishment of a Comprehensive Information System on Transnational Corporations: Government Replies*** (New York, 1977). 26 pages (E, F, S). Sales No. E.77.11.A.7. Out of print. Available on microfiche. Paper copy from microfiche: $30.

UNCTC, ***Curricula for Accounting Education for East-West Joint Ventures in Centrally Planned Economies.*** Advisory Studies, Series B, No. 6. (New York, 1990). 86 pages. Sales No. E.90.II.A.2. $10.

HOW TO OBTAIN THE PUBLICATIONS

The sales publications may be purchased from distributors of United Nations publications throughout the world. They may also be obtained by writing to:

United Nations Publications   or

Sales and Marketing Section, DC2-853

United Nations Secretariat

New York, N.Y. 100 17

U.S.A.

Tel.: ++1 212 963 8302 or 1 800 253 9646

Fax: ++1 212 963 3489

E-mail: publications@un.org

United Nations Publications

Sales and Marketing Section, Rm. C. 113-1

United Nations Office at Geneva

Palais des Nations

CH-1211 Geneva 10

Switzerland

Tel.: ++41 22 917 2612

Fax: ++4122 917 0027

E-mail: unpubli@unog.ch

INTERNET: www.un.org/Pubs/sales.htm

For further information on the work on foreign direct investment and transnational corporations, please address inquiries to:

Karl Sauvant

Director

Division on Investment, Technology and Enterprise Development

United Nations Conference on Trade and Development

Palais des Nations, Room E-10052

CH-1211 Geneva 10 Switzerland

Telephone: ++41 22 907 5707

Fax: ++41 22 907 0498

E-mail: karl.sauvant@unctad.org

INTERNET: www.unctad.org/en/subsites/dite

QUESTIONNAIRE

International Investment Instruments: A Compendium

Volume XIV

In order to improve the quality and relevance of the work of the UNCTAD Division on Investment, Technology and Enterprise Development, it would be useful to receive the views of readers on this publication. It would therefore be greatly appreciated if you could complete the following questionnaire and return it to:

Readership Survey
UNCTAD Division on Investment, Technology and Enterprise Development
United Nations Office in Geneva
Palais des Nations
Room E-9123
CH-1211 Geneva 10
Switzerland
Fax: 41-22-907-0194

1. Name and address of respondent (optional):

_____

2. Which of the following best describes your area of work?

Government	○	Public enterprise	○
Private enterprise	○	Academic or research institution	○
International organization	○	Media	○
Not-for-profit organization	○	Other (specify) _____	

3. In which country do you work? _____

4. What is your assessment of the contents of this publication?

Excellent	○	Adequate	○
Good	○	Poor	○

5. How useful is this publication to your work?

Very useful ○   Of some use ○   Irrelevant ○

6. Please indicate the three things you liked best about this publication:

_____

_____

_____

7. Please indicate the three things you liked least about this publication:

_____

_____

_____

8. Are you a regular recipient of *Transnational Corporations* (formerly *The CTC Reporter*), UNCTAD-DITE's tri-annual refereed journal?

Yes　　　　　　　　　○　　　　　　　　　　　　　　　　　No　　　　○

If not, please check here if you would like to receive
a sample copy sent to the name and address you have
given above　　　　　　　　　　　　　　　　　　　　　　　　　　　○

*